MW01616062

THE
THEORY
OF 5

Shelley

Enjoy your Journey to
Living your Theory of 5

Life!

Share Your Thoughts and Experiences!

What ideas or concepts from *The Theory of 5* speak to you most strongly? What will you take away from this book that you can put into action *today?* Share what excites you with other readers of *The Theory of 5* — or those you know could benefit! Use the **#TheoryOf5** tag for photos or quotes on Twitter, Instagram, Facebook and others and let us know what speaks to you!

Also, connect with us on social media and share your experiences with the author and your Theory of 5 peers:

- Facebook - https://www.facebook.com/CBSaraceno/
- Instagram - @TheoryOf5
- YouTube - https://www.youtube.com/c/theoryof5
- Web - https://www.theoryof5.com

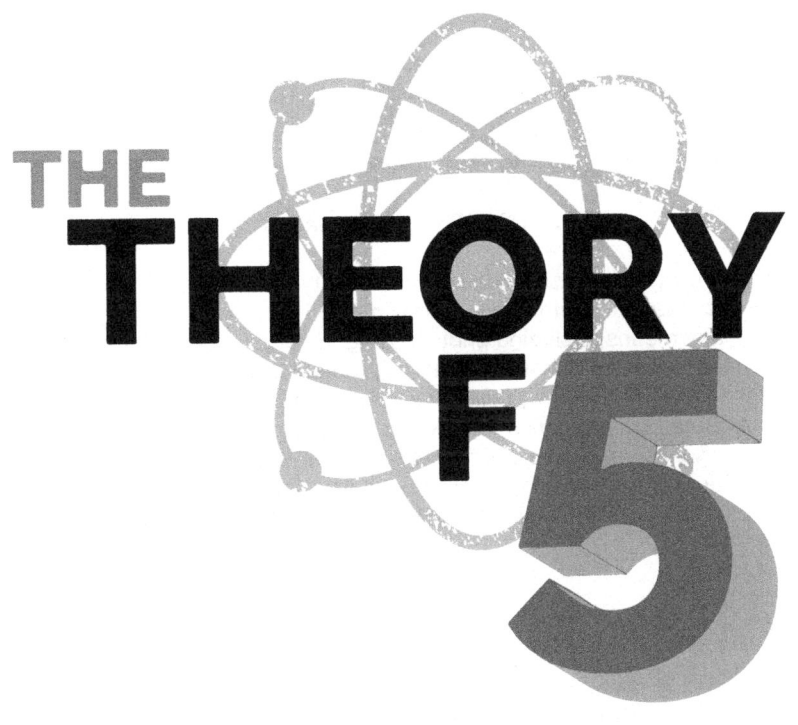

Chris Saraceno
with David Falkirk Davis

The Theory of 5 by Chris Saraceno
with David Falkirk Davis

Copyright © 2023 by Chris Saraceno

First Printing, 2018
ISBN 978-1-7323012-0-7
Library of Congress Control Number: 2018905320

SEL027000 SELF-HELP / Personal Growth / Success
SEL021000 SELF-HELP / Motivational & Inspirational

TABLE OF CONTENTS

Preface

Introduction

The Mentoring Mindset

Finding Spirituality That Works for Us

Minding Our Business and Our Finances

The Only Body We'll Ever Have

Interviews

Afterword

Acknowledgments

About the Authors

*This book is dedicated to the memory of
my nephew and godson Michael Saraceno
and my stepson Brandon Young.*

Gone, but always loved and never forgotten

Preface

WE'VE ALL HEARD SOME version of the phrase, "Birds of a feather flock together."

In the Saraceno household, the motto was, "Tell me who your friends are and I'll tell you who you are."

These two statements are the core philosophy behind The Theory of 5.

This is a book I believe will greatly enhance your life. I can say this because I have witnessed the transformation first hand both *in my own life and in the lives of those around me who have taken it to heart.*

When you open your mind to the ideas contained within the pages that follow, you will find ways to ignite the passion of your heart, beliefs and values. You will discover the tools and behaviors needed to change your life for the better.

When you adopt The Theory of 5 philosophy, it will become the ultimate playbook for positive transformation and growth in your life. It will unlock your future and aid you in setting up a *network of people* who will encourage you to excel in five key areas of *happiness* and *prosperity*:

- Spirituality
- Relationships
- Parenting
- Finances
- Health and Fitness

When you consistently follow the steps outlined in this book, you will live the life you *know* you're capable of achieving and go on to do more than you've ever thought possible.

Enjoy your journey to a Theory of 5 Life!

No matter where we start out in life, we require others to shape us, sharpen us and guide us. While we may find some level of success on our own, we'll never achieve our *true* potential and discover our best self without assistance and support from other exceptional, motivated people.

Introduction

The Theory of 5:
What It Is and How to Use It

It All Starts with YOU

IF YOU'RE READING THIS, congratulations! You're already a winner because you've won the lottery of life!

Why? Consider the odds of your mother and father finding each other in this world. Consider the odds of them conceiving the person who would become the unique, genetic "you."

Trillions to one.

And yet, here we are, winner of the biggest lottery *ever*. Excited? We *should* be.

So, what are we going to do with this amazing opportunity?

> We owe it to everyone — our family, friends, co-workers, community and ourselves — to make the most of the existence we've been given.

We owe it to everyone — our family, friends, co-workers, community and ourselves — to make the most of the existence we've been given.

One of the few absolute truths in this life is that none of us know how long we will live. Do we have decades left? Years? Months? Minutes? Another truth is that time can never be replaced or reused. Once it's gone, it's gone. *Time is our most precious commodity.*

Have you ever wondered why some individuals are so happy and prosperous while other, equally smart and talented people struggle? How do these successful people produce exceptional results when others don't? Raw talent and potential are almost meaningless; we've got to put in the long-term effort to develop the *skills, habits* and *attitude* needed to create a sustainable lifetime of happiness and prosperity.

Most who will read *The Theory of 5* strive to live a life with no regrets and to make their mark on the world. To achieve this, however, we must become our *best* selves. We must make the most of the limited time we are given to be happy, prosperous and to do something amazing. Why choose to just *exist* when we could live an *extraordinary* life?

To be remembered beyond our lifetimes and leave a legacy — for our family, friends, community and society — takes more than what many are willing to do. We remember those people who positively impact and change lives, *especially our own*.

So, how do we become the best version of ourselves? How do we become someone who will make a difference?

Here's the secret: *It's next to impossible to do it alone.*

Who are YOU?

To begin, I'd like you to stop and answer a few basic — but crucial — questions from a specific viewpoint:

- Who are YOU?
- How and why do YOU think the way you do?
- How do YOU want your loved ones to remember you?
- What are YOUR specific goals, and why do YOU have them?
- What do YOU want to accomplish in your life?

Why is it so important to understand YOU?

Because we are all unique individuals, and understanding YOU is a key element to living a happy and prosperous life.

Ready? Let's get started.

...we've got to put in the long-term effort to develop the *skills, habits* and *attitude* needed to create a sustainable lifetime of happiness and prosperity.

The "Self-Made" Man

THE MYTH OF THE "self-made" man or woman is just that — a myth.

We hold in awe those who started life without the benefit of money or resources and went on to build empires. It's almost as if they were *destined* to be giants and got there with only their own determination and talents.

When we look closer, though, behind the myth of their "destiny," we begin to see the people around them. We see the family and friends who encouraged them. We find the teachers and coaches who instructed them on how to best use their gifts. We see the trusted mentors who coached them and got the best out of them. Even those who *didn't* believe in them played a part, providing them with the challenge and inspiration to prove their doubters wrong.

In this world, we are *never* alone.

No matter where we start out in life, we require others to shape us, sharpen us and guide us. While we may find some level of success on our own, we'll never achieve our *true* potential and discover our best self without assistance and support from other exceptional, motivated people.

These mentors may come from any facet of our lives. Wherever we find them, the results are the same. We grow, we discover certainty and clarity and we learn to become more than who we were.

In the best cases, these people don't tell us *what* to think; they teach us *how* to think. They model ways we can attain our best lives through their actions, behaviors, support and guidance. They challenge us to achieve results we didn't think were possible.

So, where can we find these role models? Where do we find true mentors?

Seeking, Finding and Asking

LOOK AROUND AND FIND someone living the happy, prosperous life you'd like to achieve. Throw away any envious impulse or thought of "they must have known somebody," meaning you believe they were lucky or were given something they didn't earn and deserve. Make a brutally honest assessment of where you are and where they are. While there *are* some who simply inherited wealth, those you most admire often started out with nothing more than you have — and sometimes with far less.

When starting our quest for improvement and comparing ourselves to someone who's living our dream, it's crucial to appreciate all the concentrated effort they had to put into achieving their success. Think about the *years* it took for them to hone their skills. Think about the intense determination, focus and relentless consistent action that was necessary to reach their destination. They didn't *wish* or *whine* themselves there; they did the *work*.

The moment we appreciate their achievements is the moment we *know* what we must do.

Here's what I didn't understand until I internalized the idea that would become The Theory of 5: Those who have achieved success and have years of experience and wisdom are often more than happy to guide and teach someone who comes to them with an *open attitude* and a *willing heart*, ready to put in the effort. Many times, all we have to do is *ask*.

But what if we *can't* find someone we'd like to emulate in some facet of our life? Well, there's never been a better time to find a guiding hand or a helpful example than right now. In this modern world of online education and networking, we are all able to find mentors and role models— no matter if we're geographically isolated or painfully introverted.

Through online courses, videos, blogs, podcasts, social media, books, forums and other methods, *we can find the right mentors and role models.*

We may never meet them in person. They may never know what they provided for us. Our lives, however, will be richer because of them.

I speak from experience. In my life, I can trace my accomplishments straight back to those who took the time to teach and encourage me to believe I could be more than I thought possible when I was a young man. Some of these people became close friends while some were just brief encounters or simple observation. They all had an impact on the person I would become

Over time, the notion of seeking others to guide and challenge me in various areas crystallized into The Theory of 5, and it's been a cornerstone of my life.

Those who have achieved success and have years of experience and wisdom are often more than happy to guide and teach someone who comes to them with an *open attitude* and a *willing heart*, ready to do the work. Many times, all we have to do is *ask*.

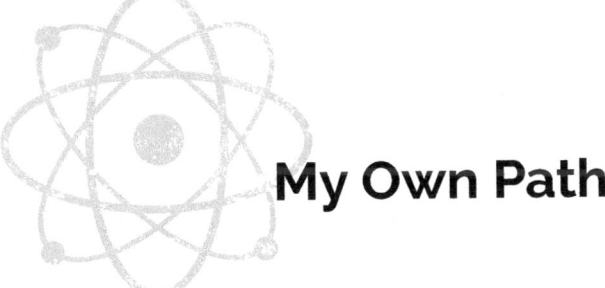

My Own Path

MUCH OF THE MENTORING I received just happened naturally because of my innate curiosity. I've always enjoyed learning and have never been afraid to ask questions. In my youthful naiveté, I believed everyone wanted to — or *should* want to — be my friend; it was only later in life I realized how empowering that belief and natural positive thinking was in building friendships with happy, prosperous people. Their way of thinking and living life was a tremendous gift to me. Once I came to that realization and thought about how much their guidance, advice and challenges had added to my life, I started seeking out these relationships on purpose.

Since that realization, the Theory has shaped how I think about the world — and myself. *With The Theory of 5 mindset I decide whom I add to my life — and whom I choose to limit or remove.* For the last three decades, I've continually refined these theories, and it is fundamental to how I now live my life.

The Theory of 5 won't keep us from making mistakes in our lives. It's not a magic spell or a miracle cure for life's setbacks. My mentors have all expressed to me that there have been times when they've felt like they've taken three steps forward and two steps back. This is, no doubt, a familiar feeling to everyone, no matter how successful he or she is. What the Theory *does* provide, however, is *a framework and a foundation that allows us to thrive in good times and survive the bad.*

We have all heard a version of the adage, "Successful people aren't those who never *fail*; successful people are those who aren't *afraid to try*, and then learn from their experience." This mindset is central to The Theory of 5. I've spoken about the Theory to thousands of people in my life and have been asked and encouraged by them to share the Theory more in-depth.

9

This book is the result of more than 36 years of research and 59 years of life experience. In recent years, however, life events outside of my control have forced me to examine what I believe and what I want to accomplish in the time left that I've been given. Some of these events include:

- My wife, Lisa's, battle with cancer
- The death of my kind, beloved 19-year-old nephew and godson, Michael, who always had us laughing and was loved by everyone who met him
- The death of my 29-year-old stepson, Brandon, a wonderful, intelligent young man with a heart of gold and a bright future
- The death of three dear friends — all of whom took amazing care of themselves — one to cancer and two to sudden heart attacks
- The separation of my parents after 56 years of marriage
- The inability of my parents to support themselves financially, as well as both of them being in declining health — they've each had two heart attacks in the last two years
- My father's diagnosis of Alzheimer's Disease, which left me as his main caregiver
- The death of my godmother and aunt, Catherine ("Kitty"), who had been the family matriarch, coordinating family gatherings over the last five years
- Complications from a surgery which has permanently limited approximately 50% of my previous daily activities

With The Theory of 5 mindset I decide whom I add to my life — and whom I choose to limit or remove.

As heartbreaking and challenging as these events have been — I will always have the sadness, loss and pain — I understand that none of these events were results of any decisions I had made. It's simply life. Sometimes life is cruel and hard. Sometimes life is *unfair* and things happen that we cannot control or avoid. What we *can* control, however, are our reactions, behaviors and attitudes.

So, I've decided that there's no time like the present to share what I've learned. Writing this book has provided me with an opportunity to take a good look at my life and beliefs. After the past few years, my viewpoints have been tested. What has *never* failed, however, is the knowledge that I didn't have to go through this alone. The Theory of 5 provided me with the necessary foundation and support I needed to get through these challenges. It also challenged me to focus on what I was contributing to the world. I want to do whatever I can do to positively influence people's lives in the time I have left, however long (or short) that time may be.

I want to be very clear that I'm writing this book from the perspective of what I've learned through discussions and lessons with my many mentors. I'm blessed to have these friends in my circle, and I'm thankful for all the people in my life who have contributed to my happiness and prosperity. I'm also fortunate to have *realized* the positive impact they've made. This realization was the seed for this book and for the examples that follow. I want to take their gifts and share them with others — *with you* — because I understand their true value and the difference it will make in a person's life.

Caring about people and wanting them to succeed has always come naturally to me. One of my absolute favorite things in life is to work with people who are *actively* reaching for their dreams, who are willing to put in the *time, effort* and *action* needed to succeed and grow. I want to positively impact everyone I meet and know. The Theory of 5 allows me to expand my reach towards this quest. I believe everyone has the opportunity — with the proper knowledge, mindset and support — to be happy and prosperous. You *can* live your best life, and the Theory of 5 is an invaluable tool for you to use in achieving that goal.

After the past few years, my viewpoints have been tested. What has *never* failed, however, is the knowledge that I didn't have to go through this alone.

What Is The Theory of 5?

THE THEORY OF 5 is a lifetime process; it only stops on the day we die.

The Theory, which can be used by anyone at any stage of life, is based on *selecting mentors in the five most significant areas of a person's life — spirituality, marriage, parenting, business and finance, and health.* These men and women will guide and support us towards fulfilling our ultimate potential in each area.

Lessons can come from observation, teaching and listening, along with some trial and error. For those of us willing to internalize the lessons, mentors can help us navigate life's opportunities and challenges.

This only works, however, *if we let them,* and if we hold ourselves accountable for our own successes and failures. Again, only those humble and open-minded enough to know they need guidance and brave enough to look honestly at themselves will get the full benefits of The Theory of 5. Those who have the passion to grow, improve and *take action* will find it to be a life-changing tool for their continued success.

The Five Areas of Personal Growth

Through my 36 years of developing The Theory of 5, I've divided life into *five key areas* critical to personal growth and success. *I consistently found the happiest, most prosperous people succeed in each of these areas.* I learned that I had to seek the advice and spend time with these individuals who excelled if I wanted to reach my full potential in this gift called "life." These were the people I wanted to emulate, and sought their support in the following areas:

- **Spirituality and Religion:** No matter what our religious convictions, it's important to have a spiritual framework to deal with life's constant ups and downs.
- **Marriage/Relationship:** Our life partner can be our greatest asset or our worst nightmare.

- **Parenting:** Our children — along with our nieces, nephews and others who will learn from us — are our legacy. Helping children grow and prosper makes us better adults.
- **Business and Finance:** A rewarding career and freedom from money woes enriches all areas of our lives.
- **Health and Fitness:** Success in other areas can be worthless if we don't have and maintain our health.

These are in no particular order, and our priorities may change during our life, based on our beliefs, values, age and the challenges we are facing at any one time. Learning to excel in all these areas, though, will be essential in reaching our full potential.

Finding those who can guide, teach and challenge us in each of these areas is the central idea of The Theory of 5. We'll go into much greater detail for each of these five categories, but I know those who master them all will live their best lives.

Your Circles

We each have a "default" circle we build around ourselves just by living our lives. *With The Theory of 5, we also develop a purpose-built set of connections that provides a strong foundation for our future success.* Let's take a quick look at each circle:

Circle I: Five Personal Connections

This group consists of the five people we spend the most time with because of work, living arrangements and personal choice. These include our spouses, co-workers, relatives and friends.

Studies have found, in most cases, our *income*, our *happiness*, our *relationships*, our *health*, our *political views*, our *spiritual views* and our *prosperity* will be greatly impacted by these people. In fact, our results in these specific areas tend to be the "average" of these five people.

When we associate with positive, energized people striving for continuous growth, it is easier to embark on our own quest for self-improvement. If we are surrounded by negative people possessing a poor work ethic, little ambition and a lack of clarity and direction, we face an uphill battle to make a better life. These self-entitled whiners are their own worst enemies. They become *victims*, not *victors*. What can they contribute to our personal growth? Think about your own circle of friends, family and acquaintances and see if

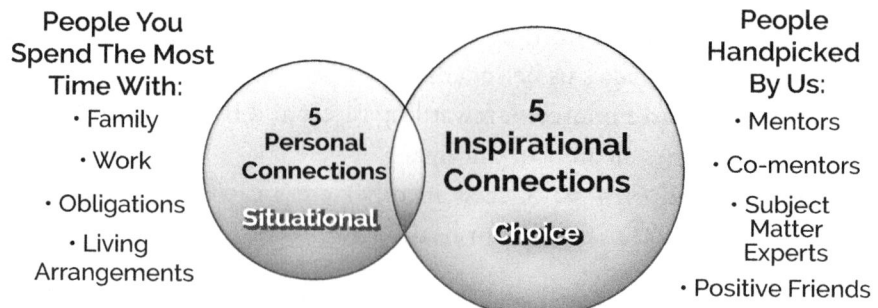

People You
Spend The Most
Time With:
· Family
· Work
· Obligations
· Living
Arrangements

5 Personal Connections Situational

5 Inspirational Connections Choice

People
Handpicked
By Us:
· Mentors
· Co-mentors
· Subject Matter Experts
· Positive Friends

this pattern holds true for your own life today.

If you have children, don't you observe your child's peer group? If they are associating with "bad influences" — children with poor attitudes, actions and behaviors — would you correct that situation? Of course you would!. Well, what's good for our child is also good for us — it's the same principle.

There are limits to our control over this circle of personal connections. Some of those around us are there because of work or family circumstances and set an example we'd *never* want to emulate. To avoid becoming the average of *these* people in critical areas of personal growth, we must implement the second circle of The Theory of 5.

Circle II: Five Inspirational Connections

This circle consists of people *handpicked by us*. They are experts in specific areas of life where we must excel to become our best selves. The word "mentor" is defined as "an expert, experienced and trusted advisor who trains and counsels." We choose these people because of their accomplishments and because we want them to be our mentors and/or friends. These people will teach us and challenge us. Here is something I've learned about mentors: They not only like us but they see something in us that intrigues them. They see raw, untapped potential. They know, with training, this person will go places. These are people who are happy to support our growth.

We should consider their interest in us as a gift — and make sure we are worthy to receive it. When we seek the advice of someone we admire we need to be ready to actively listen to them and are prepared to put their wisdom into action. They may be generous with their time and effort, but they have no desire to waste it on someone who won't take their example to heart and

"OR" Versus "AND"

MY MENTORS AND I believe most people think they are realistic about what they want in life. We understand not everyone wants to work 60 to 90 hours a week to become a multimillionaire. They don't need to earn a doctorate just to find satisfying work. They don't need to be an elite athlete to simply stay in shape. From my own experience and from the experiences of my mentors, we hear most people say, "I want to make a good living and have a balanced life shared with friends and family."

Before diving into the lessons and practices of The Theory of 5, *we would caution you to not get stuck into a limiting concept called* **"The Tyranny of the OR."** This concept, described by author and business consultant James C. Collins, comes into play when people believe they have to make a choice between what they consider to be two contradictory paths. "I can live a balanced life OR I can have prosperity," for example. "I could be a good husband OR a good father."

Collins went on to describe an extremely liberating strategy called **"The Genius of the AND."** All of my mentors subscribe to this concept. They have discovered and implemented the daily behaviors needed to have a balanced life AND create prosperity. They take the time to maintain and improve their health AND spend quality time with their families.

Does this happen overnight? No. Will it happen if we put in the proper time, extreme effort and laser focus? Absolutely. Limiting ourselves to certain options before even *considering* that we could have it all only ensures limited results.

The Theory of 5 will guide you in achieving harmony and balance in your life *while* allowing you to dominate one or all of its specific areas. It will allow you to experience the Genius of the AND while avoiding the Tyranny of the OR.

The Time Is NOW

I TRULY BELIEVE WE all are living in what is *literally the most prosperous time in the history of the human race.* Stop to think about this for a moment. There are so many opportunities available to learn through online courses and materials and to connect with people through new technologies such as social media. People are living longer than ever before. When it comes to buying homes or starting businesses, we have seen historically low interest rates. People are finding success today like never before — studies show that there are currently 1,700 new millionaires every day, and more than 11 million millionaires in the United States. And prosperity isn't just about money; there are more opportunities than ever to find ways to improve yourself, be true to your calling, to live life on your terms and find your own rewards.

So, when people choose to constantly focus on the "doom and gloom" on the news, they're missing the bigger picture. If they spend their precious time with negative, selfish, self-absorbed people who have no direction or focus and constantly whine and complain about what they don't have, they are missing all the exceptional opportunities around them.

There are *unlimited* opportunities out there for us and our families — if we want the prosperity, success and happiness that a Theory of 5 lifestyle brings badly enough and are willing to take consistent action. Read *The Theory of 5*, take notes, make your plans and get ready for the journey of a lifetime.

Before we get to the specific areas that make up The Theory of 5, however, let's first examine the key ingredient it takes to make it all work: the proper mindset. When you achieve this, everything else starts to come to life.

Let's get started!

The Mentoring Mindset

Preparation
and Expectations

This Book and Your Needs

WE ALL COME TO the table with different skills, different experiences and different goals. None of the five elements of the Theory are more important than the others — as stated previously, *it depends on where we are, what we want and what we need in our lives at any given moment.*

Perhaps you are naturally gifted at three of the five Theories and only need strong support for the remaining two. In the other three areas, you might just need to find like-minded individuals to support you and keep you on track. If you really excel in an area, maybe *you* should be the one mentoring to another — that path comes with its own rewards, which we'll also go over in this book.

It's important to note you will notice certain concepts and suggestions keep coming up in different areas of The Theory of 5. *The reason for this is that they are important to finding success.* Repetition of key ideas, viewed from different angles, is an excellent way to internalize these thoughts and reach the goals and vision we've set out for ourselves. This is an important technique of The Theory of 5.

There may be statements in this book you disagree with, and that's okay; sometimes people have to agree to disagree. I am confident, however, that the philosophy behind The Theory of 5 is one everyone can put into action in order to reap rewards. It's easier to reach our goals when we have the support of those who have accomplished what we've set out to do.

In order to get the most out of the Theory, it's crucial that our goals are just that — *our* goals. Not everyone will have children or get married, but positive relationships and personal prosperity will support a happy life. The lessons and the ideas presented in *The Theory of 5* strengthen our commitment to pursue the opportunities in areas that matter most to us. Everyone wants to have a prosperous life — to have an existence that *matters.*

A Word Before Beginning
(The Author's Mindset)

THROUGHOUT THIS BOOK, I'LL be sharing real-life lessons with you that come from decades of experience developing and practicing The Theory of 5. They represent the real-life examples of knowledge you will gain by spending time with the exceptional people and asking quality questions which generate solutions and plans for action.

It is not my intention to preach, lecture or come across as a "know-it-all"; I'm *still* looking for new mentors to both guide and challenge me, and I always will be. In this book, I simply want to demonstrate the depth of knowledge we will find when asking mentors for assistance. *I want to show you the power of surrounding yourself with those who will support you in achieving your goals. I want to share with you the difference it will make in your life.*

I'll also be sharing interviews with several of my mentors, co-mentors and friends, allowing you to meet the people who have shaped — and continue to shape — my life. You'll see why they are so important to my personal and professional development. This will demonstrate how The Theory of 5 works in the real world.

I'm beyond excited to share with you the lessons I've learned through The Theory of 5 because I'm living proof that it works. At the age of 21, I had next to nothing. Back then, I was the definition of "working poor," living by myself in a trailer with my pit bull Pepper and sleeping on a bare mattress. I existed on tuna fish, ramen noodles and pizza. To save every dime I could, I washed out the paper towels and paper plates that weren't too torn so I could reuse them. I had one spoon, one fork, one knife, one real plate and a soup bowl. Television was an extravagance that was beyond my means. I worked 12-hour days as a fitness instructor to pay my way through college and was determined to survive on my own — but I had no goals or vision beyond food, shelter and day-to-day survival.

The only motivation I had in my life at that point was sparked when a family member once told me "you'll never make it on your own." While I was committed to proving that person wrong, I didn't have a plan.

At 22, however, my life drastically changed. This is when I met my first two mentors.

Harvey Ritter, then 78, was the retired owner of the first auto dealership I worked for. Even after he handed his business over to his three sons, he would still come around almost every day to check in, see how things were going and talk to the people at the dealership. After getting to know me on these visits, Harvey decided to take me under his wing and show me how he had built both his business and his wealth.

> The people who excel understand and have clearly defined their purpose — their "Why" — in life. It's their laser focus that makes the difference.

Robert Plarr, a well-known area businessman and fitness guru — who also served four years in U.S. Marine Corps Force Reconnaissance during the Vietnam War — is *still* one of my most faithful mentors to this day. Bob was a partner in Dorney Park and Wildwater Kingdom — one of the largest amusement parks in the northeast. He also owned gyms, a dance club called Castle Gardens and was a master of marketing. Bob invited me to weight train with him — beginning at 4:30 a.m. each morning. While we trained, we also had conversations focused on personal and professional growth. It was during these morning workouts when we first discussed what would develop into The Theory of 5.

Harvey and Bob demonstrated to me how valuable it is to be around people who elevate the way we think — both about the world and about ourselves. People who challenge us and make us examine our own mindset allow us to set sail for new horizons that we never could have imagined for ourselves.

Before meeting these two men, I wanted to be a high school wrestling coach. My goal was to live in a small home or a trailer in the woods surrounded by half a dozen dogs where I could live a simple existence and stay within my personal comfort zone. In fact, at 22, I was very close to buying that small trailer in the woods. What stopped me was that I would be living too far away to do my 4:30 a.m. workouts with Bob.

My life turned out very different from what I had first imagined because of Harvey and Bob.

In addition to giving me practical lessons on how best to harness my time and energy, they also opened my mind to the idea that *I didn't have to do it alone.* They both shared a simple philosophy of why some individuals succeed in specific areas: People who excel understand and have clearly defined their purpose — their *"Why"* — in life. It's their laser focus that makes the difference.

These are the people who dream about their "Why." They talk about it. They study it. They seek counsel.

And then they live it.

Harvey and Bob shared their secret with me: People who excel in life surround themselves with exceptional people. We tend to rise to the level of those around us. If we're surrounded by mediocre people, we'll be satisfied with hitting "average" or "good enough." However, if we surround ourselves with *outstanding* people in their field or profession, we'll be internally motivated to up our game and achieve more than we ever thought possible. And, once our lives begin to change because of our efforts, we'll start to believe in ourselves. That's when we'll *really* start seeing results.

Successful people look for the mentors and role models who will support their *purpose* in life. There are people out there with the knowledge and wisdom we need — and who are willing to share those lessons. In my case, even more important than teaching me how to win, Harvey and Bob first taught me to *believe* that I *could* win. Through their examples, they showed me a world where happiness and prosperity would come to those who seek it and are ready to do the work that would make their dreams a reality.

Your individual experiences will differ from mine; your goals are your own, and the people who can guide you come from many backgrounds. Whatever your circumstances, I know the Theory will be as life changing for you as it has been for me. Once you have your own set of mentors in place, you'll see how much richer your own life will become.

In my case, even more important
than teaching me how to win, Harvey and Bob first
taught me to *believe* that I *could* win.

Role Models Vs. Mentors

WHILE THE TERMS "ROLE models" and "mentors" are often interchangeable, I'll make a distinction between them for the purposes of this book.

- **Role Model** — These are people we admire. They are accomplishing goals in their lives and we want to be like them. They might be outside our personal network, though; the truth is that we may *never* meet them in real life. We can use their lessons or examples in our own lives, but we admire them from afar. In fact, these people might not even be *alive*; history is full of role models who still have valuable lessons to teach.
- **Mentor** — This is someone who observes more talent, potential and personal power within us than we may see in ourselves. They take the opportunity to guide us in becoming the best version of ourselves, and we develop a personal connection with them that will deepen over time.

There's another kind of relationship — ***co-mentoring*** — that can also be mutually beneficial. This is where peers focus on developing each other's skills, habits and attitudes in any or all areas of The Theory of 5.

In this type of relationship, both people reciprocate, supporting one another's development through a continued exchange of ideas and concepts and the sharing of knowledge. There's no "leader/boss" hierarchy here, but is instead strictly focused on improving one another. *In many cases this just happens naturally* — in sports, for example, or when doing business — with people who want to excel.

This has been the experience of Chip Perry, the former CEO of Autotrader.com and current CEO and president of TrueCar. "I've been like a sponge around a lot of people I've worked with in the past, and I learned from everybody around me, but I've never had what you would call a formal mentoring relationship with anybody," he said when interviewed for this book. "I know people talk about mentors, and for some, it's a very important part of how they developed. I know that some people really dedicate themselves to being mentors. I work with a lot of people, and I share what I've learned. People tell me they have learned from me, and I know I've learned from others, but it's never been in the context of formally becoming a mentor or being asked to be a mentor."

Throughout the book, we will be using "mentoring" and "co-mentoring" interchangeably. We may receive guidance in one area from someone while providing them guidance in an area in which we're stronger. These are the relationships that enrich everyone's lives, and where The Theory of 5 really comes to life.

> Throughout the book, we will be using "mentoring" and "co-mentoring" interchangeably.

When we fully embrace The Theory of 5, we'll be building relationships with more than one person to mentor us in various segments of our lives. It's important to ensure the person we're asking is the best one we know for a particular area.

Who are the people we know or admire who can offer us their support and guidance to attain our goals? Will it be a face-to-face relationship? A long-distance/video conference type of connection? Or will it be someone who doesn't know us and who we'll never meet, but whose example we'd like to emulate?

To make the best use of both our time and our mentor's, it is important *to create a list of what we want and the areas where we'd most like to grow.* When we know what we want, we'll be better equipped to approach the right person.

Clearly decide what it is you want. What are your goals? Take a few minutes and write down an initial list of your specific Theory of 5 goals.

Leave Your Ego at the Door

SEEKING GUIDANCE CAN BE a humbling experience. We're admitting that our knowledge and skills are inferior to someone else's. They are excelling and have talents and refined skills we would like to learn. We're acknowledging that, at least in one particular area, they are our superior.

Our pride might take a hit. We need to get over it.

When we ask for guidance from a successful, motivated individual, our egos may get bruised from time to time. A motivated mentor *will care more about our future than our feelings*, and more about us accomplishing our goals than he or she does about protecting our egos. *Be prepared for this*. They aren't being mean. They aren't being cruel. They are giving us a *challenge*. Be open minded and ready to take action, because that's the kind of person they want to mentor. A bruised ego will heal; hard-won lessons will be remembered.

Most of us are familiar with the statement, "Pride cometh before the fall" — and no truer words have ever been written. We're *all* ignorant about something. There's no shame in accepting that. What *is* a shame is when someone is too proud to admit it — when they're too proud to ask for training, advice or education.

We also need to be honest, both with ourselves and with our mentors. Many people have a tendency to present the best version of themselves to the world — even if they have to embellish here and there to make it happen. Others may go the opposite way and actually *downplay* their skills and accomplishments. While we should show up positive and ready to learn from our mentor, we want them to know the *real* us — our strengths *and* our shortcomings. If we were already perfect, we wouldn't *need* a mentor. We shouldn't waste their time pretending to have a perfect life, but instead let them know where we most crave their guidance.

It's important to keep in mind that The Theory of 5 process *never* ends — and that's a good thing! We'll never achieve perfection, and the moment we believe we have is the moment we stop improving and start falling behind. The goal is continuous improvement.

There's a temptation as we get older to dismiss new ideas and innovation as "not important." We didn't need it to get where we are, so its value is minimal. It's trivial. Kid's stuff.

Think about this: How many people got left behind because they thought the personal computer was a toy? The Internet was a "fad"? Social media was just for kids? By the time the truth dawned on them, they were miles behind the curve. Times change, and while the basic foundations of business and life may stay the same, we should never dismiss new ideas out of hand. Social media, analytics, digitalization and the brave new world of artificial intelligence, for example, have revolutionized how we live, work and communicate. When we don't understand some aspect of this, we might need to seek counsel from a *younger* mentor and ask them to share with us some specifics we can use to achieve our goals.

> We'll never achieve perfection, and the moment we believe we have is the moment we stop improving and start falling behind. The goal is continuous improvement.

One of my best friends has said to me several times, "If you find yourself being the smartest person in the group, *run* and find a new group." Let's agree to constantly grow. To do this, we can't afford to close off avenues we need in order to reach our personal and professional goals.

We can be proud of what we have accomplished, but let's never be satisfied. *Life greatly rewards continuous action and growth — so seek those rewards!*

The Anti-Mentor

WHILE MENTORS CAN PROVIDE us with the blueprints of how to succeed in any facet of life, there's another valuable resource that we shouldn't ignore. We can also learn from the bad examples of others. Many times, learning what *not* to do is as important as learning what we should do.

> Many times, learning what *not* to do is as important as what to do.

I have a lifelong friend who is an excellent example of what properly using this mindset can mean for our lives. In his case, his anti-mentor was someone he couldn't avoid as he grew up — his mother.

My friend's mother had dominated his childhood, as she herself had lived through a dysfunctional, haunted childhood. His mother was miserable with her own life. Nothing was ever good enough, the deck was always stacked against her and the world would never cut her a break — *or at least that's what she believed.* And because she couldn't — or wouldn't — figure out how to improve her life, she took out her frustrations on my friend, his siblings and their father.

When one of his siblings left the family dog out in the front yard, for example, she had the dog — beloved by everyone in the family, *including herself* — put to sleep. She did this just to prove a point: "If you don't listen to me, I *will* hurt you, no matter the cost." During my friend's senior year, the week before a big tournament — something he'd been working towards since second grade — she kicked him out of the house because he'd gone out on a date with a girl she did not approve of (the girl he would later go on to marry). He returned home to find his clothing spread across the front yard. On that cold winter night, he had to find a new place to live.

These are only two of the dozens of over-the-top punishments, in addition to her several suicide attempts, my friend and his siblings experienced. He could have used these examples to feel bitter against the world for having such an unpredictable mother. Society is full of people who blame their parents for the shortcomings in their own lives.

My friend, however, learned a different lesson from his anti-mentor.

To this day, he puts a great importance and focus on being a good father and *breaking the patterns* he experienced growing up. He constantly looks for ways to improve his relationship with his children. He wants to provide them with the tools and knowledge they need to survive and thrive in life.

His mother's parenting skills, however, weren't the only way she proved to be an anti-mentor; she provided many examples of how *not* to live in other areas of The Theory of 5:

- **Mindset** — She constantly focused on all the things she didn't have in her life versus all the wonderful things she *did* have if she had just let herself enjoy them. She had plenty to be grateful for. She had a loyal, hardworking husband and healthy children. She had married into a wonderful, kind, close-knit family and lived in a nice neighborhood. She also held to a strict double standard of treatment in her misaligned mindset. She wanted to be shown ultimate respect, all the while disrespecting those closest to her with her words and consistently inconsistent behaviors.
- **Marriage and Relationships** — She had no interest in a partnership with her husband; she was continuously ready to yell, scream, intimidate and bully when she didn't get her way.
- **Health and Fitness** — She practiced poor eating habits and never exercised. Because of these habits, she was overweight and constantly on medication.
- **Business and Finance** — When she was angry with her husband, she regularly maxed out every credit card she had available to her without communicating with him. As a result, they are now penniless and living on Social Security.

Her bad examples gave my friend the motivation to build a better life for himself and his family. It also gave him a healthy *fear* — which is, in itself, a powerful drive — to not repeat her mistakes. "I remembered how she made me feel," he said. "I remember the sadness I felt when she kicked me out of the house on more than one occasion. I remember what it felt like to have her purposely try to embarrass me in front of people. I never want my children — or *anyone* — to feel sadness, pain or stress like that."

In my friend's case, he's managed to turn what could have been negative experiences into something positive. He believes that having an anti-mentor like her has truly been *the greatest motivator in his life.*

He's also taken this positivity and put it into effect in his continuing relationship with his mother. He reminds himself that, as a little girl, she never had the kindness, compassion, empathy and love from her own parents that every child deserves. She was raised in an environment where rage, screaming and insulting were accepted as the norm because that's how *they* were raised. These actions, if left unchecked, get handed down from generation to generation.

My friend was determined that this destructive behavior would end with her generation and not continue into his own. In order to do this, he first had to forgive her for her behavior during his childhood. He did this for himself, for her and for his family. He understood that he would contaminate his own consciousness if he allowed the anger and bitterness to take root in the inner core of his mind. It would only create negativity and inject anxiety and uncertainty into every decision he made. By forgiving her and letting go, he would have the ability to rise above the challenges in his life. To be free to live his best life, he had to accept he would never receive any of the apologies he had hoped to hear — and he has made peace with that.

He loves his mother and truly wants the best for her, but he wants better for himself and his children. Letting go of negative feelings is the only way a person will truly be able to forgive, move on and live a Theory of 5 life.

Recognizing Our Own Anti-Mentors

Many times, with family members or co-workers, we don't have a choice about being around them. For one reason or another, they may be unavoidable. Signs you're dealing with these people include:

- Your pulse starts to race when their name pops up on your caller ID. You feel that lightness in the back of your head and your face flush. Your stomach churns and your fight-or-flight system kicks into overdrive.

- You find yourself putting an exit strategy in place before starting *anything* with them.
- You dread the conversation, knowing you'll be in for hearing yet another extended round of "I'M A VICTIM."

Put this book down for a moment and picture them in your mind. Why are they so exhausting to be around? Why are they always arguing and battling with other people? When did they become so envious? Why are they so unhappy?

Anti-mentors can be motivators unlike any other.

So, what can we learn from the anti-mentors in our own lives? Like my friend, we can use these experiences as fuel to motivate, push, grow and achieve. *If we believe things happen for us and not to us,* we will make that transition into the larger, prosperous, more beautiful world we all deserve.

We're much better off to learn the lessons they have to teach us and then resolve to focus on doing the opposite. Be a *victor*, not a victim. Where they complain, *we attain.*

Anti-mentors can be motivators unlike any other.

Programming
Our Onboard Computer

WHEN MY FRIEND THINKS about his mother, the anti-mentor, instead of being angry at her, he actually finds her life heartbreaking. "She's never realized that the happiness she's always searched for was in front of her most of her adult life," he said. "She was so busy looking at what others had. She didn't realize she *already* had what everyone else was looking for."

> The most successful people I've met have learned to program their onboard computers with positive questions.

Unfortunately, she had programmed her mind — her "onboard computer" — to search only for "things I do not have," and asked herself only negative questions. The only thing this produced was bitter, selfish thoughts and actions. If she would have asked *positive questions*, she could have had more positive results and an exceptional life.

Always On, Always Learning

Our minds are wonderful machines. These onboard computers will set to work finding answers to any question we ask them to solve — automatically. Our subconscious is always listening and ready to spring into action.

The trap many people fall into is that they don't ask high-quality questions. The usefulness of the answers we receive depends on how we phrase the questions.

The most successful people I've met have learned to program their onboard computers with positive questions. Because of this, the answers they receive move them forward because positive questions produce positive answers.

Read that again and say it out loud: *Positive questions produce positive answers.*

Take the following two questions about your life and imagine what the answers might be:

- What *don't* I like about my life, my job or my relationship with my wife/husband?
- What will I do today to *improve* my life, my job and my relationship with my wife/husband?

At first glance, both of these may seem like everyday questions people might ask themselves. The first question, however, comes at the subject from an entirely negative point of view. It will only force our mind to examine and dissect things *wrong* in our current situation. Some of these items might be within our control while others will be outside of our reach. This inadvertently blames others for what we dislike rather than generates ideas that will improve our situation.

The second question focuses on only yielding positive answers to improve our condition, making our onboard computer consider the things within our control. These are the answers we will be able to put into positive action to make ourselves stronger.

The questions we ask ourselves during any event in our lives — consciously or subconsciously — determine how we think (see Figure 1). It's critical that we pay attention to the questions we ask ourselves over the course of the day and, if we catch negativity creeping in, turn it around. It takes effort, awareness and repetition to program our onboard computers to ask positive, high-quality questions so they can produce positive, high-quality answers.

This is a topic we should discuss with our mentors and co-mentors. With their guidance, we'll ask *positive questions,* which in turn provides *positive answers* that create the *actions, behaviors and solutions* we need to bring about the *successful results* we desire.

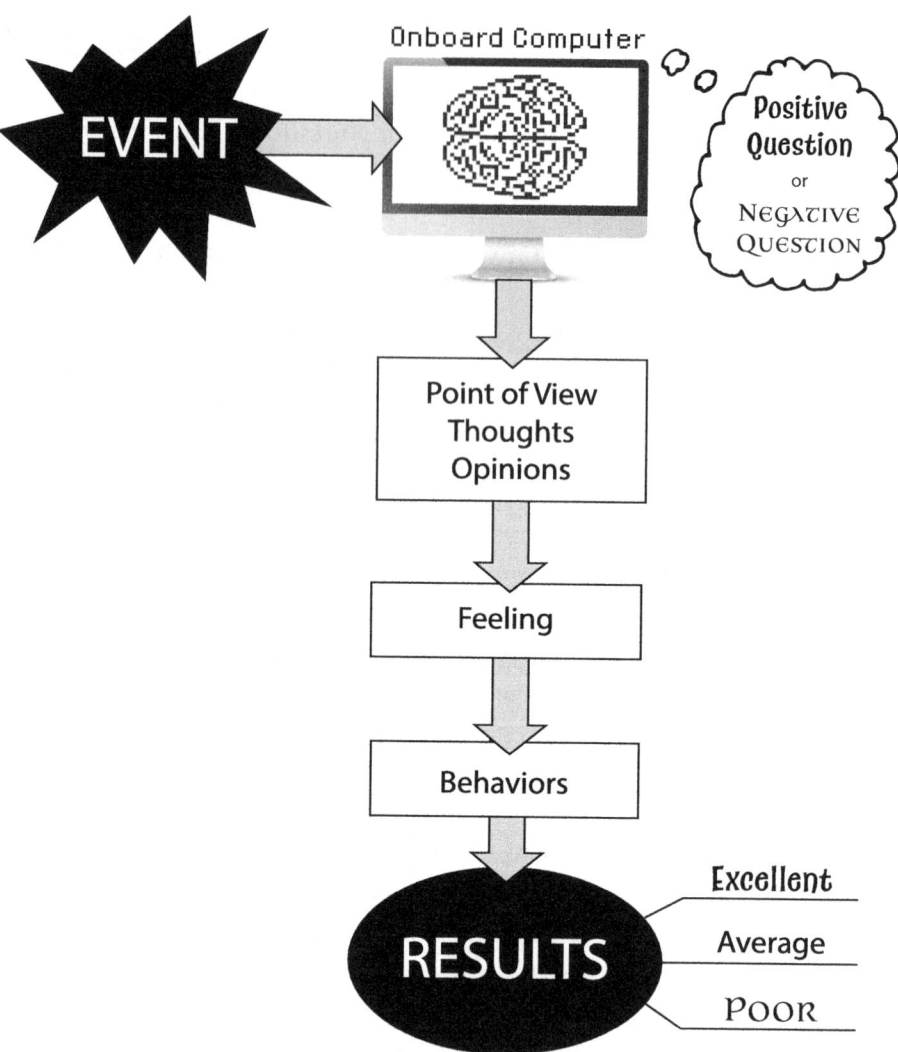

*Figure 1 — Every **EVENT** in our lives goes through our **ONBOARD COMPUTER** and is viewed through the prism of the **QUESTIONS** we ask that computer to solve. These questions are typically negative or positive ("What's wrong with me?" vs. "What am I most grateful for in my life"). The questions we choose to ask determine our **POINT OF VIEW, THOUGHTS and OPINIONS**, which in turn determine our **FEELINGS** about that event. These feelings directly influence our **BEHAVIORS**, which determine the **RESULTS**. Our results are often affected by the questions we input into our onboard computer more than from the event itself.*

Removing Self-Limitations

THE GREEK STOIC PHILOSOPHER Epictetus said, "It is impossible for a man to learn what he thinks he already knows." If our minds are full of bloated self-worth and untested "certainty," there's no room for anything else. If we refuse to learn, we can't grow — we can't *succeed*.

A closed mind is impossible to educate. "Knowing" everything about a subject keeps us stagnant and prevents us from evolving, learning and growing. My mentor Harvey Ritter was fond of saying, *"A man convinced against his will is of the same opinion still."* It's a phrase that runs through my mind — and the minds of those who have worked with Harvey — when we're exposed to new ideas or challenges. Once a person is unwilling to listen to fresh information or other opinions, they start to play it "safe," relying on "the way we've always done it before."

These are the people who avoid "mistakes" at all costs. Mistakes can poke holes in the "all-knowing" image they hold of themselves, so they never risk trying anything new. They fear looking "foolish" or anything other than perfect. The truth is that it's okay to make mistakes. Mistakes show that we're trying to master something new to us. They are a sign of growth and striving to become more tomorrow than we are today.

After a mistake, we know more. We're smarter. We're more experienced. We're *wiser*.

Think about the last trip you took to a destination you'd never visited before. Did the return trip seem much shorter than the outbound journey? Experience makes the difference. On some level, traveling into the unknown always feels perilous. You were ignorant on the way there. You know what to expect when you came back.

Now think of the last time you tried something — really put yourself out there — and it didn't work out. While it might have been disappointing, and perhaps even painful, *it had a value.* The person you became after that mistake knows more than the person you were before. Hard-fought experience is often our most valuable teacher.

We *all* make mistakes. There will be times when we'll fail, and it will hurt. The only people who never fail, though, are those who never try anything. We want to avoid associating with life's bystanders. Chances are they'll never be more than they are right now.

President Theodore Roosevelt — who is a *wonderful* role model in most areas of life — said it best: "Far better is it to dare mighty things, to win glorious triumphs, even though checkered by failure... than to rank with those poor spirits who neither enjoy nor suffer much, because they live in a gray twilight that knows not victory nor defeat."

Fear the Idea of Average

Be *anything* but average.

If you're reading this book, it's not to have an average career, an average marriage or an average life. Ask any parent what he or she hopes for their healthy newborn child. "I'm just hoping my child will be average" is something you'll never hear them say when their child is an infant.

And yet, along the way, people begin to settle for average. "This isn't so bad," they say and, in their minds and hearts, accept and justify that striving for more is "unrealistic."

> "I'm just hoping my child will be average" is something you'll never hear (parents) say when their child is an infant.

One of my co-mentors has said to me many times that unchecked ambition is a disease, invading all areas of our lives and pushing everyone we care about away. Unrestrained apathy, however, is also a sickness, consuming all around it and robbing us of energy, desire and everything that makes life worth living.

Controlled ambition is an engine. *Successful people live life with a mindset of "the sky's the limit."* They put their heart, mind and soul into achieving what's most important to them. They balance the areas of their lives and find ways to win in one area without losing in another. There are times when certain facets of life demand more attention. When starting up a business, for example, our families will see less of us. If our spouse or other family member falls ill, the business might have to make do with less of us for a while. Over time, though, if we improve our performance with The Theory of 5 in all five key areas critical to personal growth, success becomes less of a destination and more a way of *thinking about life.*

To be clear, we don't have to have a single-minded obsession about becoming world famous in our career field, or wealthy beyond measure to finally feel satisfied with our efforts. Again, that unchecked ambition can eventually destroy the other facets of our lives. As stated in the "'OR' Versus 'AND'" chapter of this book, not everyone wants to work 90 hours a week to become a multimillionaire.

What we *don't* want, however, is to live with the knowledge that we didn't put our best effort into what we've set out to accomplish. To become average, all we need to do is the bare minimum. We can be better than that. If we put our hearts and minds into whatever activity we're doing at the moment, we'll see much better results — and that adds up to living a fuller life.

Over my career, I've spoken with hundreds of people in their 60s, 70s and 80s. After seeing life from their perspective, one of my biggest fears is *regret.* I don't want to be the person who looks back at his life and says, "I should have," "I could have" or "I would have." I don't want to be bitter because I did not allow myself to forgive people, express my feelings, stay in contact with certain people, take opportunities or face challenges head on.

I know this because I see that the happiest, most prosperous older mentors in my life have few regrets because they have lived their life to the fullest — and continue to do so. They've taken chances. They've made mistakes. They've had failures. *They've learned.* Just like everyone, they've faced their own challenges and have been hurt and disappointed by people in their lives. They have embraced forgiveness. They've grown and used those lessons to excel. They've never settled for average, and they've reaped the rewards. They have *lived* The Theory of 5.

Pleasure Versus Pain, Passion and Perseverance

My mentors have modeled the philosophy that short-term, quick-fix pleasures must be set aside to build a life with a firm foundation. Some of the actions we must take might have an element of pain or discomfort to them in the short term. Those are the ones, however, that will pay off in ways which matter across our lives.

We might, for example, have to get up 90 minutes earlier to get our workout in before the day starts making its demands of us. It would feel better in the short term to stay in our warm bed. By making the time to exercise, though, we know we'll feel better about ourselves and have more energy for the rest of the day.

In business, if we get in earlier than our team members or the competition, we'll have time to plan, prepare and implement our ideas to get the results we need for that promotion or to grow our business. This will reward us in allowing us to live in a nicer neighborhood and to send our children to a higher-quality school. We'll be able to better provide for our family. We'll be able to have special moments and experiences with the additional income. We'll have less stress because we're less worried about money. The hard work, effort and actions we put in to produce superior results — effort that others *didn't* — will pay off. We set aside short-term pleasure and reap the long-term rewards of perseverance and true grit.

In discussions with my mentors, we've discovered that the "average" person gives up a new goal or dream if they don't see results in the first few days or weeks. To excel, these actions take passion and persistence. They are not "once in a while" behaviors; they must be followed through daily, weekly and yearly, decade after decade. *This perseverance is the one common trait we've seen in all successful people.*

Or, as my good friend and co-mentor David Lewis (president and founder of David Lewis & Associates) says in his meetings, "*Stop* doing what everyone else is doing. That is just a way to receive what everyone else receives — average results."

In discussions with my mentors, we've discovered
that the "average" person gives up a new goal
or dream if they don't see results in the first few days
or weeks. To excel, these actions take passion
and persistence.

Give Back and Pay It Forward

WE LIVE IN AN era of social media, the Internet and other forms of enhanced communication. With these tools come more opportunities to compare our situation not only with those around us, but with those living extravagant lifestyles. When I was a young child, I had no idea our family struggled financially; I actually thought we were rich. Now, society seems to be locked in a race to see who can live most beyond their means.

Many in today's society seem to live by the motto, "What's in it for me — and ONLY me?" My mentors have stressed the importance of avoiding these people whenever possible. If we ever catch ourselves falling into this mindset, we pull it out by the roots before it takes hold and sucks the energy from our lives.

We all need to look out for ourselves in this world; that's a given. After all, with the possible exception of our parents or other loved ones, no one will care as much about our success as we do. When self-interest is *all* we care about, though, that's a sad, short-sighted, debilitating attitude to hold. Compassion is a strong trait of The Theory of 5.

Through their actions, my mentors modeled and demonstrated to me that successful people *do care* about those around them, especially those people who have the desire and commitment to excel. They understand we don't live in this world alone. We're all connected, and the people in our lives are as vital to us as we are to them. The "Law of Reciprocity" philosophy is true throughout our lives. When we share our knowledge, *their success is our success.*

Besides the joy of doing something for someone else, mentors *do* get something for themselves in return for their efforts: The best way to understand and internalize something is to teach it. In 1993, I was one of the three lead trainers of the Saturn Corporation. One day, I was able to sit down with Skip LeFauve, president of Saturn, and I took the opportunity to ask him, "How do you stay so passionate and motivated?" His answer was simple: "I teach." He said when he is teaching someone, it reinforces the lesson within his own mind and behaviors. "It motivates me and keeps me accountable. And, if I don't do what I say when teaching, that would make me a hypocrite. The thought of someone thinking of me as a hypocrite pushes me to walk my talk."

Becoming a mentor to others is an excellent way to motivate ourselves by lifting someone else through sharing of knowledge, modeling proper behavior and providing them with encouragement. Sometimes being a mentor just means listening to them and asking the right questions.

There's an importance to rooting for each other, both in words and in action. Our families, friends and team members will appreciate our support, and will support us when we need it.

The happiest people I know actively show the people around them they love them, care about them and *always* have their backs. They *never* let them doubt it. They also make a point to support people, just as they were supported by others in the past. Mentoring isn't a one-time event, but a cycle. Sometimes, we'll need the mentoring; other times, we'll be asked for our knowledge, support and encouragement.

My mentors have found the truth in a simple but powerful statement: When a person provides value to the world, that person is rewarded with happiness and prosperity in their life. Those willing to assist others in achieving their dreams will themselves find support when they need it the most.

Life is interactive. Living a Theory of 5 life means making sure we're paying attention to both sides of the mentoring equation.

When a person provides value to the world,
that person is rewarded with happiness
and prosperity in their life.

Taking the First Step

USE THIS BOOK AS you see fit, in any order that makes the most sense for your unique situation. I would, however, urge you to read it all. Learning to excel in every area of The Theory of 5 is essential to reaching your full potential.

By living a Theory of 5 lifestyle — and that's what it is, a *lifestyle*, not a bandage or a shortcut — you are about to separate yourself from the pack. You'll move away from those who only wish, whine, complain or otherwise make excuses why they've never achieved what you're about to accomplish. You will stay ahead by consistently taking action. Where others give up, you will *get* up and keep going.

> You will stay ahead by consistently taking action. Where others give up, you will *get* up and keep going.

The first element of The Theory of 5 we'll examine is our spiritual lives. It's something that many of us don't pay enough — or, in some cases, *any* — attention to. This is a major building block of the foundation of our lives, though, whether we realize it or not. Taking the time to examine our beliefs and seeking guidance and support from others not only helps us when life's challenges seem overwhelming, but also allows us to find perspective when times are good. In this area, like all the others in The Theory of 5, finding mentors can make all the difference.

Use this book as you see fit, in any order that makes the most sense for your unique situation. I would, however, urge you to read it all. Learning to excel in every area of The Theory of 5 is essential to reaching your full potential.

**Finding Spirituality
That Works for Us**

Finding Our Place in a Larger World

DEFINING OUR SPIRITUALITY IS a lifelong process; there is no finish line. It's not something we can "accomplish" and finalize. Most successful people I've known have believed that, to become a well-rounded individual, it's critical to include spirituality as a way of life.

> People are willing to share and assist us on our spiritual journeys — some even feel *called* to do so.

Finding our way in the world by understanding that we're not at the center of it can, at first glance, seem counterintuitive. Seeing the world as a bigger place than we can comprehend and then *accepting* the idea we are not in control of everything, however, can be empowering. With a spiritual and moral framework in place, our decisions become easier to make. Those choices might not be easy to live out — doing the right thing can often be more difficult than what might feel good in the moment — but they provide peace of mind that would otherwise be difficult to achieve.

It also can be a lonely road if we walk it alone.

The great truth, however, is that *there's no reason to do so*. People are willing to share and assist us on our spiritual journeys — some even feel *called* to do so. In my opinion, this is the easiest of all five theories to find a mentor and a great place to start on your Theory of 5 path. It's just a matter of finding the right people to support and guide us with our questions — and to challenge us when necessary. These are the individuals who will be there to consistently raise our standards and remind us of our purpose: to grow and become the best version of ourselves.

The Author's Journey

BEFORE WE REALLY BEGIN to delve into this topic, I should point out that I was brought up as a Christian. It's the religion I still practice, so my examples and experiences draw from that faith; your experiences and beliefs might be different, and that's perfectly fine — it's a very personal decision. I do believe in the need of taking part in *some* form of spirituality, however, be it Catholicism, Protestantism, Judaism, Islam, Hinduism or another faith or philosophical conviction. My mentors and I believe it's critical for us to ask the important questions and see ourselves as a part of a larger world. That need is universal, and that's the main thrust of what we'll be discussing here.

> I also want to be transparent with you and say that spirituality is something that has not been a consistent calling for me for most of my life.

I also want to be transparent with you and say that spirituality is something that has not been a consistent calling for me for most of my life. I've gone through seasons of my life where my focus on spirituality has waxed and waned, depending on the challenges I was facing at the time and the responsibilities I was dealing with. What has been constant, though, is *the need for understanding something bigger than myself*, and spirituality is crucial to attaining that perspective.

One of the first times I remember having a "spiritual awakening" was in 10th grade after reading Norman Vincent Peale's *The Power of Positive Thinking*. I finished it before I was set to wrestle the top-ranked wrestler in my district's weight class. This wrestler also happened to be a senior and was the region's reigning champ. In his book, Peale mentions the Bible verse Philippians 4:13, which reads *"I can do all things through Christ who strengthens me."* That phrase lodged in my mind and heart and gave me an outlook and confidence that has stayed with me to this day.

As I prepared to face my opponent, I was nervous — and not without reason. When it comes to high school wrestling, Lehigh Valley, Pennsylvania is the top high school wrestling area in the United States. The district champs of our area would routinely defeat most state champions in the country. In preparing for the match, I repeated Philippians 4:13 in my mind so often it became something of a mantra to me. It helped me generate the confidence needed to bring my best performance to the match, and I ended up beating the champ.

Of course, this is not to say that, because I kept the verse in mind, Jesus was on my side over my opponent.

What it *did* do was change my outlook and thinking to give me a bigger world view. I'd done the work to prepare for the match. I was focused and had trained since grade school to hone myself both mentally and physically. What that verse gave me was the knowledge that I wasn't alone; I could draw from a strength bigger than my own. That belief and confidence allowed me to perform at my best for that challenge.

As a child, up through the age of 8 or so, our family consistently went to church. After that, I really didn't go regularly again until I was 22, when I got engaged. My fiancée was Catholic and, since I wasn't passionately devoted to a particular faith, I decided to take classes to convert. I went to classes twice a month for almost a year, meeting with Monsignor Murphy at St. Thomas Moore in Allentown, Pennsylvania, and *loved* the process. I had a great time meeting with him one-on-one and discussing religion and philosophies of life. The class was only supposed to last three months, but we decided to extend these discussions for several more. Both of us were enjoying the topics, debates and life's philosophical discussions.

Becoming a father reignited my desire to engage with the church. In addition to attending church, I also searched for information and lessons to help me build my own spiritual life. In the 1990s, for instance, I attended several conventions conducted by Promise Keepers, a men's ministry founded by Bill McCartney, the football coach of the University of Colorado-Boulder. These conventions were focused on ways men could unite and commit to becoming exceptional fathers and husbands. Experiences like this can give us information and a framework to structure our spiritual thoughts and beliefs.

My mentors have taught me that having a spiritual life isn't simply for those who are comfortable living their faith "out loud." Just because someone doesn't constantly discuss spirituality, quote scriptures publicly or make a point to get on their knees to pray doesn't mean they're not spiritual. Many people live a quiet but deeply spiritual life. In my own case, I rarely discuss religion with anyone except for my circle of spiritual mentors. And yet, spirituality is important to me, shaping my decisions and forming my actions and reactions to life's challenges.

The question of faith is one of the most personal decisions we'll ever make. We believe it's important to find guidance in order to live our faith. Many times, simply finding the right questions to ask will shape our spiritual journey.

Just because someone doesn't constantly discuss spirituality, quote scriptures publicly or make a point to get on their knees to pray doesn't mean they're not spiritual.

Our Focus in Life

A COMMON ELEMENT ALL the mentors in my life share is that each and every one has a strong spiritual or religious belief. Most are not zealots, by any means, but they have internalized a spiritual system that has served them well in all areas of their life.

We've had discussions on the topic and believe the reason many find it difficult or impossible to prosper in their lives comes down to focus. They only look to excel in one or two areas. They throw all their attention and energy in that direction, leaving other areas neglected. Spirituality, in fact, is one of the most often-neglected areas in our lives, and we may pay a price when we don't have it. When hit with life's setbacks or heartbreak — as we all will experience in our lives — people without the larger worldview that spirituality provides often have nothing to fall back upon.

For many people reading this, spirituality is an area of The Theory of 5 that becomes one pillar which supports us in all the things we set out to achieve. Missing this essential building block, my mentors have come to believe, limits us to what we can make of our lives.

Spiritual Vs. Religious Vs. Secular Outlooks

One of the main advantages of maintaining a spiritual viewpoint is that it takes us out of the center of our own universe. While the strictly secular point of view allows one to inquire freely about nature, morality, philosophy and other facets of the human experience, the spiritual perspective tells us there is a *higher* power. It offers the viewpoint that we are not alone. We are part of a larger picture, and that while we are responsible for our actions and the effect we have on the world around us, we are not ultimately responsible for — or in control of — everything.

As I mentioned earlier in the introduction of *The Theory of 5*, my family has endured several heartbreaking tragedies in the past few years. These are the times when most people ask "Why? How is this fair?" It's in times like these where it's invaluable to have faith to fall back on. It's been incredibly powerful to have a community and mentors to challenge us and to let us know there's a higher power. Cold logic does not and *cannot* give most people comfort; from the spiritual perspective, there's more to life than just the things we look at every day. It's in times like these that Philippians 4:13 still passes through my mind. By repeating this mantra, I'm reminded that the world is bigger than what I can see, and I'm never alone in life's struggles.

Even when things are going well, there's a lot to be gained by having a wider spiritual perspective. We may be highly motivated by nature or desire, but there will be times when we might ask ourselves if everything we're working for is worth the time, effort and energy we're putting into it. By having a moral, spiritual compass, we'll get a better perspective on the value of what we're doing and why we're doing it.

Most people long to be in control, especially those of us in business or leadership roles who are used to being the one in charge. The painful truth, however, is that *total control is an illusion*. Things completely outside of our control can change our lives in a heartbeat or over the course of years. The spiritual perspective allows us to recognize this and find solace in the idea that events outside of our influence are not our responsibility. It also provides us with a community of like-minded people to support us through the difficult times.

When Tragedy Strikes

WHERE DO WE TURN when the worst life can throw at us brings us to our knees? Even when the pain digs deeper than we believed possible, even when heartache alters the tapestry of our family, spirituality can give us the lifeline we can use to pull through these times. Many of us rely on spiritual messages and ideas to lead us to calmer waters and greener pastures of hope.

Our spiritual community also provided my family with a wonderful support system of people who cared and went out of their way to support and walk with us. If we didn't have these people, it would have been difficult to pull ourselves together and keep moving forward.

Understand that, just because somebody believes in a faith or has just started their spiritual journey, they are not immune to experiencing tragedy or loss in their lives. No matter what our beliefs or outlook are, we can never know when our time on earth will end. Living a Theory of 5 life is about living our best lives and positively impacting lives — in good times and in tragedy — with the time we have left on earth.

Living a Theory of 5 life is about living our best lives and positively impacting lives — in good times and in tragedy — with the time we have left on earth.

Finding Our Flock

A SPIRITUAL MENTOR ONCE said to me, *"The bigger you make God in your life, the smaller your problems are. If you want to live a peaceful, productive life, you have to do it on purpose."* One of the most important steps we can make toward this is finding the right church or organization to join and finding mentors to help us along our path.

And, when searching for a church to join, there's never been an easier time to make an informed decision than now. Thanks to the Internet and the increasingly effective ways churches are learning to market themselves online, we can often take a virtual tour of the facility. We can check out its programs and activities and observe the sermons and services. From the Christian perspective, a church is not only motivated to grow for growth's sake, but is tasked to move people to Christ. Because of this mandate, they have an intrinsic reason to bring people in using all the available tools. We can take advantage of every bit of information we have available to find the right fit for our needs and personalities.

When looking for a spiritual place to call home, we have to determine what's most important for us in order to keep us engaged. For me, personally, there is *power in passion* — that's what I'm drawn to. I have to see and hear the enthusiasm and conviction in the speaker's voice and actions while they address their congregation. In a church setting, the old saying "the speed of the leader is the speed of the pack" holds true. The leader of a congregation, more often than not, sets the tone and tempo for the church's activities, both for internal ministry and for ministry outreach.

When a church has multiple pastors, you can often see the difference between the passionate and "autopilot" speakers in action. The speakers with the most passion, who *truly* believe the message they are presenting, who are *on fire* with the ideas they are trying to share, will soon be speaking in front of a packed house every time. They may even be moved to the services in the hours that are more difficult to fill, and they'll fill them just the same. No one goes to church — or *any* presentation for that matter — to be bored. Some may show up out of duty or habit, but people *want* to be excited.

As someone who has regularly worked six or seven days a week for the past 36 years, Sunday mornings are precious to me. The prospect of getting up on my only morning off and listening to a speaker who doesn't engage my emotions or give me something to think about doesn't motivate me. Why *should* I go listen to someone who doesn't give the impression of believing what he or she is saying? *Going through the motions doesn't add anything to our spiritual life.* Being bored doesn't get the job done.

The delivery of the message can be as important as the message itself. The best speakers can relate spiritual messages to *our* real-life circumstances. A well-thought-out sermon can echo throughout our week — or in the best cases, our entire life. Messages that challenge us in all parts of our life — work, family, fitness, ethics and more — fully engage us spiritually, and *that's* when we'll experience the best growth.

And, as time goes on, we must make sure the church we attend continues to meet our needs. If we find ourselves not wanting to get up and listen to a sermon on Sunday, or if we have that gut feeling telling us we're not receiving what we need, then we need to take a hard look and decide if our requirements might be better met elsewhere. Most people go through ups and downs in their faith. It's not necessary to make an abrupt decision — unless there are circumstances happening in the church we believe *require* us to make a choice. If that feeling persists over time, however, it might be time to move on.

Going through the motions doesn't add anything to our spiritual life. Being bored doesn't get the job done.

Iron Sharpens Iron

ALONG WITH A CHURCH family, we need mentors to help us successfully walk a spiritual path and grow as a successful, productive person. And, because of the opportunities we have to share information online, we have options:

- **Face-To-Face Mentors** — These are the mentors and co-mentors we find at church or in other aspects of our lives who will model the correct behavior, mindset and actions. They not only give us a yardstick to measure ourselves to but also help us become the person we're striving to be. These are people who we can observe being awesome spouses, parents and business people who are living a healthy lifestyle. We can watch them deal with people in ways where their spirituality and values shine through and are in alignment with *our* visions and goals. They follow their moral and spiritual compass.

    For me, *I want mentors who carry themselves in a way that inspires me to be a better person.* I need those who will challenge me to be stronger in my faith and who makes me understand the invaluable benefits of knowing I don't have to do this alone. These are people who know me well enough to ask the right questions, listen to my reasoning and confront and guide me when I fall short.

- **Virtual Mentors** — As noted in the mindset section, thanks to the Internet and other forms of communications, we can select mentors who we'll *never* meet and who will *never* know they mentored us. In our modern world, there's no excuse for anyone — even extremely shy people who have trouble asking for help or overly proud people who don't want to be seen asking for help — not to have mentors. These spiritual mentors from afar might be the preacher across the country whose sermons we can listen to online. They might be someone who gets into the news by setting a good example with their actions or works. They might be an author whose work inspires us. It might be a podcast host who presents ideas that challenge our thinking. We need to be open to those who we believe deserve our attention and whose words or actions test our thoughts and attitudes. While they might never know what impact they've had on our life, *we will.*

Also, we should be aware that this type of mentorship can work both ways, and our own actions can have a greater impact than we might ever know. Sometimes, we don't realize that the little things we do can mean so much to somebody. People whom I've spoken to or who attended a presentation I made 10 or 20 years ago have later come up to me and say, "I remember you told me this." I had no idea someone was listening so closely, and I was humbled that it made an impression on them. That's one of the best compliments we can get in life.

> While it might be difficult to hear — our first impulse might be to become defensive — good mentors will ask the tough questions.

One of my absolute favorite Bible verses is Proverbs 27:17 — *"As iron sharpens iron, so one person sharpens another."* This maxim, one I learned as a 7-year-old from my YMCA wrestling coach Don Pryor is one that plays out in all the areas of The Theory of 5, but it's never truer than it is here. This message is the very heart of mentoring. People who want to be great must *challenge* each other to be great.

For a mentor to have an effect on us, we must be willing to be challenged and to take it in the spirit a true mentor intends. If a mentor *actually* cares about our well-being and spiritual progress, they will tell us when we're falling short. While it might be difficult to hear — our first impulse might be to become defensive — good mentors will ask the tough questions. We need to do our part to answer those questions and face up to those challenges.

As a young man, one of my spiritual mentors gave me a piece of advice that has served me well ever since. "When you make a mistake, admit it quickly," he said. "Confess and repent, which helps to rebuild trust." This went along with his "Three Stages for Mistakes":

- Admit It
- Learn From It
- Don't Repeat It

That doesn't mean there won't be penalties for our mistakes or bad decisions — there will *always* be consequences for the actions we take in life. Having the mindset of being able to admit our mistakes, however, allows us to heal and to get a fresh start on living our best lives. Admitting when we're wrong doesn't mean we're weak; it means we're *strong*. It means we are exceptional and worthy of being a role model to our friends, co-workers and family.

We all know people who never admit when they're wrong. They may be in our family, at our office or in some other area of our lives where we can't avoid them. What is your opinion of that person? The people we form strong bonds with aren't the ones who never make mistakes; we bond with the ones who apologize when they screw up and learn from it. They're the ones who change and grow *with* us.

We all do foolish, childish, selfish things from time to time. We all have those moments. We need mentors who care about us enough to listen to us, to challenge us and to correct us. Sometimes, they simply say, *"That's not you — you're better than this."* It's in this way we grow to be who we're capable of becoming.

Our Monday-Through-Saturday Path

I TRULY UNDERSTAND IT's easier on a Sunday to think about and preach about The 10 Commandments than it is to live them during the week.

This is why it's so important to surround ourselves with good people in all aspects of our life. The people we associate with during the week, during the month and during our lifetimes are the ones who will really have the most influence on us. That hour of church on a Sunday isn't going to be enough to get us through the trials, temptations and sheer grind of our everyday life.

> I truly understand it's easier on a Sunday to think about and preach about The 10 Commandments than it is to live them during the week.

And we can't fall into the trap of thinking that, if someone doesn't agree with our spiritual choices precisely, they automatically have nothing they can teach us. Most of us will experience pious people who are great at talking about religion but fall far short when it comes to walking the walk. And, we've seen others who don't talk about it at all. They might not have *any* discernible spiritual leanings but live a cleaner, healthier, kinder life than those who do nothing but talk about their faith. Ultimately, people's *actions, behaviors and attitudes* are much better indicators of *who they are* — and the influence they'll have on us — than what they say. We must keep our eyes and our ears open and choose the spiritual counsel with whom we want to spend our time.

Setting the Example

ONE OF THE ACTIVITIES that supported me in my spiritual desire to grow was raising our children. Being accountable for *their* development provided a context for me to become an active participant in our spirituality. Also, when my mentors challenged me, questions that struck me to my core were, "How would you want your daughters treated?" and "If that was your son, how would you want him to handle that?"

When we introduce our children to religious or spiritual concepts, I believe it's important that we approach it in a fun, entertaining way. When my daughters were between the ages of 2 and 10, we had religious videos that told Bible stories in a way that captured and held their attention. We had books of Bible stories written for children, religious coloring books and other material that got them thinking. We made a point to keep it at an appropriate age and spiritual level so that they could comprehend the underlying message.

As children mature, it's natural that they'll start asking questions. Our parental choice was to take a light hand and guide them. We liked to answer questions with our own questions:

- "What do you think?"
- "Why do you think that?"
- "Why do you ask that?"
- "How would you handle that situation? Why?"

Having them answer their own questions, especially those asked with innocence and curiosity, allowed them to *internalize* the topic much more than if we just told them what we believed. When children are young, they believe anything their parent tells them. As they become teenagers and start questioning, that's when they have to start thinking about it on their own.

It's also important for children, as they grow and mature, to build their own circles of accountability and find their own mentors. Like all the other facets of The Theory of 5, we *want* them to be tested. We wanted people to challenge our children while they were growing up. They needed to know that the world wouldn't be easy on them, and to be successful and vital, they required doses of reality. Parents must encourage their children to see challenges as opportunities for growth, and not obstacles standing in the way of what they want.

Parents must encourage their children to see challenges as opportunities for growth, and not obstacles standing in the way of what they want.

Concepts Learned Along the Way

MUCH OF MY SUCCESS as a businessman and in life can be traced back to lessons I've learned in my spiritual journey. My mind is wired towards business and competition — I most easily internalize information by looking at it through that lens. Different messages will resonate differently for you, depending on how your mind works, but some of the most influential concepts I've gained include:

- **Servant Leadership** — This is one of the most powerful lessons a leader can learn. I first came across this idea when I worked with the Saturn Corporation — its philosophy and major focus was on leadership — and I've carried it with me ever since. The idea of servant leadership is ancient; it's one of the foundational concepts of Christianity. Recall the story of Jesus washing the feet of His disciples. In doing this act, He demonstrated that to *truly* lead, we should have a spirit that allows us to truly *serve*. We'll discuss the concept of servant leadership more in depth in the business section of *The Theory of 5*. For now, just know that servant leaders are driven to make a difference and a connection in people's lives. People don't care how much we *know* until they know how much we care.

- **Persistence** — There are several stories and passages in the Bible that demonstrate the value of persistence, of keeping our goals in mind and our path true. Hebrews 10:36, for example, states, "You need to persevere so that when you have done the will of God, you will receive what He has promised." In all areas of The Theory of 5 — business, marriage, children, fitness and spirituality — persistence is the key to attaining success.

- **Integrity** — The "Parable of the Talents" (Matthew 25 and Luke 19) is perhaps the best-known example of using our abilities to make the most of what we're given. In this story, a wealthy man who must travel entrusts portions of his wealth, called in that time and place "talents," to three of his servants. He gives five to one servant, two to another and one to a third. When he comes back, he finds that two of the servants put their talents to work, invested and grew the wealth; the other "played it safe," hiding his talent by burying it in the ground. The two who had the work ethic to use what they had been given were rewarded and called "good and faithful servants." The one who hid from opportunity was punished and cast out. It's a story as true in business as it is in life. We must, to the best of our abilities, use what we've been given to the best of our abilities.
- **Pride** — Proverbs 16:18 tells us that "Pride goes before destruction, and haughtiness before a fall." I've seen this in practice and experienced it. There are a lot of people who let their egos get in the way — in business, in marriage or any other area of their life. When that happens, there's usually a rude awakening coming in their immediate future. Pride keeps us from learning the lessons we need to learn and asking for guidance when we need it the most.

Pride keeps us from learning the lessons
we need to learn and asking for guidance
when we need it the most.

Putting the Lessons
into Practice in Business

MOST OF US SPEND a lot of our time at our jobs with our co-workers — often, more time than we spend with our families — that it just makes sense to include this time as part of our spiritual journey. Having a brain wired for business, the ideas of servant leadership and framing business in a spiritual context are concepts I have worked to develop.

I believe the best leaders are able to create a vision and stress values that give purpose to team member's actions and efforts. They help their team generate the passion necessary to make a difference, both for themselves and for their clients and customers.

Workers feel most invested in the company's well-being when they know the company and its leaders *actively care about them as individuals,* instead of treating them as replaceable cogs in the machine. By truly being concerned for their team — not faking it with hollow platitudes — true leaders can create a sense of unity and family within their team. That feeling will translate into an elite organization with a culture that will dominate their competition.

Leaders who ignore this spiritual and human element of the workplace, on the other hand, are setting themselves up to have staff members who are, *at best,* indifferent. Their team members will be looking for other positions, for leaders and companies who are *passionate* about their team's personal and professional growth.

Taking Stock

SPIRITUALITY, UNLIKE THE OTHER sections of The Theory of 5, isn't something we can quantify. We can look at our bank balance or profit statement to see if our business is going well. We can often tell just by looking if someone is in good physical shape.

Spiritual matters, however, can be tougher to gauge, but just as important to measure. We have to keep an open dialogue with ourselves, checking in and digging deep to see if we're meeting the goals we *know* we're capable of attaining. To live a life of happiness and prosperity, it's crucial that we touch base regularly with those who are walking along in faith, love and hope with us. It's vital to keep the lines of communication open with those who challenge us and call us out when they see we're falling short. As English poet John Donne wrote, "No man is an island," and that sentiment is the bedrock of spiritual and religious undertakings.

> We have to keep an open dialogue with ourselves, checking in and digging deep to see if we're meeting the goals we *know* we're capable of attaining.

Spirituality has an effect on every other aspect of our lives and is an excellent foundation for creating and maintaining a loving, supportive marriage or relationship. In the next section, we'll take a look at how my mentors have used spiritually and many other elements in building marriages of equals.

Ultimately, people's *actions, behaviors and attitudes*
are much better indicators of *who they are* — and
the influence they'll have on us — than what they say.
We must keep our eyes and our ears open and
choose the spiritual counsel with whom we want
to spend our time.

A Marriage of Equals

"What's Left"
Vs. "What's Deserved"

OF THE ELEMENTS DISCUSSED in *The Theory of 5*, the work of creating and maintaining a successful marriage or relationship might have the biggest impact on the other four. If care isn't taken in building this critical component of our lives, its failure will affect *everything* else. Divorce splits assets. Breakups drastically increase the difficulty of parenting. Constant strife creates self-doubt and challenges the things we believe in. It can and *will* negatively impact our health.

> The happiest people I know have mastered the skill of building relationships with their spouse or partner.

And yet, personal relationships are the one area many of us pay little attention to. Work puts constant demands on us, the needs of our children often take precedence over the needs of our spouse and, of course, life in general happens. Sometimes, we only give our husbands, wives or partners "what's left" — and that might not be very much.

It might not be *enough*.

To make a meaningful change in our relationships, we have to take an honest look at ourselves and our behaviors. *In my experience, it's natural to judge ourselves by our good intentions while we judge others — often our spouses — by their actions.*

This profound idea hit me like a lightning bolt one morning. Throughout the day, we might have grand intentions — we'll plan to take our partner out for a night on the town to show our love and appreciation, for instance — but after a long day, those intentions fall by the wayside. While we were *thinking* of our partner, our *actions* didn't rise to meet our good intentions. And, since our spouse isn't a mind reader, our intentions meant nothing. Building a solid relationship requires *our actions to match our intentions.* To build and maintain a solid relationship our intentions and our actions have to match. It means we walk the talk.

A truly happy and prosperous relationship provides us with a pool of strength we can use to deal with whatever life throws at us. Knowing we have the support of a life partner will allow us to overcome whatever obstacle we might encounter or give us the stamina to endure the unavoidable. Also, life is just more fun when we can share our dreams, hopes and worldly possessions with someone we love and appreciate. The happiest people I know have mastered the skill of building relationships with their spouse or partner. More than simply being a partner or lover, they are each other's *friend.*

The 10 Elements
of a Successful Relationship

The idea of "soulmates" is a tempting one — finding that singular person we were meant to be with. Through discussions with my mentors and examining the relationships of my own life, however, *I believe the reality is that true soulmates are made, not born.* It takes consistent effort, patience and communication to make our relationship the one that lasts. The most devoted, loving couples continually put forth the effort to strengthen their bond — the bond that makes each other their soulmate.

Each relationship is unique, but there are certain attitudes and behaviors that someone can point to in a successful marriage as being key to the couple's happiness and prosperity. *My mentors have shared with me the 10 elements that are necessary to discover our "soulmate" within our own spouse or partner:*

1. **Love** — It may seem obvious, but a marriage without love is like a car without gasoline; it may look fine on the outside, but it's not going anywhere. There are different elements that go into what may at first seem like a simple emotion — infatuation, lust, friendship and others. To make a marriage work, however, there needs to be that enduring, all-powerful *desire to be with our partner*, in both good times and bad. Marriage should never just seem like a "good idea"; it should be an "I can't imagine my life without this person" type of idea. We also must let them know how important they are to us. It's the little things that we do that matter: the smile when we walk in the door, holding hands and that tender touch. Words matter, as well. Most spouses don't want their partners to only *show* them they love them — although that's vital; they also want to *hear* it. We need to make it a point to

tell them we love them. Words and actions are both necessary; we shouldn't waste any opportunity to communicate to our partner what they mean to us.

2. **Commitment** — It's easy to be with someone in the first stages of love or marriage (or, at least, it *should* be). Soon enough, though, life starts to encroach on the honeymoon phase. It's at this point we'll see what marriage, and life, will actually be: an inevitable series of highs and lows. It's here that commitment — knowing our spouse is *there* for us, we are *there* for them and we are a *team* — really comes into play. A marriage where one partner doubts how committed the other is to them is a doomed marriage.

> We should maintain the ability to be awed by our partner and keep our eyes open for both the "wow" occasions and the everyday moments that enrich our lives together.

3. **Respect** — *Successful marriages are unions of equals, but each partner brings their own set of skills, talents, expertise and knowledge to the relationship.* The happiest couples find value in what the other adds to the relationship. One partner might be better at finances, for example, while the other is handier at repairing things around the house. One might be better at maintaining relationships with family and friends, while the other is better at organizing the home. Both partners contribute to the wellbeing of their lives together; they are just stronger in different areas. They also are not shy about voicing their respect and letting the other lead in areas where they are the expert. We should maintain the ability to be awed by our partner and keep our eyes open for both the "wow" occasions and the everyday moments that enrich our lives together.

4. **Support** — In a successful marriage, each partner feels supported by the other, to the point that there is no doubt that, if they need encouragement — if only to listen — that reassurance will always be there. There are times when we'll need to be there for the other person, depending on what's going on in his or her life, and there are times when we'll need to hold onto each other. Relationships will either fall apart in hard times because of a lack of support

or be made stronger because we both know we have each other's backs through anything. Support is a key component of commitment; it's the two of us against the world. In many cases, the only thing we might be able to do is just listen to them and let them talk about their feelings; it's still crucial that we do this and never let our spouse doubt that *we're their biggest fan.*

5. **Humor** — Living life without a sense of humor can be a long, painful experience. The ability to make each other laugh is a gift that lets oxygen into our relationship. That's not to say our lives together should be a stand-up comedy act, but we must make sure that our lives together aren't grim exercises in survival. Laughter is exceptional medicine, literally. Research has proven that people with a sense of humor have fewer symptoms of physical illness. Humor also helps a couple bond; it's harder to stay mad at someone who makes us laugh. In many discussions with my mentors, humor has been a key ingredient in their relationships. Humor puts things in perspective, reduces levels of stress, mitigates burnout and is healing. It's a wonderful experience. Bottom line: **Life's more fun with humor.**

6. **Communication** — As in sync as we might feel with our spouse or significant other, it's important to realize that they are their own person, with their own feelings, drives, desires and goals. Keeping the lines of communication open is critical to keeping in step with our partner throughout life. We must set time aside to talk and make sure they know we'll always listen when they have something to say, and say what we need to say to them, as well. Neither of us can read the other's mind; we have to speak our truth and be honest with each other.

7. **Patience** — It's not just a virtue; it's a *necessity.* Two people living together will inevitably get on each other's nerves from time to time. It might be something they're doing, or we might just be in a touchy mood at a given moment. When we feel that irritation creep in, we should take a moment, breathe and decide if it's something worth a discussion. If it is, we should have that discussion (going back to "communication"); if it's not, we need to let it go. Remember: Our spouse is the person we love and want to spend our lives with, and we should be generous when it comes to cut-

ting them a break. We also need to keep in mind that *we're* not perfect, either.

8. **Common Core Values** — While we don't have to agree with our spouse on every subject (and, honestly, it's probably healthier if we don't; otherwise, we're probably not being completely honest with ourselves), it *is* important to agree on the big things. Attempting to spend our lives with someone we fundamentally disagree with on important issues (and we need to decide what's important to each of us early on) has a much greater chance of ending up in heartbreak.

9. **Forgiveness** — *Everyone* screws up and makes mistakes. That's just part of being human. Continually holding our partner's mistakes over them, however, or keeping a running tally of all the times they've fallen short of the mark will erode our relationship into a bitter struggle to see who comes out on top. In the big picture, these behaviors help *neither* of us. If something our partner has done truly bothers us, by all means tell them (again, *communicate*) but we shouldn't hold grudges or keep score.

10. **Gratitude** — It's almost impossible to notice every single little kindness our spouse does for us over the course of a lifetime. If we're determined to keep score in a marriage, though, *this* is the area we want to focus on. I personally have found that people who are grateful for what they have — but continue to push to improve their lives — are the happiest, most enjoyable people to be around. We need to let our partner know that we appreciate them and we don't take them for granted. We must thank each other for acts both large and small, and do it often.

For many of us, it's not easy to live up to each of these expectations daily — but it's important to keep them in mind. That's why mentors are so important for maintaining our focus and challenging us to constantly strive to be better. Iron sharpens iron.

For some of us, putting in the work to make a committed relationship a success is second nature; for others of us, it may not come as easily. It may even be one of those life goals that threatens to fall into "The Tyranny of the OR" that we discussed in the introduction of *The Theory of 5* ("I can be a good provider OR I can be a good husband"). If it was easy for

> I personally have found that people who are grateful for what they have — but continue to push to improve their life — are the happiest, most enjoyable people to be around.

everyone, the divorce rate would be closer to zero, rather than hovering around 50 percent. My business partner and friend Greg Kelly — who I consider to be an exceptional husband based on his actions, along with the quality and longevity of his marriage — has said this to me on different occasions: "Chris, think about the alternative — to be alone in life, to grow old without a partner." This thought drives me to make the effort necessary to build upon our relationship — even in those moments when business or other distractions happen. I truly want to be an exceptional husband. That's why I seek advice from my mentors, and I always will, and why I'm confident the effort we spend into this part of The Theory of 5 is always worth it.

Mistakes Made and Lessons Learned

WE UNDERSTAND IT CAN be much easier to talk about the proper ways of creating and maintaining an exceptional relationship with our spouse than it is to actually live them. This is one of the elements of The Theory of 5 that did not come naturally to me earlier in my life.

I'll be the first to admit I've made my fair share of mistakes when it's come to my relationships. These mistakes weren't made out of not caring about my partner; they were simply results of my *cluelessness*. My intense focus was always on my children (I always wanted to be there for them), my business (with its long hours and extensive travel demands) and working to maintaining my health, which made all my other efforts possible. It didn't leave a lot of time or energy for romance and fostering my relationships, and I hadn't yet internalized the reality that my partner needed these things from me.

If my 59-year-old self could speak to the 30-year-old version of me, one of the most important things I would tell him is this: "Stop making excuses. All the reasons you are doing what you're doing for your family won't matter if you're not maintaining your relationship with your wife. My experience has taught me that a person can't focus on only one element of their life and expect the others to be exceptional."

I've since improved my attentiveness in this area — both through experience, focus, conversations and commitment and from the lessons and examples of my mentors. I've worked to find a better balance that has allowed me to build a stronger bond with my wife. That being said, I still need to remind myself not to neglect this critical facet of my life. One of the reasons I'm so compelled to share The Theory of 5 with you is because I've experienced firsthand how it has supported me, allowing me to establish and improve the balances in my life.

I believe that, when people get married young, they're often more interested in surface matters ("I like the way you look" or "We like the same activities") rather than things that allow a marriage to deepen and grow stronger over time. Most of us (especially males) are *not* deep thinkers about relationships in our late teens and early 20s. And I speak from experience.

I met my first wife when I was 17 years old. She was my first real girlfriend, and we dated on and off — mostly on — through college. We married when I was 23 years old and had two daughters: Tia, when I was 28 and Taylor, when I was 31.

My wife and I rarely argued (when we did, it was usually over finances — I required more structure than she did to be comfortable). Both of our families got along. Everything seemed to be going well, other than some everyday differences of opinions that didn't seem important at the time. And then, in 2000, when I was 38, my wife asked me for a divorce *while we were at a company function.* I was shocked. I was saddened.

Blindsided.

I had no *idea* she was unhappy. *It never entered my mind that I would fail in a marriage and go through a divorce.* It was impossible to wrap my mind around the thought of it.

As the initial shock passed, the reality of my new world shook me to my core when I came home to an empty house. Much of the furniture was gone. The place was bare, containing only the memories of happier days. I had to travel out of town for business in those days, and usually, when I came home, I had been greeted enthusiastically every evening by my two daughters, along with my beloved dogs Rocky the boxer, Bingo the beagle and Teany the rat terrier. It was the general commotion of a happy family, and I felt like a rock star every night when I was home.

Now, suddenly, there was just silence.

And, as painful as this was, the future looked even bleaker when I thought of what would happen with my relationship with my children. Having to consider the possibility of some other man could eventually enter into my daughters' futures — a man who would co-raise them with me — brought more pain. The vision of this absolutely crushed me. The idea of not seeing my daughters consistently, of having to share holidays and being an "every-other-weekend" dad made me both spiritually and physically ill. I'd never felt pain and sorrow like that before.

As I laid in bed over the next week, unable to sleep, I had plenty of time for self-assessment. I thought about our relationship. In retrospect, I could see that we were growing apart and that our values — what we wanted out of life — were not aligned in any way. We had very different visions of what our future should look like. I had assumed we looked at our life the same way — we had two healthy, exceptional daughters, our families got along well and we rarely argued. We were doing well financially, we had plenty of friends and we *were* friends — or at least I thought we were. We had our health, and she was able to stay home with the kids, which is what we had both wanted. What else did we need?

I realized that my view was incomplete, though, because I wasn't seeing the entire picture; *she had a very different opinion of how things were going in our marriage.* That difference in our viewpoints had doomed the relationship.

This is why I'm such a believer in what follows in this section. I've learned that it's so important to find the right partner and have discussions *beforehand* and *constantly throughout the relationship.* I hadn't done this. At that time, I didn't have the mentors to guide me or the knowledge to sit down with her and ask:

- What do *we* want out of life?
- What gives *us* joy?
- What makes us *truly* happy, both as individuals and as a couple?

I didn't know to ask my wife, "What is important to you and why is it important?"

Once I had the time to process these thoughts and some of the acute initial pain faded, I knew I wanted to get remarried someday. I enjoyed being married and being in a monogamous relationship.

Five months after my divorce a common friend introduced me to Lisa, and it went well; so well that, after our first meeting, I somehow knew that we would be married. And, apparently, that prediction wasn't just my imagination working overtime. It was amazing how many of my friends reached the same conclusion after seeing us together. "You're both done," one friend said to me. "She's it, Chris."

When I was 41, we were married and gained full custody of my daughters that same year. Together, Lisa and I have created a blended family. We went into this relationship knowing that, statistically, the odds were against us — couples with children of our own but no biological children together have a divorce rate of close to 80 percent. While that's not a happy figure, it was good to know, because it told us we had to keep a constant eye on the health of our relationship. And, as in any relationship, there are challenges. There's also the wisdom that we both brought to this relationship, however, and lessons we've learned through our own experiences and through seeking the counsel of mentors.

To this day, I still catch myself falling into some of the same traps of focusing more on business and work than on our relationship. I'll catch myself about to cancel vacations or starting to pay more attention to my text messages, emails and phone calls than to Lisa when we're out. This can be the challenge of people like me who are business/work-centric because we can — or will attempt to — justify this behavior in our minds by rationalizing that "this is how we pay the bills for our lifestyle." For us, business isn't really work; it's competition. We love winning. It's our sport. It's *fun*.

This is just an excuse.

What most of our spouses will believe is that we'd rather be at work than be with him or her.

Many of my business mentors have faced these same challenges, but they've found ways to overcome it. A simple step is to *put our phones away*. Another method is to plan time — a date — with our spouses as we would a business meeting and then respect that time as we would with that meeting. Business may always come more naturally to me than working on a relationship but being *aware* of the situation is necessary to overcome those challenges. *I'm not a marriage expert, but thanks to The Theory of 5, I have access to people I know — based on their behaviors, actions and results — who are.*

It's ironic that something as important as our relationship with our spouse or partner can be taken for granted. This doesn't *have* to be the case for us though. Even if it doesn't come easy for us, there are people who can guide us in building a healthy, kind, loving, exceptional relationship. Just know, as I've mentioned several times before and will continue to say, that we don't have to do it alone.

Avoidable Grief:
Not Finding the Right Partner

Two people in love might not be the most rational of beings. The idea that "love conquers all" is certainly a strong notion. There are discussions that need to take place, however, before reception halls are booked and rings are exchanged. These aren't discussions about things that "might" happen; these things *are* going to happen, and we need to be on the same page when deciding how we're going to spend our lives together.

It's possible to have a healthy relationship even if there are fundamental disagreements between us. If this is the case, however, we need to be aware of that going in. It's going to take extra effort and understanding to keep our relationship on track.

I'd like to point out here that there is a small percentage of people for whom, no matter how much we give, it'll never be enough. They've programmed their minds to focus on what they don't have and are not getting, instead of the blessings they *do* have. These are the people who hold the "I, Me, Mine" mentality. They don't want to be equals in a relationship, but rather want what's best for *them*, personally and financially. Nothing will satisfy them. They have to win every disagreement. They hold double standards. They take credit where they don't deserve it. They minimize what they receive and magnify what they give. They insult and jab their partners both privately and publicly. They compete with their partners and are envious of their success. These people will find something bad or negative to complain about daily. They are completely selfish and self-absorbed. They'll typically be miserable — and will want to spread their misery around.

It's important to explore our own relationships with clear eyes and recognize if our intended partner fits this description. If they do, it's better for both to make the tough decision now and *RUN* — before things get too serious and we'll be hit with even more grief and agony down the road.

Life's Big Questions

WHILE EACH COUPLE BRINGS with them a unique blend of assets and complications, here are eight of the most common, potentially conflict-laden areas for discussion:

- Money
- Values
- Religion
- Living Arrangements

- Division of Labor
- Intimacy
- Children
- Extended Family

Money

Money and finances are one of the main points of contention a couple will have in a marriage or relationship, and it's easy to see why. Decisions made here affect the couple's security, lifestyle and future plans. And, since many of us aren't taught good money skills as we grow up, our shortcomings — and those of our partner — can cloud our financial future. Communication before, during and after the wedding is key to our own mental wellbeing as well as having a happy partner and a happy life.

In my experience, I've found many couples fall on different ends of the spectrum when it comes to spending and/or saving money. Some people are more prone to building up a nest egg and feel better when the bank account is fatter than thin. Others see money simply as a means of getting what they want out of life and aren't afraid to spend it to get it. Some simply lose their money while others know how to both invest and grow it. There might not be a big difference between us and our partner in this regard, or we could be on opposite ends of the scale. Whatever the case, we need to have an honest discussion about our habits and our financial viewpoints.

We also have to be truthful with each other; we can't say we're a saver because we think that's what our partner wants to hear, or vice versa. It takes both kinds to have a well-adjusted life. Too far on one end and you're a miserly money hoarder. Too far on the other end, and you're an irresponsible bankruptcy in the making. Successful couples know when to save and when to go on vacation, and they constantly communicate.

When I first married at the age of 23, we literally tracked every single penny we spent during our first few years of marriage. I was a natural saver and constantly looking for ways to grow our net worth and she was not, but together we decided to set financial goals we wanted to reach. By doing this, it kept us *focused on a single-minded objective*; when people have the same or similar goals together, it's easier for both to pull in the same direction. Our goal was to build a new home, and we learned to sacrifice in the short term to reach our long-term goals. I drove a 10-year-old Oldsmobile station wagon — complete with the woodgrain side panels — with 230,000 miles on it. We didn't go on vacation for years; we focused on having fun with family and friends. We rarely went out for dinner; we enjoyed cookouts. We kept our eyes on our goal and did what we had to do to reach our destination. There was enthusiasm and excitement in reaching our goal.

And it's important to have shared goals, plans and vision — this is a lesson I learned from my parent's unfortunate financial example. My father was one of the hardest workers I've ever met. He regularly worked two or three jobs and, statistically, made an average or slightly above aver-age living providing for his family. He and my mother never had a plan, however, when it came to money and their finances. As a result, money was always a constant issue, and a constant argument, between them, especially as they got older and weren't able to pay all their bills on a consistent basis. Now, as elderly individuals, they don't have the means to care for themselves. My father worked as a barber from 18 to 81 — Alz-heimer's finally forced him into retirement — and now has no savings or financial means to provide for himself other than Social Security. I don't want anyone reading this book to share his fate. Hard work is necessary, but it isn't enough; *we all need a plan to be financially secure.*

Constant communication is key to working together. My mentors and I have found that it's important to discuss what kind of lifestyle we envi-sion for ourselves early on in our relationship. These questions are critical and ongoing:

- What *really* matters to us?
- What are our financial ambitions?
- What are our goals?
- How will we save for retirement?

If this person is to be our life's partner, we need to let them know what we envision the future together will be. We also need to listen to what they want from their life. There will almost certainly be compromises, but if we work together to build a future we can both be excited about, we'll have each other's support and encouragement. We'll be partners in the truest sense of the word.

In addition to the "big picture" vision we share with our partner, these day-to-day finances and expense questions should be discussed, as well:

- Will we keep one account ("our" account) or will we each have separate accounts?
- If we have separate accounts, who will pay which bills?
- If one partner makes substantially more than the other, how are the bills sorted at that point?

There's no one right answer; each couple must figure out what works best for them. For instance, while having one account might keep us on the same page financially, other couples might start to question each other over each and every purchase. There could start to be resentments because, as adults, we shouldn't feel like we're "seeking permission" to buy small items. This could be solved by having a main account for bills, and then separate accounts for smaller "splurge" items.

The question of joint or separate accounts will become even more complicated when entering into a second or third marriage. This is especially true when there are children from previous marriages or relationships, financial obligations or other facets to deal with. These are serious questions that need to be communicated beforehand — otherwise, there will be battles down the road. This is all avoidable grief if we discuss it and, if necessary, put it into writing.

Another serious question that needs to be discussed is whether or not to have a *pre-nuptial agreement*. When we both are starting out with nothing, this is a non-issue. However, when one partner comes to the relationship with a substantial amount of savings and income from their own money, trust, inheritances or insurances, a pre-nup agreement should be discussed. Either party or concerned family members may raise the question.

Several decades ago, these agreements used to be fairly rare — and were considered "planning to fail" by some. Today, a pre-nup agreement is a common and relevant practice for several reasons:

- In the later stages of life, when both partners have children from previous relationships and do not plan on having children together, because of age or choice
- When one partner makes substantially more than the other or brings significantly more assets to the table
- One or both partners have already experienced a nasty divorce and have paid (or are paying) large sums of alimony and/or child support

Stop, for a moment, and ask yourself what advice you'd give your adult son or daughter who had worked for many years and had built up a substantial net worth. What would you want them to do? Stepping away from the emotions of our potential relationship and looking at it from a more objective point of view can give us a valuable perspective when considering such a major life decision.

In these situations, entering into a pre-nup agreement is now viewed as smart financial planning, much like having a will or power of attorney. Again, communication is crucial, and reasonable, logical people can find reasonable, fair agreements. Many of my mentors have handled this by using insurance policies or financial advisors to put the spouse with minimal funds at ease. This way, they know they are loved and cared for. They feel secure and know they will be able to pay the bills if something suddenly happens to their spouse.

At the risk of sounding cold or cynical, if we both are unable to come up with a logical, fair decision on the subject of pre-nups, we may want to rethink our decision to be together, or at least ask ourselves if our partner might have ulterior motives; it wouldn't be the first time someone wanted to marry for money or status rather than for love. This would be an excellent conversation to have with several of our trusted mentors — someone outside of the relationship who can see things with clear eyes. They can let us know if we are being unreasonable or if they, too, see reasons for apprehension. I'm not advocating pre-nups — I'm only pointing out that this will be a conversation that will occur in the situations described here.

Discussions about money can become emotional, but they are *absolutely* necessary. Setting expectations and ground rules about this topic early in the relationship — a topic that will come up again and again in a relationship — will help defuse potential arguments down the road. We'll go into much more depth about money and money matters in the Financial section of *The Theory of 5.*

Values

This usually isn't a matter of "right or wrong" as much as it is how we see the world and what beliefs and behaviors are acceptable to us. The important values we hold near and dear to our hearts aren't usually up for debate. We don't have to agree with our partner on every detail of every topic. There are couples, for example, from different political parties who have very happy marriages and, on occasion, lively debates. We should, however, be able to see "big picture" concepts through each other's eyes.

In the successful relationships my mentors have modeled for me, a common theme has been that their values mesh — or at least mesh *enough* — to create harmony in their marriage. A shared perspective, I believe, is necessary to navigate the twists and turns that life will throw at us.

It's vital that we communicate to each other how we see the world, listen to what our partner is saying, and decide what's important to each of us. Which behaviors and beliefs are acceptable to us — and which aren't?

We should be cautious if we have the thought that we can "change" our potential partner down the road. "Good" girls who fall for "bad" boys — or vice versa — can throw a lot of energy down that particular pit and have nothing but disappointment or heartache to show for it. Opinions may evolve as life goes on, but the bedrock values, or lack of values, generally stay the same. While we can improve and evolve in some areas of our lives, on many fronts we are who we are. If we're not happy with who our partner is on a fundamental level, it's rare that things will get better. In fact, the relationship has the potential to get much worse as we become more invested.

Religion

We discussed the place of spirituality and religion in the first section of *The Theory of 5,* but discussions on this topic need to be had early on if we'd like our relationship to last. When one partner is devout in one religion and their partner devout in another, or not devout at all, this could cause a major problem as things get serious.

In the beginning of a relationship, topics like religion can be overlooked because the bloom of love is all that matters. Our ideas and feelings about spirituality, however, often run deep. For many of us, they are an integral part of who we are and how we interact with the world. No matter what the religion or belief — atheists can be as protective of their philosophies as the most devout Catholic — it's part of our identity.

> No matter what the religion or belief — atheists can be as protective of their philosophies as the most devout Catholic — it's part of our identity.

Religion can go along with values — it certainly can shape our morals and ethics — but it also can run deeper than that. People respond in several ways to the question "What are you?" Some may answer "American," "a salesperson," "a parent," or something else. Some will answer "Christian," "Jewish" or "Muslim." The depth of our spirituality varies from person to person; my mentors have always recommended that the question needs to be asked and the discussion entered into. We wouldn't want our partner to try to change our mind; for the health of the relationship, we shouldn't expect to change their mind, either.

Living Arrangements

Where do we want to live as a couple? Just because we met in a certain geographic area doesn't mean we'll be staying there. My mentors have taught me that determining the location and circumstances of where we want to live is vital before plans for the future can be made. We should discuss with our partner where we see ourselves in the future, and if that vision will require compromise.

There are a lot of question to ask and answer when it comes to living arrangements. A few of these include:

- **Location** — Do we prefer cold climates to hot ones? Arid climates to rainy ones? Town or country? Mountains or ocean? Do we want to travel and live abroad for a while, or do we want to put down roots?

- **Career Path and Transfers** — Will our careers collide? What will happen if there's a transfer? Does one job take precedence over the other?
- **Housing** — Would we rather live in an apartment, or do we want to buy a house? If so, would we want to wait and save for a big down payment or take the plunge early on? Do we ultimately see ourselves in a big estate, a tiny house or something in between?
- **Education** — If one or both of us are in school, or plan to continue our education at a later date, will we have to move to make that possible? If we have or plan to have children, what about their education? Does the area we are in offer good schools? Would we be willing to move if it meant better educational opportunities?
- **Family** — Do we want to move closer to our family? Does our partner? Would that move take us away from our family? As children age and become independent, move out and have their own children, many do not want to live too close to their parents or in-laws. (If this is the case with *your* children, remember: It's *their* time to fly on their own, and they're just a flight, phone call or video chat away.)
- **Smoker Vs. Non-smoker** — When a non-smoker dates a smoker, they might be able to overlook the habit to some extent. When they live together, however, it becomes a different matter. Where will that person be allowed to smoke — on the porch, in the garage or in the house? Will the non-smoker be able to deal with the smell — in the house, on their clothes and on their breath — on a long-term basis? Will they pressure the non-smoker to quit even if he or she doesn't *want* to quit? Smoking literally affects the atmosphere of the house; it deserves to be discussed.
- **Dog? Cat? Fish? Bird?** — Do both of us want a pet? If so, what kind? Are allergies an issue? When is the best time to take on this obligation? Who will clean, bathe, groom and pick up after the animal? Will it sleep in our bed? On the floor? In a crate? You get the picture. Ask lots of questions before taking on the responsibility.

Also, while these are fundamental questions for a young couple to answer before entering into marriage or a long-term relationship, it's just as important for couples of any age to find common ground. On a flight many years ago, a well-dressed woman in her late 60s sat next to me. I was looking at some photos of my family on my phone, and I noticed her glancing over. She shared a photo of her own children and grandchildren and then made a comment about her life that was very surprising to me. "Sometimes," she said, "I feel like a prisoner without a jail cell."

Cautiously and respectfully, I asked her why she felt this way.

She explained that she had gotten remarried a few years earlier and was now part of a blended family. She and her husband had no children together — something very common for people who get remarried beyond their mid 40s — and most of their finances are kept separately. Fortunately, she said, they were able to live and pay all of their expenses on her husband's income. She knew they had a comfortable life, free from the financial stresses most couples face today. His job, however, required them to live on the West Coast, far away from her children and grandchildren.

She loved her husband and knew he was a good man. Still, she felt like she was a captive of his job and his life, even though they bought a second home just two hours away from her children. Because of his career, permanently moving to the same town as her children would not be an option for several years.

As a result, she felt like a prisoner, because she wanted to be the kind of grandmother who all the children and grandchildren could visit whenever they wanted. The idea of "just dropping by" was very important to her — it was the kind of life she always dreamed of having. Her reality, while happy, had turned out to be something different.

When it comes to the discussion of living arrangements, some questions might at first glance seem simple. It's crucial however, to be honest — both with our partner and with ourselves. What's "just fine" or "no big deal" now might become an intolerable situation later.

We all know that the circumstances of our lives together will change over time. We might change jobs, our adult children might move away, our focus on what's important will evolve and so on.

This conversation on what's most important to us is not a "one-time" discussion; it's something we must reevaluate on a consistent basis.

In the case of my "trapped" friend, I believed a possible solution to her challenge might have been as simple as investing in a flight once a month to visit her family or flying family members to visit them now and again (money did not seem to be an issue in their case).

As our conversation continued, I made sure to keep my tone friendly and body language relaxed, and then made sure I understood her situation. "So, let me make sure I understand," I said. "You are remarried, you love one another and together you make a good living with all the bills easily paid. You respect and treat one another well. Your children and grandchildren all get along well, and you see your children and grandchildren 70 to 100 days a year… and you feel like you're in a prison? With respect, I believe 95 percent of the population in your age group would love to be in your prison."

I then took the opportunity to offer some advice, just as others had advised me. "From what you've told me. I believe you are focusing on what you *don't* have, rather than all the great things you *do* have in your life."

There was a pause which seemed to last minutes — but was probably only a few seconds — as she processed what I had just said. She shifted in her seat, her body language telling me she was both frustrated and surprised I hadn't agreed with her, as I assumed so many in the past had done. "So," she said, "it sounds like you're telling me I'm not doing myself or my family any favors by thinking this way."

As we traveled on, she thought about it more. Reluctantly, she came to the conclusion her thinking may have put her in that mental prison far more than her actual situation. Like many people, she had put herself in a cell because of her own self-imposed boundaries and had programed her mind to ask the wrong question. Instead of asking, "What don't I have?" a better question might be, "How can I make the best use of what I *do* have?" Because she was programming her onboard computer with negative questions, her onboard computer could only produce negative answers.

She told me she would sit down with her husband when she returned, discuss the issue and, together, she was sure they'd be able to find a solution. Communication is the key to overcoming any challenge.

Life is always going to be unpredictable, so it pays us to stay flexible and communicate with our partners. We should regularly spend some time sharing our visions of the future with each other and make sure there's a common ground both of us will feel good about.

Division of Labor

Each of us will bring different talents and different habits to the relationship. One of us might be a better at keeping an eye on short-term goals while the other might be better at keeping things organized so we can meet our long-term goals. There will certainly be a period of learning which arrangements work best for us when we move in together. Clear communication can keep the process on track as we both adjust to our "new normal." This identification of each partners role will dramatically enhance a relationship and minimize future conflict. Once the roles are *clearly identified and agreed to*, it is crucial that both partners *support and relinquish control* of this specific task/decision/role — unless our partner seeks input, advice or counsel.

The upkeep of the household will quickly become a topic of discussion once we are living together. What's cute at the beginning ("Oh, he leaves his workout clothing in a pile by the bed.") can become a point of contention later ("Why won't he ever pick up his damned workout stuff?"). If we are neat freaks — yes, I'm guilty — and our partner is not, we'll probably have to agree to meet in the middle. Sloppy people can pick up after themselves and cleaners can learn to breathe if something is out of place. We shouldn't depend on our partner to clean up after us; they're not our parents, and that's where resentments can find a foothold.

This is another item my mentors have talked to me about. Cleaning habits were a point of contention in my previous marriage. With Lisa, however, we're a perfect fit, and that goes a long way toward marital harmony. It was actually one of the many reasons I was attracted to her in the first place; she gives me a run for my money in this area.

Another major conversation that needs to be addressed early on is the matter of work and income. Will both of us have careers? Will one of us be the primary breadwinner, especially if/when children come into the picture?

As society has evolved, gender roles are nowhere nearly as defined as they used to be, and that's a good thing. Each couple has unique skills and abilities, and if one partner is better at a task, or enjoys it more, then go with those strengths. In today's society, if she makes more money — or has better prospects because of talent, education, etc. — it's accepted when they agree that husband will be the children's primary caregiver. Today, the younger generation is better at breaking down the gender stereotypes than older couples. Whatever our age, though, we should be open to living our best life by making whatever arrangements work for us.

Intimacy

This may be an uncomfortable topic of discussion, or it might be the most natural conversation we'll have. It depends on our upbringing, attitude and personal preferences we each bring about intimacy.

This area is an integral part of a romantic relationship and one where emotions can run high — both for good and bad reasons. For many, it's natural for the intensity of our desire to ebb and flow depending on what's going on, how we physically feel, etc. If our drive is naturally much higher or lower than our partner's, however, this is a topic that needs to be discussed early on. Are we *attracted* to each other? We have to be honest with ourselves as much as with our partner when it comes to this topic.

The initial natural excitement of living with the one we love will fade as we become more accustomed to each other. Also, circumstances change as we age. While these are natural and part of an evolving relationship, it's important to keep the lines of communication open — even when it might be uncomfortable at times. It's better to talk about our concerns than to keep those feelings in until they fester and grow unmanageable.

For a long-term relationship, my mentors and I have discussed how important it is to be attracted to someone for more than their purely physical appearance. No matter how we fight it, time marches on and youth fades. If there's not something connecting the two of us beyond simple physical attraction, it's going to become an issue. How important is it to us that our partner maintains his or her looks? We shouldn't let ourselves go once the ring is around the finger — for our partner and for our own health — but change is inevitable. Wrinkles, lines, lumps, bumps, less hair in one place and more in another... the person we fell in love with at 20 is going to look different at 60. Hopefully, we'll age gracefully together. If we're not okay with that, though, it's a warning sign for the long-term health of our relationship.

As we all know, intimacy means different things to different people. Are you a hugger but your partner is more reserved or standoffish? One of you may feel smothered while the other could feel rejected. Clear communication of what makes us feel loved early on can support both of us with understanding each other — and help protect feelings. Positive questions to ask about this language may include:

- Do you need to hear compliments and kind words?
- Does the thoughtfulness of gifts make you feel appreciated?
- Does spending quality time together make you feel closer?

- Do you need physical touches and smiles?
- Do you show your love through fixing things around the house or other acts of kindness?

Everyone is different, so we should know how we can make each other feel appreciated and loved.

My marriage mentors have shared with me that talking about this topic — and talking about it away from the bedroom, where tensions can run high — is a must for a happy, fulfilling marriage and relationship.

Children

Again, we'll go much further in depth about children and parenting in the next section, but this is a discussion we *must* have early in the relationship. Most critically, we need to find out if both of us *want* children. When one partner does and the other doesn't, it's the recipe for disaster. One of us could be bitterly disappointed with our life if we compromise on this point. Children are — or at least *should* be — an "all-in" situation. We can't try to change our partner's mind about it; a reluctant parent is probably not going to be a good parent.

If we both want children, how many do we see in our family? Sometimes there are problems in conceiving, and sometimes the conceiving goes a little *too* well. Would we rather have a small family or a large one? Where's our comfort zone, and where is our partner's?

What if there *are* problems in conceiving? Would we be open to adoption or other alternatives? If we discuss these "what if's?" early, we can take some of the sting out of a difficult situation if it comes to that.

What about discipline? Will we be strict or will we be free spirits?

How about education? Public school? Private? Religious? Home school?

How were we raised? What was/is our relationship with our own parents?

All these things will come into play as we start to build a life for ourselves and our family. We don't have to hash it all out in one conversation; this will take some time. We *do* need to communicate our feelings and desires, however, before life and/or circumstances take the decisions out of our hands.

Decisions about raising children are too important to completely make up as we go along. We must make sure we want to make the trip in the first place, and then decide together what course we want to take.

Extended Family

How close do we want to be to our parents, both in location and relationship? How close do we want to be to our in-laws? Before we even think about specifics on where to live, these are questions we need to ask ourselves and get *honest* answers. Some people may love the thought of living next door or within walking distance of their parents or other family members. For others, this would be a nightmare — and possibly a deal breaker.

Even if we have a good relationship with our parents and in-laws, sometimes a little distance is necessary to keep that relationship positive. Different people have different boundaries, and those boundaries must be respected, even — *especially* — if our partner has different ideas on what's acceptable. I have friends where the husband's side will drop by unexpectedly — and uninvited — but he loves it. His wife, on the other hand, does not. It's not that she doesn't get along with them — she does — but "drop-ins" make her uncomfortable. It's a point of contention with them, and one they have to continually work on.

Are there family members who might come between us? Do we have a brother with addiction issues? Do we feel a responsibility to look after him? Does our partner have a sister with special needs? Will aging parents be something we have to take into consideration? Very few people come into a relationship unattached to family. The best relationships are those where the partners can discuss anything with each other, and family is a topic that cannot be ignored.

While there are no right answers to these questions, we need to be honest with ourselves and our partner if there are areas of disagreement. Some of these discussions might not take a lot of thought, while others may make a couple reconsider their entire relationship. It's critical to have them, though. A happy, prosperous marriage must be built on a solid foundation, and this is where we begin to build that foundation.

While there are no right answers to these questions, we need to be honest with ourselves and our partner if there are areas of disagreement.

Fighting Fairly
and Disagreeing Well

NO MATTER HOW COMPATIBLE they are, two people living together are *going* to butt heads every now and again, so let's decide on our "rules of engagement" early on. Do we never want to go to bed angry? Do we need the opportunity to "cool off" after a time, or are we the "have it out until it's decided" kind of couple? There's no right answer; *what works for one couple could be poison to another.* We *do* need to discover what our particular type of conflict resolution needs to be, though.

This is an area that took Lisa and me years to figure out — and we still are finding ways to improve this facet of our relationship. Personally, I'm a believer that, in most cases, we need to take a little time. My preference is to take a walk or go work out to break up a heated debate or argument and take some time to think logically and cool down. Time and distance, I believe, can help calmer heads prevail. Lisa, however, prefers to lock the door, thrash it out to get it done and move on. Those styles, natural to us, don't naturally work together very well, and we've both had to make compromises. We're much better at this than we were at the beginning of our relationship, but it's a constant work in progress.

It's tremendously helpful if both parties go into disagreements with the proper mindset. My mentors have shared with me that successful relationships are built on serving the other (again, however, this only works if *both* hold this mindset). Partners with a "What can I give?" mindset will both come out ahead every time over couples who hold a "What can I get?" attitude.

It can be hard to hold this outlook when tensions are high and tempers are flaring. If this attitude is part of our everyday life, however, I've found we are far more likely to win *with* our partner — instead of winning *over* our partner. As one of my friends and mentors once said, "Learn to disagree well and choose your battles wisely."

Years ago, when I was working with the Saturn Corporation, the company brought in a speaker who talked with us about *conflict resolution*. The points he made during that seminar have stuck with me and are effective in many different situations. For me, however, the lessons seem to fit with martial disagreements best of all.

He shared with us six core behaviors people tend to use when faced with conflict — behaviors that do us or our partners no good. While we might not display all six — we all have our "favorite" behaviors we tend to fall back on — most of us are familiar with our natural impulses. **Here are six of the most common behaviors that occur during conflict:**

- **Walk Out/Storm Away** — When things get heated, we unilaterally stop the discussion, possibly after saying something we'll later regret. We then walk away, leaving our partner alone with another reason to be angry.

- **The Silent Treatment** — The argument stops, but we both know it's not over. It hangs over us and festers as we refuse to talk with our partner about it.

- **"You're Wrong/I'm Right"** — This mindset may look like the argument is over, especially if we don't say those words. If we still hold them as truth, however, this delay in resolving the conflict allows it to grow further.

- **Labeling the Other** — This is the name-calling phase. "You're stupid," "You're selfish," "You're always/never…," etc. *This* is where the original conflict morphs into a different argument — one that will be harder to repair.

- **Venting to the Wrong People** — This is usually venting to friends who are sure to take our side and *will help us vilify our partner*. While they want to support us, they ultimately don't have our best interest at heart as a mentor would. Instead, they'll give us the "moral authority" by saying we're right, even if we're not.

- **Vicious Attacks** — This is the worst and most unfair stage, where we get vulgar and cruel with our attacks. In the worst cases, the attacks become physical. These attacks are designed to cause as much pain as possible.

So, why do we display these behaviors to someone we love? I believe it's because we're angry and we're afraid. Deep down — sometimes so deep that we're not even consciously aware of it — we fear that we *can't* be loved. We fear that we might have chosen the wrong partner. We fear that we're inadequate, that we're not enough to make our partner happy. Some of these fears may come from childhood or perhaps from past relationships. *Whatever the cause, we all can act "crazy" from time to time; we each just bring our own "brand" of crazy to the table.*

Knowing that these core, negative behaviors are always close at hand when conflicts inevitably arise, my mentors have developed better responses to use instead. We *can* train ourselves to be better. **Better ways to resolve conflicts are:**

- **Stay and Solve** — We take the time to work things out with our partner and find a solution. If we need a break, when our emotions are running too hot and our logic might fail and we might say something we will regret, we can tell our partner we need a time out. We should be sure to let them know, however, that we still are committed to working this conflict out because we love and respect them.

- **Ask Questions** — We should seek to understand where our partner is coming from. What we see as conflict might simply be a misunderstanding. We ask why they feel the way they do and get their side of the issue. We seek to understand so we can be understood. Even if we still don't agree after hearing what's on their mind, we'll at least be working on the same problem together. Robert Kelly shared a wise mindset with me many years ago. "Chris," he said, "in most cases, there are three sides to every conflict: Person A's point of view, Person B's point of view and the actual truth or resolution, which usually lies in between."

- **The World's Not Black and White** — This is when we ask ourselves, *"Why can't we both be right?"* Sometimes, we'll just have to agree to disagree, and there's nothing wrong with that. We're two separate individuals who won't agree on everything all the time. That's actually a *good* thing. I've found that the people who choose their battles wisely and not "major" on every minor issue have truly learned how to disagree well. As long as we agree that we both love each other and have the other's best interest at heart, that's what matters.

- **Focus on Specific Behaviors** — Instead of labeling our partner as a villain, we focus on the specific behaviors that hurt us, and why they hurt us. "When you did this, this is how (your actions/behavior/words) made me feel," rather than, "You always...." We owe it to our partner to tell them how what they did or what they said disturbed us and learn what their intention was in the first place.
- **Go to a Trusted Mentor** — Here, we ask someone who holds us accountable to be our best self, rather than someone who will blindly take our side in all things. Someone who will challenge us can help us organize our thoughts, and will have the best interest of both us and our partner at heart. They'll encourage us to go back and talk and to do so in a way where we won't be ashamed of our behavior down the road.
- **Fight Fairly and with Respect** — We all need to learn how to navigate these moments of conflict, where our relationships are made or broken. These will be the moments where we keep or lose the love of our lives. We need to learn from our experiences and find ways to communicate when we disagree in such a way where we still are listening to each other. For instance, I've found that — when used correctly and *appropriately* — humor is a good way to lighten the mood and defuse a tense situation. This keeps it from escalating beyond our ability to remain logical. Whatever works in our unique relationships, the willingness of both of us to disagree well and keep each other's well-being in mind will make the difference.

As a young, engaged man, I attended a marriage workshop. An older Italian man shuffled up to me during the event and grabbed my arm. In accented, broken English, he asked me, "Young fella, do you know what the biggest destroyer of relationships is?"

"No, sir, I don't," I said.

He tightened his already strong grip on my elbow. "Focusing only on yourself," he said. "The more you focus on yourself, the more you distance yourself from your partner. She'll feel unloved and unimportant. At the beginning of the relationship, there's passion, excitement, enthusiasm. You'll do anything to be together and to make her happy. After a week, a month, a year, though, people stop doing the little things. Also, *never* keep a scorecard. As soon as you do, this weakens your relationship. Don't measure what you get from a relationship — that'll be the *death* of it. It's not about what you get from your partner, it's what you *give*. If a couple did the things they did at the beginning of the relationship at the end, there would *be* no end!"

He shared with me that he and his wife had been married for 60 years before she passed; in that time, he said, many of his friends had gotten divorced. He then patted me on the back and, as he shuffled away, said, "Life is not about *me*; it's about *we*."

This, obviously, was a man who knew what he was talking about.

I had just that one brief encounter with him, but I've carried his wise words with me to this day. In just those few moments, he became a mentor to me.

"Don't measure what you get from a relationship —
that'll be the *death* of it. It's not about what you get
from your partner, it's what you *give*."

The End (?)

DIVORCE IS A TOPIC that many authors will not discuss. I don't want to focus on this subject — the main objective of this section has been to *grow and improve* your relationship. It's a part of modern life, however, that can't be ignored, since 50 percent of marriages in the U.S. end in divorce.

In most cases — except when there's physical harm or the threat of it — it's best to attempt reconciliation through communication and counseling. Working with each other, counselors and relationship mentors can remind us why we wanted to be married in the first place. What was it we once loved about each other? Where did things get off track? Did something between us fundamentally change, or did our marriage simply fall into disrepair? Many times, if we *both* put our heart and soul into reconciliation, we might discover what went wrong and find ways to fix it.

Sometimes, however, it's apparent that reconciliation isn't going to happen. Maybe one partner has moved on already with another relationship, or has zero interest in resolving the issues in the relationship. One partner, no matter how much he or she wants to, can't repair a relationship.

There also must be some form of passion to rekindle the spark of love. When asked what the opposite of "love" is, most people would answer "hate." The reality is that the opposite of love is *indifference*. When one or both of us stop caring, that is typically the beginning of the end of any relationship.

If we're not both fully invested in making the relationship work, divorce might be the best option remaining.

"Staying together for the children" is often a reason to put a marriage on life support and grind away at life. Children, however, need to see *healthy* relationships modeled for them; two people miserable in a marriage isn't going to do them any favors. Damage is done both in the present and for the future when they enter into their own relationships.

It will be painful for everyone at the time, but don't confuse short-term pain for a lifelong grief.

If reconciliation isn't possible, it's time to settle and move quickly. Once the final decision is made, the longer it takes, the more complicated things will get. More people will get involved with their opinions that can cloud our minds. Friends and relatives might have our best interests at heart, but this decision is between ourselves and our spouse.

We've all heard the horror stories of people taking five or 10 years to settle a divorce. Many attorneys relish emotional couples who are out for blood. When a divorce gets contentious, only the lawyers win. Their client, their client's spouse and their client's children all lose.

As I mentioned earlier in this section, I've been divorced. In that experience, we signed papers within a week of the time she asked for the divorce — she had no interest in reconciliation — and that worked out for the best. Lawyers, friends and relatives never had the chance to get involved and start the "blame game." From my perspective, it allowed me to quickly move on with my life, start the healing process and focus on my daughters. Had it been drawn out and turned into a battle, the divorce would have become like a chronic illness to be *survived*, rather than an injury to be *healed*. The advice and caring I received from my mentors allowed me to get my life back together and find love much sooner than I would have otherwise been able to do.

Because of this experience — a quick, seamless divorce and our agreement to quickly move forward and not destroy our lives — I've had several opportunities to mentor other individuals going through difficult times. Rather than battle, it's usually better to move quickly and make it as much of a win-win as possible, *especially when children are involved*. Some of these couples were able to save their marriage. Others, when there was no chance of putting it back together, were able to move quickly through the settlement process.

One of the best pieces of advice I've ever received was from one of my spiritual mentors, Steve Munyan. He told me, "If you're going to stay *bitter*, you will never get *better*." This statement applies to any relationship that ends — friends, lovers, coworkers or anyone else. I'm a believer that — excluding tragic accidents or deaths — many things that happen to us happen for a reason; they happen *for* us and not *to* us. We can learn from these experiences to make the future better.

Getting Guidance and Learning from Others

WE SHOULD MAKE A point to learn from couples whose lives we'd like to emulate. If our parents or our partner's parents have a thriving relationship, we can ask them some questions that might not have come up while they were raising us: When were their most difficult times? How did they argue? How did they decide what was important to them? As children, we can be oblivious to the challenges our parents faced because they wanted to protect us. Now that we're all adults, we can have conversations about our lives. (And, by the way, if your parents *didn't* have a good relationship, there's always something to be said for learning what not to do.)

Find older couples who have been through life's highs and lows and are still each other's best friends. We can often tell these couples by the little things: their body language, their communication styles and the little gestures that show they still love and care for each other. Churches and other religious institutions are often good places to find mentors because they're reminded of higher ideals on a weekly basis.

We also need to recognize that if the couples surrounding us *don't* model good behaviors, it can be a risk to our own relationships. Drama-addicted couples can make bad choices seem like the norm and constant arguing a valid communication choice. It's much easier to appreciate what we've got and maintain our relationship if we hang around the people who are successful in theirs.

Finding Our Relationship Mentors

WHEN LOOKING FOR MENTORS who can support us and our partner, or even guide us before we find a partner, there are some criteria we should examine and some questions we should ask.

- Who has the relationship we admire the most?
- What is it about their relationship, behaviors, actions and results that we admire?
- What are the little things we notice about them that we admire and would like to duplicate?
- What questions should we ask to support and improve our relationship? (How do they handle conflict? How do they manage holidays? How do they deal with finances?) Take the time to be prepared and write questions down.

There are married couples all around us, but from which ones should we seek advice?

Becoming a Mentor

PART OF THE PLEASURE of finding a mentor is preparing ourselves for the day when we can become one ourselves, to give back to the world what we've received. It's an important duty and opportunity, one where we must be honest and transparent with ourselves before helping another. If we think we would make a good mentor, here are some questions we should ask ourselves:

- Do I and my partner have a good marriage or relationship? Are we both happy and passionate about our relationship?
- Are we able to laugh and learn from our mistakes and experiences?
- Are we invested in growing our own relationship or marriage?
- Are we both 100 percent committed to each other?
- Are we both willing to be honest and open about the times where we've struggled to work on our relationship — and times where we've fallen short?
- Are we both willing to share some of our time in discussing how we've built a marriage of equals and the 10 elements that got us there?

If we can answer "yes" to these questions, we'll be able to provide the guidance that we received — or deeply *wished* we'd received — when we were starting out or navigating through difficult times. We can make the world a better place by helping a relationship blossom or maintain its strength for both those in that relationship and those around them.

In the next section, we'll explore a topic that often goes hand in hand with a healthy relationship, in the best of circumstances, and yet requires skills and a mindset all its own to be successful: the power of parenting.

The Power of Parenting

Our Gift to Society

RAISING CHILDREN HAS BEEN the greatest joy and privilege in my life. The Theory of 5's point of view is that once we become a parent or involved in raising a child, the main goal is to nurture, guide and influence them to be a respectful, productive, self-sufficient adult. In order to do this, we have to ensure they have the knowledge, skills, attitudes and behaviors needed to thrive on their own.

I've raised two daughters of my own — Tia, now 31, and Taylor, now 28 — and was involved in raising Ashton, the youngest of my three step-children, now 27. (Madison, now 35, and Brandon, who would have been 34, were already adults before I had the pleasure of joining their family). For all the challenging times, the heartaches and the sleepless nights children inevitably bring, the rewards have been far greater than anything I could ever have imagined.

Imagine the kind of world we'd have if every child was raised by caring, loving and focused parents. Raising a well-adjusted, highly contributing person is the ultimate gift to a society. While we can't control how other children are raised, however, we *are* utterly and ultimately responsible for how we raise our own.

And it's not just the parents involved. Those without their own children — by fate or by choice — often have a role in raising the next generation. Aunts, uncles, godparents, friends and other family members all play a part in nurturing and teaching children while supporting those children's parents. *Preparing children to be adults who make a positive difference in the world is a job — and a privilege — where many people may lend a hand.* So, let's discuss what the most successful parents have done to provide this ultimate gift to society.

What to Do
(and What Not to Do)

As with the other facets of The Theory of 5, finding mentors to help us in the critically important task of raising children can help us successfully navigate a path to success. We want to take advice and be open to the suggestions of parents who have raised healthy, happy, independent children who became prosperous adults. It can be easy to find these parents when we see them interact with their adult children. They have a close, happy, loving relationship; people cannot fake this.

In addition to these mentors, it's also useful for us to find like-minded parents with kids the same or similar ages as ours to become our co-mentors. They'll find themselves in some of the same situations as we do. While great parenting advice never ages, there *are* new circumstances that come up with each generation. Parents in the early 2000s, for example, didn't have to tell their kids, "Never text and drive." Also, some of the problems of the past have gotten worse. Drug addictions and fatal overdoses have increased dramatically in the past few years. Having a peer group we can brainstorm ideas with as situations arise can be invaluable.

We want to take advice and be open to
the suggestions of parents who have raised healthy,
happy, independent children who became
prosperous adults.

The Guiding Principle

As with any important undertaking, it's best to begin by imagining what the best outcome will look like. My friend and parenting mentor Evelyn Longsworth (who is interviewed later in this book) once shared an excellent analogy with me about raising children:

The main responsibility of every parent is to successfully set each child up to excel in life with the skills, knowledge, education and life skills necessary to be independent and thrive.

"Look at it this way," she said. "Imagine if you knew you wouldn't be around to be there for them and protect them after they became 18 years old. How would you raise your children differently? You'd be firm but fair with them; you'd be loving, but you'd want to make sure they were set up for success. You'd want them to know what they were doing and how to handle the key aspects of having a successful life."

She likened the relationship to that of a mother bird with a nest of hatchlings. There will come a day where those birds will need to be able to fly on their own; not preparing them for that moment when they will take to the sky will rob them of a productive, happy life.

The age of 18 is a good target goal for them to internalize the knowledge, skills and ability to survive on their own. By that age, our children are adults, at least in the eyes of the law and society. We can't protect them as much after that age because they are their own people, with their own outlooks, resources, rights and responsibilities.

Evelyn's advice stuck in my mind, and I have thought about it every day, with every decision I made in dealing with our children. I don't know if I'll be around tomorrow — no one does. Understanding this, my goal always was to provide them with the tools and skills to survive and thrive without me.

Eight Traits to Parenting Success

I'VE LEARNED FROM MY mentors — and my own experience — that, to raise children into productive adults, the following traits are necessary:

- **Love** — Love is the engine that makes all the rest possible. Love is what gives us that extra bit of energy we need just when we think there's none left. Love is what allows us to take that deep breath and be patient. Love is the root motivation of every positive action we take with our children.

> Love is the root motivation of every positive action we take with our children.

- **Rules, Regulations and Consequences** — It's important for parents to be *parents* and not their child's "pal." They have friends; they need us to be their parent. Rules and regulations tell children we love them and want to develop them into good citizens.

- **Patience** — Children will try our patience, be it the homework they don't want to do, the room they don't want to clean or any of a million other annoyances. We need to be patient, even when we don't think we can (*especially* when we don't think we can). If we need to, we should take a walk and take a breath. Then, we go back in with the goal in mind of molding a productive, self-sufficient child who will become an amazing adult. Why? Because we love and care about them. Their successes as adults reflect our successes as parents.

- **Dedication** — Little things mean a lot; they can make the difference between raising an outstanding child who becomes an outstanding adult and a child who "grows up" and can barely survive on their own. Take, for instance, getting up in the morning of their own volition — a child who is raised with this ability becomes responsible and proactive. My wife and I made sure our children made their bed every day after getting up. It might not seem like a "power" move for a parent, but we told them that, by making their bed first thing, they start the day having *accomplished* something. A little victory is a great way to kick-start every morning. The "easy" thing would have been to close the door on their mess of a room; this, however, would have robbed them of that feeling of accomplishment and a valuable life lesson.

- **Determination** — Raising a child can be a battle of wills. It can boil down to "either I'm going to win or they're going to win." The best outcome is a win/win, though, where we guide them to do the right thing. As a result, you'll both win in the long term. We know what's best, but when the child "wins" — when a parent gives up and gives in — good things rarely happen, both in the short and long term. *We can't give up.* If we raise a child who has common sense, we'll be raising a child who'll be able to avoid a lifetime of pain.

- **Self-Control** — There are times when we'll just want to reach across the table for them or to say something insulting. While we might be the parent, we are also human beings with breaking points. It's important for us not to simply react and do something we can't take back. We can take that walk or send them to their room, breathe and then come back with an action created out of love, kindness, caring and respect.

- **Communication** — It has to be constant and ongoing. It's absolutely critical to keep the lines of communication open. Even during times when the child doesn't seem to *want* to talk with you, they should always know that they *can*. In his interview for this book, David Boice, one of my friends and parenting co-mentors, said, "There are a lot of situations that they'll go through and they need to have somebody in their corner at all times who has their back and their best interests at heart. They need to know you are someone who they can really count on."

- **Discipline** — We have to be disciplined in providing a structure for our children and a framework that allows them to thrive. We have to stick to our guns when necessary, even when it would be so much easier to give in. Brushing their teeth, going to bed on time, making their bed, picking up after themselves, teaching manners and respect for elders... each activity might not seem to be that important on its own, but each is a building block for the greater whole. Children are learning machines; at some level, *nothing* we do goes unnoticed, even in those times when we'd swear no one is listening to us. It's important to share with the child — and remind them again and again — *why* we're doing these important tasks. When they start finishing the statement — "I know, I know, because this is going to make me a better person" — we can recognize that the message has been received and internalized. This is when we will know we've changed the culture of our family well into the future.

Children are learning machines; at some level, *nothing* we do goes unnoticed, even in those times when we'd swear no one is listening to us.

Proper Motivation

AS PARENTS, WE ARE responsible for our young children's actions. As they get older, more and more of that responsibility must be transferred to them, and helping them develop a sense of motivation is crucial. There are two ways to motivate a child (or anyone, for that matter): intrinsically or extrinsically.

- **Intrinsically** — Someone does the right thing because they have their own sense of responsibility and understands the benefits of correct behavior. This could be referred to as their "inner compass," and is both a product and a generator of self-esteem.
- **Extrinsically** — Someone does the correct thing because they are *told* to do it ("… or else"). They either have no choice in the matter, or the immediate consequences of bad behavior simply outweighs the reluctance of performing good behaviors.

Both of these motivations can be useful at different age ranges. As the child gets older, however, the intrinsic, internally motivated school of thought will be the most valuable and serve them best. When a child *never* moves from extrinsic motivation to intrinsic — whether they are unable or unwilling to do so — they are being set up for failure in life. When they are out of the house, they won't follow through on positive behaviors because they don't *truly understand* the benefit of them.

Real Love Is Tough Love

SPOILED CHILDREN ARE NOT used to hearing one simple word: "*No.*" They are not made to act intrinsically, deal constructively with failure or develop a *true* sense of self-esteem. Think, for a moment, about what "tough love" really means. "Tough" means we are being challenged, and that there are *consequences for unacceptable actions or behaviors.* We are holding the child accountable, but we're not doing it out of meanness or indifference. We're doing it because we love them, and we want the best for them.

It's important not to kill our child's spirit with *too* much tough love, though. *Tenacity is a great quality to have in life and is something to be encouraged in the right circumstances.* When our children asked something — and especially when they asked repeatedly — we wanted to give them our decision. At the same time, though, we let them know that it was okay to fight for what they believed. Persistence is a valuable quality that will help a person in life. If the answer for today is "no," however, let them know with a positive, loving conversation or appropriate consequences. They'll get the message.

We are holding the child accountable,
but we're not doing it out of meanness or
indifference. We're doing it because we love them,
and we want the best for them.

Equal Treatment of Unequals

OUR CHILDREN ARE UNIQUE individuals, but the temptation is to treat them equally in all things. We don't want to seem unfair, or appear to favor one over the other. While the impulse may be noble, this is a mistake. I'll go into this topic deeper in the business section of *The Theory of 5*, but the reality is that there is nothing more unequal than the equal treatment of unequals. It sends the wrong message to everyone. If one of our children puts in the work to excel in a given activity while the other coasts through without extending the effort to try, treating them the same does each of them a disservice.

For argument's sake, let's say we have two children. One does their homework and has exceptional grades. He's respectful, kind and loving. He cleans up after himself and constantly puts forth his best effort. Our other child constantly lies. He has a bad attitude. He's self-absorbed. *Everything* is a battle.

Do we love both of these children? Yes.

Do we want the best for them both? Yes.

Will we put our effort into both? Yes.

Will we reward both children the same? No!

Again, our goal is to raise them into adults who can achieve their dreams and stand on their own when we're no longer around. By rewarding the misbehaving child the same as his motivated sibling, we're telling him that the world doesn't care about or reward performance, attitude or results. *We're setting him up for failure.* Not only that, we're sending a negative message to the motivated child. He could "learn" that he's trying too hard and that his extra effort and outstanding results will not be recognized or rewarded in life. Why work hard? Take the easy street. Why should he put out extra effort if the reward is the same?

In the end, the only things we have control over are our attitudes and our behaviors. Parents who teach their children early on that actions have consequences — both positive and negative — are training their children to live in the real world. They are giving them the tools they need to succeed.

Parents who teach their children early on that actions have consequences — both positive and negative — are training their children to live in the real world.

Parenting Is a Joint Venture

As we mentioned in the marriage section of *The Theory of 5*, a couple needs to be on the same page when it comes to raising children and present a united front. One parent cannot undermine the other and still have a healthy result. United we stand, divided we fall — and fail. Exceptional parents have discussions about their viewpoints on parenting before the child ever enters the picture. This way, the first time they put the baby in the crib, there are few surprises about where each parent stands. Most major differences were already discussed and agreed to. It's called the "united front"; one parent *never* contradicts the other.

No matter how in tune we are with each other, though, everyone has their own natural style when it comes to parenting, and that's fine. My mentors have taught me that it's not necessary for each parent to act in lockstep with the other. Different people bring different talents and different temperaments to the table.

For example, I grew up fearful of my mother — and the consequences that would occur if I did something wrong or not up to her standards or satisfaction. My father, on the other hand, was kind, calm and logical with me. This had the effect that incurring his disappointment was *worse* than getting yelled at and punished by my mother; it always made me think twice before doing something that would lead to disappointment or embarrassment in his eyes. I know they both loved me, but they *enforced* their desire for me to do the right thing using extremely different approaches.

That being said, my mentors and I have found that it's important to maintain the child's respect for each parent. It's dangerous to use statements such as, "Wait until your father/mother gets home," because it weakens our credibility. *It makes one of us appear weak and incompetent while making the other look like a bad person.* Children are quick to pick up on this, and their relationship with each parent could be damaged. It's much better to say that "When your father/mother gets home, we're going to discuss this with you." We should make sure they know we are a *team*, not two individuals with different ideas of what's acceptable.

My mentors have taught me that it's not necessary for each parent to act in lockstep with the other. Different people bring different talents and different temperaments to the table.

Adult Children
and the Blame Game

PARENTS ARE RESPONSIBLE FOR their children, but once those children grow up, many young adults — or older adults, for that matter — still cling to roles that don't fit anymore. More than ever before, my mentors and I have noticed members of society blaming others for their own deficiencies, inadequacies and failures. It seems to us that, in many cases, too many young adults blame their parents for being *parents*. They have their go-to excuse for not excelling in life or for treating people with disrespect. "My parents got divorced and I didn't see as much of my dad," is an excuse someone once gave me for his bad behavior in the workplace. "That's why I have issues."

That excuse didn't work for me. I made sure to remind him that he was responsible for his own behaviors and it was *him* — not his father — on our team.

People holding onto this sentiment must let go and take responsibility for their own actions, behaviors and results in life. When we say the behaviors of others are responsible for our decisions, it's an attempt to take ourselves out of the loop. *We are responsible for our own decisions.* The Theory of 5's point of view is to stop the whining, move on and learn from our experiences as well as improve ourselves. This is how we grow and change.

In cases of *true* abuse or neglect, counseling may be necessary to help people move on from their past experiences and focus on the future. The Theory of 5 is about surrounding ourselves with the people who will lift us up and will believe in us. We're either going to stay bitter or get better. If we need professional assistance, then let's get it and get started. It's time to leave the past behind and achieve the life we want and deserve.

For those of us who simply disagreed with some of our parents' choices, however, it's time to let go of all the excuses that keep us from excelling. We can't change the past and we can't win a 20-year-old argument. Holding onto perceived slights, insults and criticisms does nothing to build the future we desire or deserve — unless we use them to positively power our actions.

There's another way to look at this. If we are going to blame our mom or dad for the poor choices and results in our lives, then we should give them credit for all the exceptional things in our lives, as well.

We should examine all the things they said or did that made us stronger, that made us better, that built the desires and passions we hold. We can use it to build a "never say die" attitude and focus on continuous improvement.

Many children who had difficult childhoods fail to recognize that their parents were mortal. They were flesh-and-blood beings who made mistakes but did the best they could with the tools they had. Life is not simple. It is not a "black or white" experience. It's made up of decisions — both small and large — made by people often trying to figure things out as they go through life and raise children.

Being a parent may not come naturally to some people. As I mentioned earlier, my mother had an in-your-face personality. She would quickly dispense a whooping when any of her three sons behaved poorly, talked back disrespectfully, did not put forth the effort she felt was needed or didn't hold themselves accountable for poor results.

As I got older and matured, though, I started to see her not just as my mother, but as a person with her own challenges. She had three sons within four years of each other when she was 21 to 25 years old. Also, my father worked two to three jobs at a time and she had no help from her own parents or in-laws. It was not an easy situation — probably one of the reasons she developed a short fuse.

Despite not being what could be termed as a "nurturing" mother, however, I knew she always wanted her sons to do well. She attended every sporting event and was the first person to stick up for and protect us when she felt someone was unjust or had attempted to take advantage of us. She was brutally blunt — you never had to guess what she was thinking — but she would regularly remind us to never to back down from a challenge.

I credit her for making sure we were surrounded by other children when we were young who had the expectation to succeed, dream big and go to college. When I was a small child, we lived in a rough neighborhood

> "...if we would have had the 'perfect' parents we wanted, we may not have become the people we wanted to be. Life is always happening *for* us, not *to* us."

— one that she knew was heading in the wrong direction. She pushed my father to move the family to a neighborhood that, quite frankly, they couldn't afford. She did this so my brothers and I would be in better schools and be around other children and families who were positive influences. She wanted us around children and parents who were focused on building a bright future rather than those to felt they had to settle for less. *My mother clearly understood that our surroundings would make the difference in our thinking, attitudes, behaviors and future success.* In our new neighborhood, we learned that a person must *earn* what they get out of life, instead of the belief in our old neighborhood that prosperity was something just given to someone or passed down from parent to child. It was a valuable lesson.

So, rather than focusing on and blaming our parents for our poor results and behaviors as an adult, we can credit them for all the exceptional things we have in our life. For example, we have:

- The passion to grow and achieve more
- The desire to feel and care
- The ability to love family and friends

(How do I know this applies to you? You wouldn't be reading *The Theory of 5* if you didn't have these qualities.)

Stop reading for a moment to really think about what you could give your own parent *credit* for, instead of what you can blame them for. In my case, I give credit to my father for *modeling* an exceptional work ethic, serenity, love and kindness. He was one of the best listeners I've ever known. I credit my mother for *preparing* all her children for the real world, for our discipline, our competitive spirit and for the lesson to not back down from a challenge, but instead to embrace it.

I look back at my childhood with fond memories, with times such as pickup games of basketball and football and swimming all summer with great friends in an exceptional neighborhood. Were my parents perfect? No. Did they say and do things I disagreed with as a child and now as a parent myself? Absolutely. That being said, I had a great time growing up and that was because of the good people who surrounded me. I wouldn't have had them in my life if not for some of the decisions my parents made. I love them both.

One of my mentors shared a thought with me years ago. "Chris," he said, *"if we would have had the 'perfect' parents we wanted, we may not have become the people we wanted to be. Life is always happening* for *us, not to us."*

Steps

We live in an age when many children, through divorce and remarriage, might have four or even more parents in their lives. It's essential to get all those involved in the child's upbringing together and pulling in the same direction. No matter how acrimonious a divorce might be, no matter what kind of jealousy and resentments there might be, all the adults should keep in mind that the children are the innocent party and should be their first priority. The decisions made *will* affect them for the rest of their lives.

With children who move between households, the rules and accepted behaviors of each home should be harmonious with one another. Having a "fun" house and a "strict" house sets up bad expectations and does not serve the child well. Both parents, of course, must agree to this. While what goes on at the other parent's house might be out of our control, we need to do our best to influence it and to provide structure under our own roof.

They might never say it, but children crave stability, structure and discipline in their lives. Going back and forth between warring households may make the children grow up too fast to protect themselves or might prevent them from *ever* maturing to the point of self-sufficiency.

Even when there is bad blood between divorced parents, we need to keep in mind that, when speaking negatively about the other, the children are *always* listening. Unless one of the parents is a threat or danger to the child —if that's the case, don't be afraid to get authorities and legal system involved — we should never *force* a child to choose between parents. When we insult an ex-wife, we're also insulting our child's mother. When we belittle an ex-husband, we're also belittling our child's father. Children, regardless of their age, take everything to heart and incorporate it into their self-identity.

I was fortunate when it came to my stepson's biological father. We genuinely like and respect one another — he is a good man and a good parent, and he feels the same about me. It made it easier on my stepson to see this respectful relationship between his father and me. If we do have a good relationship with the biological parent, it's important to let them know we believe they're doing a good job and that we respect their position.

Decide on the roles the stepparents will play in the child's life as soon as possible.

While minors should respect the adults in the house, will those adults have as much authority as the birth parents? It's my strong belief that the punishment should come from the biological parent *whenever possible, depending on the relationship and temperament of everyone involved.* It's too easy for children to put the non-biological parent into the "wicked stepparent" category. To date, I've not found any data or research that makes a logical case for the stepparent to take the lead in punishment when the biological parent has a good relationship with the child. The younger the child, the easier it is for the stepparent to step in; with older children, punishment is better accepted from the biological parent.

And, before they *even become* stepparents, parents must have the discussion with their potential partner about children. Are they comfortable around children in general and *our* children in particular? They *will* have a relationship with our children; we must make sure it's a positive one. *We may have more than one spouse in our lifetime; our child will only have one set of biological parents.* It's up to us to make good decisions, both for our children and for ourselves.

We may have more than one spouse in our lifetime; our child will only have one set of biological parents.

Is Bullying Just a Fact of Life?

BULLYING HAS ALWAYS BEEN an issue in all societies — it's an unfortunate but embedded element of human nature. I'm sure it happened during the days of the cavemen.

I'm sure most of us can remember confrontations with bullies from our childhood and how much we dreaded having to deal with belligerent classmates. In the past 10 to 15 years, childhood bullying became a much more prevalent and discussed subject. It's also spilled from the physical world into the online world through social media — something people of my generation never had to face as children.

Even in adulthood, many of us still have to contend with bullies. While the threat may not be physical, many people in the workplace attempt to bully others through their position or their knowledge in certain areas. They try to make others feel weak or stupid to make themselves feel better. Any real or imagined power they have over others is a tool to bend people to their will.

All children *will* have to deal with bullies at certain points in their lives. We need to give them the tools and confidence needed to stand up for themselves and not become victims.

As parents, we are the most influential sources when discussing bullying with our children. They look to us to see how to behave when interacting with others, and they model their ideas of appropriate interactions and communication from us. For example, children learn how to resolve disagreements and conflicts by seeing how we, as parents, treat each other, family members, friends, neighbors and others. We should never forget that, even when we think our children aren't paying attention to us, they are.

Discussing bullying with our children needs to start at an early age. We need to share with them what is acceptable and unacceptable behaviors, based on both school and family guidelines. It's crucial to teach our children how to take a joke or handle teasing within reason. We should be prepared to step in, however, when we see our child has become a target of unrelenting bullies.

> It's crucial to teach our children how to take a joke or handle teasing within reason. We should be prepared to step in, however, when we see our child has become a target of unrelenting bullies.

Much of what's termed "bullying" today would have been called "teasing" or "joking around" in earlier times, and our parents taught us that the best way to deal with it was to laugh it off. There's some truth to the old adage, "Sticks and stones will break our bones, but words will never hurt us." The truth is that words *can* hurt us, but *only* if we let them. If we let words hurt us, it can affect our own self-image and self-worth. Words certainly can take their toll.

One of my friends from junior high and high school — I'll call him "Marcus" — experienced that first hand. Marcus and I were in the same large group of friends as kids and, as boys will tend to do, we teased and kidded each other. Everyone gave as good as they got. Marcus, however, couldn't shake it off, and it started to affect him. Worse, once others in the school saw this "weakness," they joined in and piled on. Several friends and I tried to coach him into not letting it get to him, or at least not letting others see that it *did* get to him. Marcus, however, just couldn't do it. He was a tough guy and a good wrestler. He could have easily fought back if the bullying had become physical, but this verbal and mental bullying ruined his high school career.

My mentors and I believe bullying is always going to happen in some form. Sociologists have studied the behavior for decades, and term it "dominant behavior," which is something every social animal — humans included — will display. Dealing with this "alpha" mentality is unavoidable in life. It's up to us to make sure our children know it's okay to stand up for themselves and that we'll support them when they do. Although many parents would like to constantly protect them, we cannot cover our children in bubble wrap. We have to coach them how to stand up and defend themselves, emotionally, verbally and, if need be, physically, because we do not want to raise a society of victims. *In most cases, people will treat you the way you allow them to treat you.* We need to make sure children know it's okay to stand up for themselves, and that we are there to support them when they need us to.

Bullies love to see their victims get angry, hurt or upset. They love to have power over others. If we don't get upset, we win; the bully loses and will leave us alone.

In many cases, the verbal bully simply goes away when we:

- Ignore it
- Laugh with them, or handle it with humor
- Compliment them
- Agree with them
- Pull the person aside to firmly let them know "enough is enough," "it's not funny anymore" or "let me make this clear to you; don't mistake my kindness and laughter for weakness. Now stop it."

We're not saying this is easy — it's not. When it comes to verbal bullying, though, this strategy is logical, and in most cases, it works. When it comes to physical violence, however, we *should* get upset. It is a crime — it's battery — and crimes should be punished. If our child is afraid for their safety, it's time for us to reach out for assistance.

There are several different types of bullies. Some are more common in childhood, while we meet others in adult life:

- **Verbal Bullies** — They want to make us feel bad and hurt us with their words and attitude.
- **Cyber Bullies** — They carry out their attacks through social media and other online methods to get everyone against us, which spills over into the real world.
- **Physical Bullies** — They use their physical size to intimidate, overpower and dominate us.
- **Intellectual Bullies** — This bully, seen more often as adults in work situations, uses their intellect or their position to intimidate us.
- **Financial Bullies** — They use the knowledge that we can't afford lawyers and court costs to inflict their will upon us.
- **Overreacting/Bad Tempered Bullies** — This bully blows up and/ or is easily offended whenever anyone attempts to confront them

over their bad behavior, to the point that no one wants to address it. They can often be found in a workplace, or can be a family member.

Two of our children had their own experiences with bullying on separate occasions when they were young; in both cases, an older neighbor child had started picking on them. Each time, we gave them the advice I shared earlier on how to face down a bully. While we also let them know we would go speak with the children's parents if they wanted us to, we never had to. In both cases, they simply stood up for themselves and the other child backed down. As I mentioned before, this is often all that's necessary with a bully. When someone stands up to them, they'll move on to easier victims.

If we do have to step in as a parent, we don't have to handle the matter on our own. We may need to work with other parents, the schools, social networking sites or seek support from appropriate health services. In extreme cases, especially with older children, we may have to get the police involved.

Most times, assertive children won't get picked on. They don't have to be the biggest, strongest kid around, but when they project an air of self-confidence, it will discourage bullies. We shared with our children how to walk — shoulders back and eyes up — to let people perceive and believe they would not back down from a confrontation. Little things can make a big difference and displaying confident body language sets us apart.

There are several different types of bullies. Some are more common in childhood, while we meet others in adult life.

The Danger
of Overprotection

Overparenting is often a primary factor in some children never making the turn from extrinsic to intrinsic motivation. This micromanaging behavior — sometimes termed "helicopter parenting" — *will* hinder a child's growth and development. Shame on the parents who don't teach their children the basic life skills before college or moving out on their own.

College is full of 18-year-old men and women who have *no clue* how to balance a checkbook, do their laundry or dishes, or how to cook or clean. They have trouble imagining how their actions will affect them in the future because they don't know how to think beyond their day-to-day life. They've never had to develop common sense because everything has been done *for* them by their parents, or they were told how to do everything.

Some of these people may be "book smart," but they can't thrive in the real world on their own without their mommy or daddy hovering nearby. They were never taught the basics of being an adult. They were never allowed to fail. Their parents were always quick to coddle their little princes or princesses when everything didn't go their way.

"Sheltering" children from the realities of life does them no favors. It actually erodes their self-confidence and the ability to make their own decisions.

The Theory of 5 goal is to raise children to be confident, competent and self-sufficient so they will survive and thrive on their own. Part of this is teaching them how to treat others, how they should allow themselves to be treated and how they can be capable, competent, confident adults. *Just as we are responsible for teaching them to never bully another or allow someone to bully them, we must teach them the skills, knowledge and behaviors to stand on their own, make good decisions and excel in this world.*

The Positive Aspect
of Failure

AS PREVIOUSLY STATED, SOME of the best lessons we learn in life are taught to us by failure. "Protecting" our child from taking the risks and learning the consequences is robbing them of an essential experience that will serve them throughout their lives.

Of course, if a behavior is going to physically endanger them or be destructive in a way they can't recover from, then we have to step in and protect them from themselves.

In less-dire situations, though, there's nothing wrong with standing back and giving them suggestions.

As we get older, we acquire profound knowledge — we *know* what's going to happen if our children don't listen. But there are moments when we have to sit back, give our advice and then just watch. When they *do* fail, we facilitate. We talk with them and ask, "Why do you think that happened? What could you have done differently?"

Most times *asking* questions, rather than *telling* them everything they need to do — or worse, *demand* they do it our way "or else" — will go a long way in developing their intrinsic self-worth and inner compass. These are the children who will ultimately be able to make their own decisions and enjoy the results.

Sharing Our Own Struggles

ONE OF THE BEST teaching opportunities parents have is sharing with their children their own struggles and challenges — and how they overcame them. When children observe or hear about their parent's trials and tribulations, they learn the value of persistence, effort and hard work in order to accomplish a goal. We shouldn't be afraid to share with them the times when we've failed, as well; we want them to learn from our failures and how we turned them into successes. There are valuable lessons to take away from any experience.

There's nothing wrong with letting our children know how we've struggled in our lives or what obstacles we've faced or are facing (although we should never *burden* them with our worries — they deserve to feel secure and not be worried if you're having trouble making rent that month). We can share with them stories of challenges we've faced and how important determination can be. These stories show them that there will be times in life when they'll fall down — or get pushed down. They'll learn the lesson that the most important thing they can do is continue to get back up. They'll have challenges in life to overcome; it will help them to know how their parents overcame their own obstacles.

They'll have challenges in life to overcome;
it will help them to know how their parents overcame
their own obstacles.

Life's Not Fair

YES, THAT'S A FACT of life. The race of our lives isn't run on an equal, level playing field. There are many factors that determine where we begin our journey through life, including:

- Family wealth
- Parental support
- Raw intelligence
- Health
- Physical size
- Natural athletic ability

There are many aspects of life that children have no control over. They'll face challenges that have nothing to do with any behaviors or decisions they've made. We should remind them that, while this is true, there are factors *within* their power that, when put to work, will narrow and close the gap. Their work ethic, persistence, determination and willingness to build valuable relationships are important tools they can use to improve themselves and their condition.

There will always be people who begin life ahead of us, and there are those who start out behind us. The sooner a child understands and accepts that fact, the better off they'll be *to face the real world*. We shouldn't hide this essential truth from them because they'll discover it on their own very quickly as they grow and start interacting with their peers. They may have a more difficult road than some of their classmates who start out advantaged. This doesn't mean they can't accomplish what they set out to do. By developing the work ethic, desire and drive to achieve their goals, they'll build the character and fortitude — the *passion* — necessary to face any challenge, even over their peers who had "all the advantages."

We have no choice about where we were born or who our parents are. We have no control over injustices that our parents, grandparents, great-grandparents and previous generations faced, nor can we change our own past. By focusing on the challenges that happened before, we rob ourselves of what the vast, unwritten future will hold. While we, at this very moment, are the products of the choices we've made and the obstacles we've faced, our future will be shaped by what we decide to do *next*. So, let's honor the struggles and sacrifices of those who have gone on before us by making choices, taking actions and living lives that would make our family proud. Build a legacy of *happiness* and *prosperity* that will benefit all our future generations.

As children, we have few choices during our first few years. As we become teenagers and adults, however, our choices become almost un-limited. We have substantial ability to influence many of our personal outcomes based on our daily actions, behaviors and attitudes. Think of the millions of people who overcome poverty, addictions, abuse, divorce, physical and mental illness — almost every challenge known to mankind — who have gone on to live their best life and achieve their dreams.

The first time we hear our child, or a child we're involved in raising, say "that's not fair" or "life's not fair," my mentors believe we should tell them, "*Yes*, you're correct." Then, share with them how to move beyond this. Let them know how millions of people around the world have *created an "unfair" advantage through hard work, a positive mindset, an eagerness for learning and persistence* — in other words, living a Theory of 5 life.

We have few choices during our first few years. As we become teenagers and adults, however, our choices become almost unlimited.

Respecting
Our Children's Differences

TAKE TWO CHILDREN, RAISED in the same house, with the same parents and the same rules, and you can still get two wildly different individuals. All children are individuals, and what works for one might not work for the other. While the rules were the same for both of my daughters when they were growing up, I had to take a different approach to discipline with each of them. With one, if I raised my voice or she saw I was getting frustrated or angry, she would literally break out in hives. I knew I had to be calm and logical when explaining to her why I was upset or disappointed. My other daughter didn't take me seriously *until* she saw me get upset. And my stepson responded best to a combination of logic, showing disappointment, humor and — although it was rarely necessary — raising my voice.

We have to look at each situation and each personality and understand how to deal with them as individuals. In a large family, we'll have an overall set of principals, but how we handle each child will need to be slightly different, depending on their personality and what works for them. To get the best results, we need to tailor our responses and actions to our child's personality. While we want the same outcome for each — to be productive, happy, capable adults — we might need to take a slightly different approach for each child to ultimately reach that goal.

Benevolent Brainwashing

CONSISTENCY IS A KEY to communicating our values and what we expect from our child while giving them the structure to achieve the results we (and they) desire. Repeating certain phrases — what I like to call "brainwashing statements" and others call "programming" — is a way to drive home this consistency.

"Tell me who your friends are, and I'll tell you who you are."

Note: I've had several friends challenge me about using the term "brainwashing" in this book, but one of the definitions of the term "brainwashing" is "to condition, persuade and influence." *This* is the motive behind this statement. The Theory of 5's goal is to condition, persuade and influence our children into creating their best possible lives.

One of the popular statements at my house — and a statement my wife also grew up with — was, "Tell me who your friends are, and I'll tell you who you are." When our children say, "I know, Dad," and begin to finish the statement before we do, we know it's finally sinking in. My children, for example, never had any doubt that they'd be going to college. "You would always talk about when we go to college; we didn't think *not* going was an option," they said.

Another repeated saying in our house was, "An idle mind is the devil's workshop." In high school, our children were actively involved in sports, music, athletics, jobs or some other social activity; this was a *requirement*. Open-ended questions were important. It wasn't, "Do you *want* to do a sport?" It was, "*Which* sport or activity would you like to do?" These questions made them make a choice. This had the benefit not only of making them better-rounded people, but it also limited their time, so they had to *focus* on what they were doing; their grades improved when they had a full calendar. It also prepared them for the active lives they'd live as adults.

This practice of brainwashing is especially important when providing punishment and discipline. One of my "brainwashing" statements was, "I'm making this decision because if I didn't, you wouldn't think I'd been a good parent when you're older." Another was, "I'm doing this because I know it's the best thing for your future and I want you to excel at life." In their teens, I also made sure to add in, "Because we love you and care about you."

As negative as discipline and consequences feel at the time, putting it in those terms let them know — on some level — that we were doing it because we loved them. We wanted to protect them, and we let them know what we were doing would be a *positive* thing for them down the road. We always tried to take time and explain to them, if necessary, why we were doing what we did; "because I said so" isn't a response that builds relationships. By letting them know we did these things because we loved them, the lessons had a better chance of taking hold. These are the lessons they'll remember and value as adults, and eventually pass along to their own children.

By letting them know we did these things because we loved them, the lessons had a better chance of taking hold.

Discipline and Anger

IMAGINE IF YOUR BOSS was always screaming and cursing at you, flying off the handle for every perceived slight or misdeed. No matter how loud they got, would you pay much attention to him after a while? Now, imagine if your boss was gentle, thoughtful and rarely became upset. If *that* boss raised his voice or expressed disappointment in you, would he get your attention?

The same holds true for parenting. Children *will* make us angry — it's going to happen. How we react, however, will set the tone for what's to come. When we're angry, it's okay to pause. It's okay to tell them to go to their room while we think. Telling them, "We're going to talk about this later because I'm so disappointed by what you did," or "I'm hurt because of your actions" is much more effective than screaming.

It's crucial to be calm. Our tone needs to be calm; our body language needs to show disappointment or sadness; *that* is more devastating to a child who loves and respects us. When we scream all the time, the child will just think there's something wrong with *us*; they won't take us seriously. If it's rare when they see us get upset, they then realize, "I really made a bad choice" when we do.

When deciding on punishment, we must set up logical and reasonable consequences. Some parents punish *themselves* when they say things like, "You're going to be grounded for a month" instead of a weekend. The parent is punished because *they* really can't leave the house; the punishment means nothing if the parents aren't there to constantly *monitor* and *manage* the situation. It quickly becomes unsustainable.

Another mistake is to say, "a month" or "all summer," and then ignore those consequences after a weekend; now the child will never take them seriously because their punishments are ridiculous, and ultimately not

130

followed through. In today's world, taking away their computer or TV — or especially their phone or tablet — for a time is a much bigger consequence than it might have been a few years ago. It's also something the parent can easily enforce.

We need to re-think discipline. It's okay to think about it for the day. The child will wonder what's going to happen. We need to take time to think and be reasonable. The statement, "I'm going to think about it overnight or over the weekend and I'll let you know," is its own kind of punishment.

The goal of discipline and consequences is to positively influence and/ or correct our child's behavior *while maintaining or even enhancing their self-esteem.* We never want them to leave thinking they're a loser. We want them to be thinking, "I'm better than that. My mom and dad are right — that was a bad choice on my part. I'll never do something like that again." If they can take away from the encounter that "I'm not bad, but my choice of actions were wrong," then we've done a good job. These can be the best teaching moments.

It's at this time that parents need to offer support without transferring accountability to themselves for the child's behavior. Children have to realize they are responsible for their *own* actions and behaviors; again, this is how they will learn to be motivated intrinsically.

Children have to realize they are responsible for their
own actions and behaviors...

The Trust Tree

ONE OF THE LESSONS we've developed through The Theory of 5 is sharing the importance of building and maintaining trust in any relationship.

Every good thing a person does — every time we keep our word, each time we are where we said we'd be and do what we said we'd do — nurtures and grows trust. On the other hand, every time we *don't* live up to our commitments, don't do what we said we'd do or in some other way deceive others, the trust they have for us is damaged. In extreme cases, it might even be completely destroyed.

With our children, the level of trust they built up with us directly impacted the privileges they received.

We also shared with them this essential truth: *It takes much more effort to build trust than it does to break it.* Once someone's trust in us is lost, it is not easily regained. It takes a lot of work to rebuild it to the point where it was before we let that person down.

Harvey Ritter described trust as a well-trimmed decorative tree going through a wind or rain storm. After the storm, the tree will lose many leaves and branches, altering or damaging its carefully cultivated shape. It will take many months of nurturing, watering, sunlight and skillful trimming to regain its formerly pristine shape.

This description gave our children a visual way to comprehend what can be an abstract idea of "trust." It was important for us to share with them the vast benefits of building, growing and nurturing trust — and the consequences of a lie or not doing what they say they're going to do. Lies can cut through trust like a tornado can destroy a town.

Bottom line, we wanted and expected them to commit to and do what they said they would do, and we let them know they could expect the same from us. Without truth, there is no trust.

Their Side of Things

IT'S IMPORTANT TO ALLOW the child, especially as they get older, to explain their point of view. It's amazing what we can learn when we listen and *truly* seek to understand. Too often, I've assumed that I already knew the answer, but then, fortunately, listened to their answer and thought, "Oh, man, I'm really happy I didn't just jump to a conclusion. I'm glad I asked because I assumed the wrong thing."

By allowing the child to feel "heard," even if the decision ultimately goes against what they want, we can build respect. We can strengthen our relationship with them and sometimes short-circuit a problem before it gets blown out of proportion.

> By allowing the child to feel "heard," even if
> the decision ultimately goes against what they want,
> we can build respect.

The Good Times

IT'S IMPORTANT TO REALIZE that teachable moments are always around us. As essential as proper discipline is, it's critical in my opinion to catch them doing something *right*. There's an old saying that, "What gets recognized and rewarded gets repeated." While it's great to let our children know we are proud of them, it's very motivating to be *specific* with our recognition and praise. "I'm so proud of you for all the time, effort and focus you put into getting that 'A' in trigonometry. That was an excellent job." We should notice the individual things they do, in sports, scholastics, or just behaviors to a friend or neighbor.

> "What gets recognized and rewarded gets repeated."

We tend to stop doing it as they get older, when they are teenagers and not as cute or huggable — or sometimes as lovable. That, however, is when they need it the most. They feel awkward as they mature and develop. They are dealing with powerful emotions that, in even the best of circumstances, they can barely control. Letting them know we're proud of them when they do the right thing might just mean the world to them.

My mentors caution, however, that parents should be proportional with praise. Recognition is excellent when it's earned and deserved. Too much, however, will inflate the child's ego and set them up for failure. Making a big deal over every small accomplishment dilutes the power that it has when the child truly accomplishes something. Telling an older child "You did a good job cleaning your room" is fine; telling them "You did an amazing job! You're the best! Outstanding work! I'm so proud of you!" doesn't give us anywhere to go when the child *does* put out an outstanding effort in accomplishing a goal. There's a delicate but important balance between proper encouragement and over-recognizing every minor feat.

When we have more than one child, we believe it is essential to take the time to give each of them one-on-one attention. Every child deserves special moments with a parent; let's put in the effort to make it memorable, pre-think about what we want to do, and treat them as individuals.

We're at our best when we take the time to create great memories for life. Never underestimate the importance of *fun, humor, laughing and special one-on-one time with our child.* Think back to your own treasured memories of your childhood. Remember how a brief experience or moment was integral in defining the person you are today. As parents, we have the power to create with our child their own favorite, defining moments.

And the best thing about these moments is that they are *shared* — we'll appreciate them just as much, if not more, than they will. And, God forbid, there are times when those memories might get us through every parent's nightmare. As I mentioned earlier, my wife and I lost her son, my stepson, a few years ago. The moments shared with him are something we'll treasure for the rest of our days. Just as we raise our children to survive without us, it's important to build our own memories for our own survival.

As parents, we have the power to create with our child their own favorite, defining moments.

The Time Machine Mentality

THERE'S A METHOD, A frame of mind, we can use to set ourselves up as our *own* mentor. When we have young children, imagine if we could get our hands on a time machine. Imagine if we were 30 years older and could observe our parenting methods with our adult children at our side?

- Would we be satisfied with how we handled a challenging situation?
- Were there things we would have handled differently?
- What behaviors and lessons would we want to teach and model through our actions and words?
- Would we change our actions or decisions if we were looking at the situation with our adult child?
- Would we be *proud* or *embarrassed* by our parenting?

When the decisions get hard and the energy gets low, looking at our present situation by imagining our future can reframe the discussion. It can help us keep our eyes on our ultimate goal of raising self-sufficient adults we can be proud of and who are proud of themselves.

I'd like to share a personal story here, one where I made one of the best decisions of my life. It was 2001, almost a year after my divorce, and I was offered executive positions at two different publicly traded automotive groups. One was headquartered in Florida, the other in North Carolina. Either of these jobs would have increased my income by more than 250 percent at that time

I turned both jobs down.

Most of my friends told me I was crazy, that I was sabotaging my career. It was an opportunity of a lifetime, they said, and I would never get another chance to work with these amazing companies if I turned them down. My reasoning was sound, though; my daughters needed me. If I accepted either of those positions, I would have had to move away from Pennsylvania, and away from my daughters. This wasn't a "Tyranny of the OR" situation, where I faced a *false* decision of "being a good father OR accept the new position." State law, at the time, said that children their age (9 and 11) couldn't be moved like that in a joint custody arrangement. It would be another year and a half before I received full custody. While it was an incredible opportunity to move my career forward, my decision was an easy one.

Both of my daughters were having a rough year after the divorce. Their mother was engaged to be married again, and they were having problems adjusting. If I had accepted either of those positions, I would have only seen them on holidays and a couple of weeks during the summer; I would not be part of their life on a consistent basis. That wasn't acceptable. I had always told my daughters they were the most important part of my life; if I would have left to follow money I would have been a hypocrite. It would have shown my daughters that I cared more about money and my career than I did about them.

It took me another 15 years to work up to the income level that I was offered with either of those positions, but I've *never* regretted my decision. I look at the wonderful people my daughters have become. I think back on the times we shared as they grew up in our house. I look at the relationship we have now. I know that decision — that moment of truth — to forgo the money and position wasn't a sacrifice; it was an *investment* in our relationship and an investment in their future. That investment has paid off infinitely more than any career advancement or raise could ever bring. If I had a time machine and could go back to that moment, I wouldn't change a thing.

When we're facing a decision — either a life-changing choice or an everyday judgment call — we should think how we might feel about it years or decades later. Time machines don't exist; we only get one shot at raising our children, so we need to make the choice we'll be proud of when we look back. I do believe that my *next* 15 years financially will be substantially better for me than if I had gone to work for those publicly owned companies 15 years earlier. I'm confident I'll make up any additional money I would have made. I'll have the best of both worlds. *It was an investment in my daughters — the best investment a parent can make.*

Teaching
Money Management

PART OF RAISING SELF-SUFFICIENT children is to discuss money and finances with them as soon as they're intellectually capable of understanding some of the concepts. Then, as they get older and are able to comprehend more complex ideas, keep the education going. When we "shelter" our children from the realities of budgeting, home finance, salaries, retirement, investing and other money management lessons, we aren't "protecting" them. *We're hurting them.* Children not raised with a firm foundation of how money works — and how easy it is to make mistakes with money — are starting out adult life with a severe, *avoidable* disadvantage.

There are certain cultures, my mentors and I have found, where the philosophies of money management — mainly growing net worth — and the mindset of the wealthy are taught early on. These cultures embrace educating their children so they not only can create and grow wealth for themselves and their family but so they can have enough wealth to share with those less fortunate and to build their community through charities and donations.

No matter what our net worth, we can leave a financial legacy to our children — a legacy that will have an incredible impact on their financial future. I know families who do not have lots of extra money but who have taught their children the value of savings. These children were taught never to spend more than they make. If we can teach them the importance of this one thing about money, they'll be better off than half the population.

We can't depend on the schools to teach our children about financial matters; most never touch on the subject, even though it's critical that they learn how to balance a checkbook, create a budget and handle money with forethought. Instead, we should sit down with them and make a theoretical budget for their hypothetical income. We can run down the bills and expenses they'll have (food, electric, taxes, auto, rent/mortgage, etc.) and show them the difference between gross and net when it comes to their paycheck. We need to provide them with real-world lessons because that's what they'll be facing when they get out on their own.

The lessons found under the "Financial Philosophies of the Wealthy" heading of *The Theory of 5's* Career and Finance section is a great place to start. Instilling these ideas — focus, budgeting, paying yourself (savings), protecting our assets and so on — early on in our child's life will reward them as they get older. I guarantee that children will appreciate this training when they're adults. These lessons can be passed down for generations and change the culture and prosperity of our family tree for decades, and possibly centuries. They'll see the difference between managing their money and having their money manage them by watching their friends and peers who didn't learn these lessons struggle throughout their lives.

No matter what our net worth, we can leave a financial legacy to our children — a legacy that will have an incredible impact on their financial future.

Little Things
That Make a Big Difference

PART OF GETTING ALONG and making a name for ourselves in the world is being able to make a good first impression. This is also not something taught in school, but it is a skill that makes a huge difference as our children interact with others.

I've interviewed hundreds of people for positions in our company and many of them make a *terrible* first impression. They don't introduce themselves or look me in eye. Their weak, limp handshake reminds me of a dead fish. They may be smart and they may have talent, but it's hard to overcome a first impression *that* negative; they're starting from a hole that they've dug for themselves.

Children aren't born knowing these rules and behaviors. They must be modeled by the parent who recognizes the worth of a great first impression. When our children were young, we would practice with them. We would shake hands over and over, getting them to look at us in the eye as they introduced themselves with a smile using their first and last name. Perfect practice makes perfect.

These little things — along with proper manners, respect for elders, a nice smile, inside voice vs. outside voice, etc. — may seem small. They can make all the difference in their lives, however, and they are things that *must* be taught. When we teach them the proper ways of manners, they can separate themselves from the pack from the very beginning.

No One Thing

THERE'S NO SILVER BULLET to raising a self-sufficient, productive, happy, independent child. It's the things, both large and small, we do daily on a consistent basis — selecting certain family-oriented neighborhoods; encouraging them to engage in sports, activities and clubs; choosing better school districts; meeting the parents of our children's friends and meeting parents with children who might become our own children's friends — that prepare the path to make this happen.

> "The reflection a daughter sees in her father's eyes is who she will become."

Along with these efforts, though, are the attitude we hold towards our children. When my daughters were 1 and 3 years old, my mentor Evelyn Longsworth told me about the impact a parent will have on his or her children long after they've grown into adults. "Chris," she said, "the relationship a father has with his daughter is the most important relationship in her life. The reflection a daughter sees in her father's eyes is who she will become. *If a daughter sees in her father's eyes someone who's smart, who they believe in and who will excel in life, that's who she'll become.* If they see in their father's eyes someone who's unimportant, who's a nuisance, who doesn't deserve their attention, they'll seek that attention elsewhere but it'll never fill that void."

Being a parent is an awesome opportunity but also an awesome responsibility. The steps we take now and the effort we put in while they grow up makes the difference between someone who'll take on the world and win and someone who will be victimized by everything that comes their way. Put in the effort; we're the only parents he or she will ever have.

Finding Your Circle

As MUCH AS WE'D like to believe that we, as parents, have the *ultimate* influence on children, though, we also know other people will play a part in their development. The people our children associate with on a daily basis will directly impact their beliefs, thoughts, opinions and actions in the future. It goes back to one of the statements we reinforced with our children: "Tell me who your *friends* are, and I will tell you who *you* are." Finding our circle — and our children finding *their* circles — is critical. There are good parents who have children who fall in with the wrong crowd with disastrous results. Then, there are children who have the deck stacked against them with negligent parents and difficult surroundings who go on to accomplish great things. Their circle is an *essential* element to their prosperity.

For this reason, we believe that, at the right time, every parent should discuss the importance of Theory of 5 with their children. It's important to emphasize just how vital it is for them to choose their friends wisely. When we provide them with the best opportunities we can — the neighborhood we raise them in, the schooling we provide them and the people we surround *ourselves* with — we give them the greatest chance of finding their own positive circle of friends, peers, mentors and associates.

When the Child Becomes the Parent

IT'S FATHER'S DAY, AND I am sitting with my father, Angelo Saraceno. I am reminded of something important Evelyn shared with me many years ago.

She had a deep love and respect for her father, and during the last few years of his life, she had to care for him after he had a stroke. She told me, "The way your children watch you treat your aging parents is the way they will treat you when you age."

My father was diagnosed with Alzheimer's a few years ago and has also developed congenital heart failure. The man I once knew, who I believe could have outworked any man on this planet, is now just a shell of himself.

This man I looked up to as I grew into a man myself is now unable to handle his finances or remember what medication to take. He needs to be reminded when to eat, when to bathe and when to brush his teeth. This intelligent man now can't remember a conversation you had with him 20 seconds ago.

> "The way your children watch you treat your aging parents is the way they will treat you when you age."

Caring for a loved one with Alzheimer's is doubly painful, because not only can they not take care of themselves, but you also watch the person you know and love disappear a little at a time, until they are finally gone.

We're not quite there yet, as I write this, but the day is coming. Still, there are things to appreciate, if you know where to look for them. When my father is gone, I know I'll miss our Saturday lunches at Perkin's and our Sundays on the patio listening to Italian music and streaming the Frank Sinatra station. Dad tells me stories of hanging out with Frank Sinatra, Dean Martin and the rest of the Rat Pack, and each time he tells the stories — Frank gave him the nickname "The Little Bambino" —

they become more elaborate. Dad tells me that he was the member of the Pack who, for some reason, no one remembers.

It doesn't bother me anymore that his stories never happened except within his mind.

I've learned to appreciate my father on the level where he is now, instead of trying to drag him back to where he was. I'm happy his new world is much more exciting than his reality. So, I smile, listen and ask him questions. I will lovingly remember these times the rest of my life. I'm thrilled we have this time together, and I know one day I'm going to miss our Sundays and his stories.

Changing Relationships

People are living longer, and the relationships we have with our parents will change over the years — and may even reverse. In some cases, we just need to help our parents from time to time, or with certain tasks; in other cases, we have to assume complete guardianship and become their caregivers.

When we have aging parents, it's best to ask questions *before* a crisis, while they are still healthy and have revenue coming in. By having an open and frank conversation — the "Just in Case" talk — about preparing for a caretaker scenario, we can avoid a lot of potential pain in the future. This talk should cover areas including:

- **Finances:** We can start with a list of all our parents' bank accounts. While we are doing this, we should consider becoming a co-signer; this will greatly facilitate managing their money if the unexpected happens. Also, if our parents list us as beneficiaries on their account, we can immediately claim ownership to the account after their death (with the proper documentation), avoiding a lot of legal red tape and tax implications — something we should also consider doing for our own children or other heirs with our own accounts. We need to gather all the information about their finances, including retirement accounts, investments, Social Security and other assets.
- **Insurance:** We should have a discussion about all their insurance policies — health, life, long-term care and any other items. If they don't have one or more of these, we should find out why and discuss if it is worth reconsidering.
- **Trusts, Wills and Powers of Attorney (Both Medical and Financial):** If the worst should happen, the last thing we as their

loved ones should be worrying about is going to court or fighting with others over how to handle what is already a difficult, stressful situation. Laying legal groundwork before it becomes necessary will make it easier on everyone when the time comes.

- **Medical Circumstances:** It's crucial to ask about any medical conditions they have, the medication they take, their regular doctor appointments and other health concerns. Make sure to have a list of their doctors (including dentists, optometrists, specialists, etc.) with their addresses and phone numbers. This could be a good time to review their prescriptions with a pharmacist to look for ways to simplify things. If our parent goes to several different doctors, we might not be aware of what the others are prescribing. Ultimately, we might have to become our parent's healthcare manager and we will want to record all this information.

- **Their Wishes:** It's not a pleasant topic, but we should also discuss with them how they would want to handle extreme or end-of-life healthcare decisions. How aggressive would they want doctors to be if serious problems would arise? This is a good time to talk about wills, living wills and other necessary documents.

Depending on our relationship with our parents, or their attitudes about sharing their vital information, these might be uncomfortable discussions. It's still vital we have them before we *need* to have them. We might be surprised; they will probably be more willing to have this conversation than we are.

If they are reluctant, however, we should share with them the benefits of giving us this information. It will help us take better care of them if it becomes necessary, and it will save us effort and allow us to make better decisions in what could be a stressful situation. If they're not comfortable giving this information to us, we can have them give it to an attorney with the understanding that it be given to us at a specific time, date or in the event of a disability. We will need to at least know who to contact to find out about them in case of an emergency. A lawyer? A broker? A financial adviser?

Getting older is an inevitability. By making plans well before they're necessary, we take a lot of the pressure off both our parents and ourselves. We need to have the discussions, make the decisions and give everyone the peace of mind of knowing that our family is in good hands.

Our Child's Journey

JUST AS GOAL SETTING is essential for succeeding in any other part of our lives, setting goals and having a vision is meaningful and effective when raising a child. Think about the benefits, values, skills, attitudes and behaviors we desire our child to possess. The Theory of 5 is a wonderful tool to use on our parenting journey. We need to think about how to share with our child the benefits of living this lifestyle. When should we bring up different elements, and how can we best communicate them to the child as they grow? The best legacy we can leave is by raising a productive, self-sufficient member of society who thrives and has the ability to support others in achieving their dreams. The lessons and philosophies of The Theory of 5 can help us in reaching this important goal. The best investment parents can make is investing in their child.

Teaching our children the lessons that will allow them to succeed in life is perhaps the most valuable gift we'll ever give them. Knowing what to do once they succeed, however, is an entirely different set of lessons. In the next section, we'll take a look at how to build a career to be proud of and how to take care of our money so it takes care of us.

The best investment parents
can make is investing in their child.

Minding Our Business
and Our Finances

Skills and Vision

INTELLIGENCE, TALENT AND EDUCATION won't guarantee us success in life. While these attributes are important, *the world is full of unemployed geniuses and talented, educated, penniless individuals.* For this reason, *The Theory of 5* includes ways my mentors and I have found to manage our businesses and finances.

> While some might find their passion early, few school-age children know what they want out of life. The adults around them are often little help because they also lack a clear vision of their own life's goals.

Financial knowledge, skills and commitment are essential to building success and peace of mind. Money, or the lack of it, can become a major source of stress in all parts of our lives. That's why it's crucial to focus on handling our finances and excelling at building our personal wealth. Likewise, our careers also determine much of our happiness and fulfillment. Career and finance intertwine, and successful people pay close attention to both.

But how do we *build* financial skills? How do we make decisions that lead us to a rewarding career? Many people, professionals included, struggle to answer those questions. Part of the challenge is that the skills needed to excel in these areas aren't *taught* in school. While some might find their passion early on, few school-age children know what they want out of life. The adults around them are often little help because they also lack a clear vision of their own life's goals.

Most of us learn financial habits from our parents, but that's not always a good thing. As much as we love and respect them, parents who live paycheck to paycheck without a financial plan aren't capable of modeling financially prosperous behaviors for their children. Mistakes, poor habits and bad attitudes get passed along to the next generation. As much as some people may think it is, *Social Security is not a retirement plan*. These are reasons why much of society wonders why they constantly struggle with this area of their life.

There's no doubt that our financial health, just like our physical health, will affect our overall comfort and security. That's why the area of business and finance is one of the five core elements of The Theory of 5.

...parents who live paycheck to paycheck without a financial plan aren't capable of modeling financially prosperous behaviors for their children.

Freedom and Independence: The "Why" of Business and Finance

BEFORE WE TAKE THE time and effort to build our business and financial skills, we should consider, for a moment, *why* we're doing it. The simple answer, "to make more money," doesn't go deep enough. *Why* do we want more money? By focusing on the real reasons we want to succeed, we'll propel ourselves with increased intrinsic motivation to keep pushing when we meet with the inevitable resistance.

Let's define a couple of words that my own Theory of 5 mentors and I believe are at the heart of the desire to succeed:

- **Freedom** — "The power or right to act, speak, or think as one wants without hindrance or restraint"
- **Independence** — "thinking or acting for oneself; not subject to another's authority or jurisdiction; autonomous; free"

Those definitions shouldn't come as any big shock to us, but let's stop and *seriously consider what they mean — or could mean — to us.* "Making a lot of money," in and of itself, won't make you truly happy and prosperous. Freedom and independence, however, *are* worthy goals. Think what that would mean for our lives and for our families:

- Freedom and independence from financial stress
- Freedom and independence to live where we want, to go on vacation when and where we want
- Freedom and independence to send our children to schools that are best for them

- Freedom and independence to support family members, as well as to share our financial and business knowledge with those who could benefit — people tend to listen when they observe success
- Freedom and independence to spend more time with our spouse, our children and other family and friends
- Freedom and independence to say "no" when we want and when we should
- Freedom and independence to stop spending time with people we don't want to be around

Is it easy to do the things that will build a successful career and lead to financial independence? Of course not. Is it worth it? Speaking for myself and my mentors, we couldn't dream of any other way to live. And that is what The Theory of 5 is all about.

By focusing on the real reasons we want to succeed, we'll propel ourselves with increased intrinsic motivation to keep pushing when we meet with the inevitable resistance

---

Our Relationship with Money

MONEY IS AN EMOTIONALLY charged subject. Most people are often reluctant to say how much they earn. Finances are often one of the biggest causes of stress in marriage. Some people who work jobs they despise have shared with me they continue because "the money is too good," while others stay because of a lack of confidence in themselves to find more money elsewhere. *Money is naturally on the minds of those who have very little.* When we consider our goals — leading a certain lifestyle, providing for our family or supporting our community — it's clear that it's much easier to accomplish our objectives if we have the monetary resources to make it happen.

When taking a deeper look at money, we see it is a measure of success for some. It becomes the way they judge their worth — or the worth of those around them. For others, it's a way to keep score for the love of competition or accomplishment. For many, it's their way to leave a legacy for their family and to share their wealth with those less fortunate in their community and society. There are people for whom it's a combination of all of these factors. We all have a personal relationship with money, but we seldom examine how that relationship influences our decisions.

There are two types of income in life. In most cases, our *financial and material income* is a direct reflection of our work ethic, attitude, actions and, most important, the results we achieve. *Psychic income* is everything else we receive from our efforts. This is the satisfaction — or dissatisfaction — we get from our career or activities. The *truly* prosperous among us have learned to benefit from both types of incomes. They earn enough to achieve their goals while getting the satisfaction of a job well done and making a positive mark on the world. If one of these aspects is lacking, our lives get out of balance. We're either constantly thinking about finances or we have the sinking sensation of "selling our time" for the paycheck.

Money and Morality

THERE'S A TOPIC WE believe is important to address prior to enlisting the aid of mentors in this area. In many people's minds — and in much of our culture today — the very idea of wealth, on at least a "gut" level, has been villainized. In my experience, however, nothing could be further from the truth. Most of the wealthy people I've known have been kind, caring, generous people who have worked extremely hard for what they have earned.

> Most of the wealthy people I've known have been kind, caring, generous people who have worked extremely hard for what they have earned.

So, why is wealth villainized? Because of a few bad eggs? Because of envy? Whatever the reason, if you're reading this book, you already know *intellectually* that wealthy people are not the villains. Do you know it in your *heart*, though? It can be hard to aspire to build a career and material wealth if a little voice is constantly telling you that amassing wealth is a bad thing.

Rather than seeing wealth as some kind of moral failing, think about how many more moral opportunities we might have if we're working from a place of financial independence and prosperity. When people are barely scraping by, there's no time for anything else other than survival. We shouldn't let the fear of losing ourselves and our moral compass keep us from doing what it takes to achieve great things.

If we view money as a means to amplify *good — rather than our reason for living — financial prosperity can lead to other forms of prosperity.* It will lead to the freedom and independence to build our lives into something truly special, both for us and those around us.

Find Someone Who's Done It

It's up to us to give ourselves the greatest chance for success, and one of the best things we can do, both for ourselves and our families, is to connect with a business and finance mentor. Find someone who can teach and guide us, answer our questions and model the behaviors, actions and disciplines it takes to be happy and prosperous.

I've been fortunate to connect with many mentors at different phases of my career. As I mentioned in the mindset section, at the age of 22 my first job out of college was working at a car dealership. Harvey Ritter, the retired owner who was then 78, took me under his wing and revealed how he managed his money and his business. He — along with his three sons Dale, Larry and Ron — shared with me how they built wealth and how I could make the most of the opportunities ahead of me.

Some of the lessons Harvey and his sons shared with me included:

- **Make a habit of saving 10 percent of your earnings** — There will be times when having money in the bank will keep us from disaster. *Also, by habitually saving 10 percent of our net income, we will be able to grow our net worth by taking advantage of future investment opportunities that come our way* — i.e. investment properties, starting our own business, etc. — instead of just *wishing* we could have.
- **The history and origin of credit cards** — When they were first developed, credit cards were meant to be paid off monthly. When companies saw they could make far more profits from interest and penalties, however, the way these products were marketed began to change. As a requirement for his guidance, I had to show Harvey that I paid all my credit cards off in full on a consistent basis.
- **Guard against waste** — Harvey was a big believer in the phrase, "Waste not, want not." He would "recycle" faxes by turning them over and using them as notepads. Instead of eating out every day,

he packed his own lunches. There were tons of little things he did that went beyond him simply *telling* me not to be wasteful; his everyday actions *modeled* this lesson for me.

- **Envision your goals, and then write them down** — This includes putting money in the bank, buying a house and making investments that will put our income to work. Dreams are great, but the key to achieving our goals is to make them concrete and work out the steps it will take to reach them.

Perhaps one of the most important lessons Harvey taught me was that, "A man's ambition will many times put him at odds with complacent people." When we're motivated and aspiring for more, the people around us who are willing to settle for less won't like it; there *will* be a battle. People at our work, for instance, will be upset with us because of our work ethic and extra effort will make them appear as if they aren't trying as hard. They will resent us, criticize us, make jokes about us and attempt to distract us, rather than face their own laziness and self-imposed limitations. It's easier for them to bring us down to their level than to attempt to step up to ours.

> "A man's ambition will many times put him at odds with complacent people."

In my mid 30s, I became the vice president of Kelly Automotive Group. The founder, Robert Kelly, reinforced Harvey's lessons and shared his own points of view. Robert was also talented with his favorite "one-liners" that I carry with me to this day. I made a point to share them with my children once they were old enough.

Some of these "Robert Kelly One-liners" included:

- "The difference between having an average life and a great life is (the end of his thumb and index finger held close together) is doing *this much more* with everything you do." In every area of our lives — our relationships, our children, our careers, our health, our finances and anything else we want to excel in — putting in that *extra effort consistently* will separate us from those who aren't willing to do the same.

- "Nobody will be as happy about your success than you are," meaning we don't brag or share successes to make ourselves look big. "Stay humble."

I'm now a partner with the Kelly Automotive Group, but Robert Kelly continues to coach, mentor and challenge me, just as he does his two sons involved in the business, Greg and Tim. I count myself blessed to have had Harvey and Robert take such a personal interest in my financial success.

The Benefit of Experience

Besides offering specific instructions and advice, great mentors will alter the way we *think* about the world. The best mentors will challenge us to expand our point of view. They'll hold us accountable when we are tempted to take the easier path. They give us a safe space where we can bounce ideas around with them and examine the best plan of action.

Effective mentors, in my experience, will also be blunt. *They'd rather show us the path to success than protect our feelings.* Let's put our ego aside because the benefits of growth are absolutely worth it.

Quality mentors, co-mentors and friends are themselves always learning. Their education is a continuous part of their lives until the end. There might be times when they need *our* assistance with an unfamiliar topic or skill. Interactions like this enrich the relationship and offer deeper understanding and commitment toward one another.

If we can, we should find more than one mentor in areas where we'd like to excel. Multiple viewpoints give us more options when building our own strategies. *We must pay special attention when different mentors are giving us similar advice.* That's when we know we're receiving a valuable lesson. That's where the truth is. That's the "sweet spot" of success.

You *Are* Your Inner Circle

As we get our mentors in place, we should also pay attention to the other people around us. There's a school of thought that states our income, as with other elements of our lives, will be the average of our five closest friends — *for better or worse.* That's why it's crucial to make the absolute best choices about friends and acquaintances as we search for financial independence and business success.

A key concept of this thinking, and one that holds up under scrutiny, is that *successful people in any area of life think differently than unsuccessful people.* They take responsibility for their lives and are always looking for ways to improve. They focus on how to *get things done,* instead of looking for reasons they can't, or making excuses for why they *didn't.* Successful people are not *victims;* they are *victors.* A winning mindset is a key philosophy of The Theory of 5.

...successful people *think* differently than unsuccessful people. They take responsibility for their lives and are always looking for ways to improve.

The Changing Role of Risk

MENTORS IN DIFFERENT STAGES of their lives or careers can provide us with important information not available to the others. When selecting an experienced mentor, however, we should understand that the mindset that worked for them might not work the same in the current business world.

From discussions I've had with extremely successful businesspeople, I've learned that the ability to innovate at a high level has changed. These changes may run counter to the thought processes of leaders who are closed minded to the new realities of the analytic, technological, data-driven business world.

> "Change, whether good or bad, is resisted with equal intensity."

During his interview for this book, my friend and co-mentor David Boice summed up this challenge with one of his personal mottoes: "Change, whether good or bad, is resisted with equal intensity."

We have found that many of these leaders were taught that risk and failure were things to avoid. Some, in their own minds, downplay or have forgotten the risks they took when starting out because those risks were rewarded with continuing success. In today's world, we'll most likely experience both risk and failure before succeeding in the long term.

Our attitude plays a strong role in how we perceive risk. If we run from possibilities, if we are frightened to step out of our comfort zones, we'll miss out on opportunities that the bold use to build their success. One of my business mentors has said to me many times over the past decade, *"Chris, when you are oriented toward abundance, you care less about being in control and stop dissecting every expense. This is when you will take more calculated risks."*

Many great leaders have ultimately prospered by taking calculated risks — and that means failing from time to time. The best performers analyze both their wins and their losses so they can replicate success while not repeating mistakes.

Even though they might see the element of risk differently, however, seasoned mentors in the business world will *absolutely* teach us important lessons, so we should always be open to their recommendations and counsel. The fundamentals of sound business practices never go out of style.

The fundamentals of sound business practices
never go out of style.

Younger Generations and Experienced Partners

ONE OF THE MOST valuable lessons The Theory of 5 offers is that our education is never complete, no matter our experience level. Creating a co-mentorship with younger mentors (10+ years younger) who are creative, motivated and ambitious has inspired me in new ways with their fresh ideas. I find that younger generations — Millennials in this case — often get a bad rap. Many of these young professionals are idea machines. They love to brainstorm and they just think differently. They may, however, need guidance in bringing their ideas to life, and that's what experienced partners can offer with their viewpoint. Co-mentoring is ideal because the experienced veteran is learning about new technologies, which is second nature to the younger generation.

In addition to our children and sons-in-law, all in their mid-20s to late 30s, I have two such young co-mentors. Joseph Berrios is in his late 20s, while Mike Kaunitz is in his early 30s. Their youthful energy, enthusiasm and desire to grow personally inspires and challenges me to continue to push forward. We are *constantly* challenging each other and pulling from our own unique experiences to be better today than we were yesterday.

Once we've put together our circle of mentors and co-mentors, both older and younger, we can gather information and their advice. We can allow them to give us a broader view of the world.

Bottom line: Stretching one's comfort zone requires risk and change; this is also where we will see our biggest growth and become the people we were meant to be.

Major Decisions

I've had my own experiences dealing with risk. When I was 30, I was making a good living. One day, however, the company I worked with decided to make a change to my pay plan, and it altered my outlook. This change had me feeling like I had lost control over my own destiny, something that was important — *intrinsic* — to me.

I asked myself, How can I regain that feeling of control and purpose?" My answer: Own my own business. That way, I could control my income and pay plan.

I was facing a fork in the road. There were a lot of elements to take into account, my family being my primary concern. At

> "You're older than you've ever been, and you're as young as you'll ever be."

that time, I had two daughters — Tia, who was three years old and Taylor, who had just turned one month old. My wife was a stay-at-home mom, and there was no one to back me up financially if I didn't make it.

Should I take the risk and start my own company, or should I play it safe?

Even after the pay plan change, I was still doing well financially in comparison to other people in my age group. Was I overreacting? If I started my own business, I'd have to put in more hours than the 60 hours a week I was currently spending at work. There would also be extensive out-of-state travel. It would take *massive action* on my part for several years in order to make the same amount of money that I was already making.

Despite the challenges, the allure of running my own business was too strong to ignore or dismiss. The opportunity, if it worked out, could change the course of my life, and the lives of those I loved most in the world, for the better. The question of what to do — the potential risks versus the possible rewards — swirled in my mind.

I decided to go to one of my mentors and ask him if he thought the timing was right to pursue this opportunity. His comment crystallized the choices in front of me: "You're older than you've ever been, and you're as young as you'll ever be." He told me that playing it safe now would mean a lifetime of wondering what could have been.

After hearing that, my decision was clear.

On a Sunday night, the night before I went in to resign, both my father and father-in-law came to our door. Them showing up on a Sunday night, something they *never* did, told me they had something on their minds. They knew what I was planning to do, and wanted to talk me out of it. They reminded me of the good relationship I had with my current company. They also warned that, if I did this and it went badly, I would have a family to support with no revenue coming in. They wanted to be clear that they could not help me financially if things did not work out. It was an *intense* scene.

I sat them down and walked them through my specific vision and plan. I explained to them why I was making this decision. I shared that, if I failed, I could always go back to selling cars — it was something I was very good at. They both knew I made a good living at this before. I also agreed with them that I had a good relationship with the owners of the company I worked with — and then explained that, if necessary, I was fairly confident they would welcome me back.

While I believed my plan would work, I had no guarantees. What I *did* know was that I didn't want to be an old man looking back at my life thinking, "I shoulda, coulda, woulda." I wanted to do it then, when I was young. I knew the time was right.

I took the risk, started my own business with two partners and within two years I had increased my yearly income by more than 350 percent. I truly believe that the experience of running my own company has led to great opportunities. I met many of the great mentors I now have in my life because of the choices I made. I'm happy I made that decision to go out on my own because it gave me far more options than I would have had by "playing it safe."

The lesson I learned from this experience was, when faced with a decision that involves risk, to weigh the best-case scenario against the worst-case and take a good look at all possibilities. In this instance, I was young and had options open to me. If I failed, I would have gone back to selling cars. Even then, however, I would have gained the experience of running my own business, which would only make me a better, more experienced businessman.

But most of all, because I made the leap, I've never had to live with the regret of wondering "what might have been."

The risk takers who change the world know that both the head and the heart need to be involved when plotting a course of action. Our hearts give us the passion, while our heads work out what needs to be done to achieve success. When our hearts are imagining what can be done, we need to make sure that our heads don't kill the idea before it has time to bloom. I once overheard a mother talking to her adult son express this idea the best:

"There are times in our lives when we are presented with an opportunity that may make no sense on paper but makes total sense in our hearts."

...I didn't want to be an old man looking back at my life thinking, "I shoulda, coulda, woulda."

The Struggles That Strengthen Us

LEAN TIMES MAY COME, and they may be uncomfortable, but the struggle builds character. The determination needed to get through difficult circumstances *forces* us to develop valuable *mental and emotional toughness and grit*. These are traits necessary to persist and consistently grow. The goal — the struggle — to become more than we started out with is what builds ambition and motivation. We believe goals must be written down because, without *stated* goals, it is rare to achieve the focus necessary to put our energy to its best use when we wing it.

> While we can't control all the circumstances around us, we can — and must — control our attitudes, our outlooks, our beliefs and our convictions.

High achievers understand that it's important to use our struggles to build ourselves up instead of letting them drag us down to the point where we forget our dreams. *Often, we have found that people who don't have written objectives, who are content to "hope for the best," end up working for people who kept their own goals in sight.* Again, it's all a part of building the mindset that gives us the best chance of success. While we can't control all the circumstances around us, we can — and must — control our attitudes, our outlooks, our beliefs and our convictions.

Let's spend some time digging deeper into setting the goals that will encourage and inspire us to do great things.

The Clarity in Setting Goals

GOALS AND VISION are essential to developing a sound business and financial foundation. My mentors have drilled this concept into me, and it has served me well throughout my life and career.

Most financial deficiencies come from *a lack of planning, action, effort, good daily habits and strong vision*, not money. Monetary goals are easier to set when there's a financial target — saving for a new car or a home, for instance. Nearly every life goal requires some sort of financing, so plan accordingly.

What do we want out of life? What's our purpose? Chances are, the answers we seek are already there. Anything worth achieving starts with an idea. Either consciously or subconsciously, *results happen in our minds before they happen in reality*. Daydreams and inspiration are key to building a vision. They provide the blueprints needed to take constant action, and action is what makes it real.

But to achieve our goals — and this is what most people in our society *fail* to do — we must take the next step and transform these dreams into specific goals. As my mentors have told me many times, *"It's crucial to put goals in writing."* Once we do, they become real. Abstract concepts become specific targets, and they challenge us in a way vague notions can't. *We can't hit a target we haven't clearly defined.* It's like taking a vacation with no destination in mind. When we have a clear goal, all our actions can be directed toward reaching that specific target with no wasted effort. Having a clear vision keeps us on the right path.

One of my good friends, Lee Kemp, is also one of my health and fitness mentors, and there's no bigger advocate for setting, visualizing and achieving goals. Considered one of the greatest wrestlers of all time, Lee has experienced the power of stating your goals and reaping the harvest of results.

Lee came to wrestling comparatively late — he started in ninth grade when most competitive wrestlers start in elementary school. At a summer wrestling camp after his second year in the sport, he got the opportunity to do something he never dreamed possible: meet his idol and role model Dan Gable. At the time, Gable was known in the United States as "The Greatest Wrestler of All Time." It was a boxer meeting Muhammad Ali in his prime. It was a basketball player meeting Michael Jordan at his most dominant.

Lee's heart pounded at the thought of being in the same room with Gable, who was the featured speaker and ran a workshop. Gable spoke about the importance of both short- and long-term goals, and Lee listened, taking notes and absorbing every word. Meeting the champ started a fire within Lee, and he wanted to see just what he could accomplish if he put his heart and soul into the sport.

Taking Gable's message about goal setting to heart — "Do not set limits on one's ability or goals" — Lee wrote down his *specific* goals. He envisioned himself winning a state wrestling title while in high school, winning a national title in college and, eventually, becoming a World Champion and Olympic Gold medalist in the sport. All these goals went down on paper — with specific actions he knew he must take to reach them — and were put in places where he had to see them on a daily basis.

Lee believes that writing goals down and reviewing them daily makes them more real — more tangible — and therefore harder to take back because there's a record of it. Merely *talking* about a goal allows it to fade from memory.

Lee's "obsession and relentless belief" — his words — with his goal setting led to the following results:

- He became a two-time Ohio State Champion, finishing his junior and senior years with an undefeated record of 55-0-0, with 24 pins.
- He went on to attend the University of Wisconsin-Madison on a full athletic scholarship, winning three NCAA titles at 158 pounds and placing second as a true freshman, losing on a split referee's decision in overtime. After his freshman year, he didn't lose another collegiate bout, posting 108 victories and one draw against his collegiate competition.
- Lee is known as one of the greatest wrestlers in United States history. He was a three-time Gold Medalist in the World Champion-

ships, a four-time Gold Medalist in the World Cup of Wrestling, a two-time Gold Medalist in the Pan American Games, a seven-time National Champion and was named the United States Wrestling Federation "Man of the Year" in 1978.

- He was inducted into the National Wrestling Hall of Fame in 1989, and 28 years after the United States-led 1980 Boycott of the Moscow Olympic Games — where Lee had been a favorite to win the Gold — he then got a chance to fulfill his Olympic dreams by being selected to coach the 2008 Olympic Wrestling Team competing in Beijing, China. It was also there during a ceremony at the Beijing Games that Lee was inducted into the United World Wrestling and the International Wrestling Hall of Fame — one of only six Americans to receive that honor to date.

But Lee's most memorable victory came when he was 18 years old, just 28 months after that life-changing encounter with his idol. During the finals of a prestigious tournament, Lee faced the one and only, greatest wrestler of all time — Dan Gable.

And Lee WON.

To this day, Lee still has many of his written wrestling goals archived and occasionally will look at them, confirming their power. "The power of writing clear, specific goals down is undeniable," he said. "No dream is too big. Open your mind and open your heart to the possibilities. Trust that, if you write it down, one day you'll have a better shot at making your goals happen."

For more information about Lee, his mindset and his path to success, he has written the wonderful book *Winning Gold: Success Secrets of a World Champion*. I highly recommend it for further inspiration about the power of setting goals.

A Map to Our Dreams

Goals can serve as a GPS for our life's journey. When motivation lags, when the easier path temps us, these objectives provide the guidelines to keep us on the right track. I've found that:

- Goals provide daily focus on the actions and behaviors needed to succeed
- Goals enable us overcome procrastination

- Goals assist us with time management
- Goals give us a sense of daily purpose and vision

I've been writing down my annual goals since I was 12 years old, and it's been a driving force in much of the success I've enjoyed in my life. We're focusing on business and financial matters in this chapter, but just like Lee Kemp, our goals include all our personal dreams and ambitions of what we want for our short- and long-term future. Finances are a major factor in this, but it's all part of the whole.

Our goals could be as small as losing five pounds or as large as building a multibillion-dollar business. Some we can achieve in a week; others may take a lifetime. The benefits of having a clear vision, however, remains the same, no matter the scale.

Think S.M.A.R.T.

I first encountered the idea of "S.M.A.R.T." goals when I worked with the Saturn Corporation and, because it's such a strong concept, I've have heard it used by several trainers, coaches and teachers since that time. This concept states that goals should be:

- **Specific** — Be as detailed as possible when stating our goals.
- **Measurable** — Make it something we can quantify on a consistent basis that allows us to gauge our process.
- **Achievable** — Our goal should be attainable, but it should also be a stretch so we maintain a positive pressure to perform.
- **Relevant** — It should be something that feeds into our daily purpose and vision.
- **Timely** — We want to achieve this goal in a specific time period ("next month" instead of "someday").

Tangible and trackable ideas are the core concept of S.M.A.R.T. Getting our goals out of our head and onto paper or into our computer or smartphone is the initial step.

To achieve a S.M.A.R.T. goal, we must think *specifically* about what we want — and steer clear of what's "comfortable." Setting goals that make us comfortable can *ruin* us. We need to choose objectives that make us uncomfortable but *put positive pressure on us to perform and compete.* We also need to keep revisiting those goals as our income changes and our careers advance, using them for continued motivation and drive.

When writing our goals down, we should include every ambition we can think of — every practicality, creature comfort or fantasy we can imagine. Again, we should *be precise*. Instead of "I'd like to purchase a house someday," we can ask ourselves *specific* questions that will bring our goal into focus:

> In a world of possibilities, however, we combine a vision with our goal and make life unfold to reach successes beyond our dreams.

- Where do I want to live? By the river? On the beach? Near the woods? In a development? Farmhouse? Condo?
- What square footage would I like? (Be specific — instead of "big" or "small," decide if it should be 1,500 square feet, 5,000 or some other number.)
- What features would I like? Three-car garage? Pool? Walk-out basement?
- How big should the property be? A half-acre? Five acres? More?

A clear vision of our goals will make them easier to achieve and provide us with intense motivation.

Confronting Ourselves

Goals hidden away on the pages of a journal won't generate the motivation necessary to make them a reality. My mentors taught me to put written goals in places *that force us to confront them daily — and where they confront us.* This might be our bathroom mirror, our closet, our office desk, our car, our smartphone or anywhere else where they'll be in our faces. We all need constant reminders of what we're working towards.

My wife has pointed out that I don't achieve all my yearly goals; in fact, there are years when I don't hit half of them. I'm confident she says this to challenge me, and that's one of the many things I appreciate about her. The other way of looking at that situation, though, is that while I didn't achieve half of them, I *did* achieve the other half. As for the goals I might have missed, I know I came closer than I would have without writing them down. High achievers understand they must continue to stay focused on the goals they haven't reached. They reexamine them to see if those goals are still relevant and, if they are, move them to the next year until they *are* achieved.

We have found that it's helpful to divide our goals into three categories:

1. **Short-term** (within the next year) — Buying a car, saving for a vacation or getting a certain amount of money saved in the bank
2. **Intermediate** (within the next five years) — Having a child, buying a home or planning to start a business
3. **Long-Term** (five years or more) — Saving for a child's college education, planning for retirement or supporting aging parents

Get Things in Order

Once we've set our goals, it's crucial to *prioritize* them, defining what is most urgent and important.

We'll have quite a list after writing down all our objectives. If we attempt to tackle everything at once, we'll get overwhelmed and be tempted to give up. When we select what's most important, we're setting an agenda for ourselves and we'll make traction on attaining our goals.

Be Accountable

Another value of having written, defined goals is that we can share them with mentors and trusted friends. They can hold us accountable for our progress — or *lack* of progress. When we have *external* pressure from the expectations of those whose opinions we value and admire, we have extra passion and inspiration when our natural motivation lags.

It's Our Life, Period

One last thought on this topic: *Our goals should be personal — not what others may want for us (our parents, spouse, friends, family, boss or others), but what WE want.* We must be honest with ourselves, and then become fanatically obsessed with making our goals a reality. It takes a lot of effort to achieve our dreams; we must make sure they are actually *our* dreams.

We don't want to wake up years down the road and realize we're living someone else's "best version" of our life. It's our life, the only one we'll have, so let's commit to making it our *best* life.

Our goals should be personal — not what others may want for us (our parents, spouse, friends, family, boss or others), but what *we* want.

Checking Our
Financial Attitudes

IT'S EASY TO STICK to the plan when things are going well. Those who know *real* success — in business and in life — are able to power through adversity. They may adjust their plan when necessary, but they never abandon it.

> Those who know *real* success — in business and in life — are able to power through adversity.

By overcoming obstacles, we discover who we are and what we're made of. We must use our passion, enthusiasm, belief, focus, care and creativity to maintain the mental fortitude that will steer us through life's difficulties. Always drive towards success.

Here are *10 key concepts* I've learned both from my mentors and from my own life experience to maintain a success-oriented attitude. The common element to each of these is that we have to *take action:*

- **Surround Ourselves with Mentors/Role Models** — We should build a circle of positive people who dream and think bigger than we do. *Whenever possible, we should dump or minimize the time we spend the negative people who are always whining about why they can't get ahead.* Avoid professional victims. Instead, we can find and befriend people who have accomplished more than we have. *This is the core of The Theory of 5.*

- **Our Purpose, or Our "Why"** — Understand *why* we want to accomplish our goals and vision in business, finance and life. One of my most valued mentors believes this is one of the most important aspects of success in all areas. Our purpose — our "why" — moves us, motivates us, gives us conviction and gets us up every morning — but only if it's truly *our* purpose. Having that daily focus is the reason why some people are able to achieve much more than others who are just as smart and hard working.

In reality, there's no right or wrong purpose, but it must come from our hearts. Right now, take a moment, put this book down, and think about *your* "why." What motivates you to get up every day? Is it family? Financial freedom? Helping others? Competition? Discover your "why" and put it to work for you.

- **Set the Stage** — Let's give ourselves every advantage we can as we set out to achieve our dreams. When we get the training we need and surround ourselves with those who will support us and who have achieved the results we desire, we give ourselves the best chance for success and believe in ourselves.

- **Crawl, Walk, Run** — When we first start out, whatever the activity, we might not excel at it. The temptation to quit is greatest at this point. Any improvement takes time, effort, stamina and the belief in ourselves to achieve what we want to be. *When we compare ourselves to those we respect and admire, we're not comparing equals.* We can't compare ourselves at the beginning of our journey to someone who's already walked the path for years. *Remember* that they, too, were once beginners. It took hard work and dedication to build themselves into the person we admire. We have to give ourselves the opportunity to improve, but start the process *now*.

- **Stay Hungry** — When we're comfortable with where we are and what we have, it's impossible to reach our full potential, both in business and as a human being. We grow only when we strive to be more than what we are. Gratitude and appreciation are healthy; *complacency* is debilitating and has no place in The Theory of 5.

- **Be Relentless** — It is crucial that we know what we want and what it will take to get us there. Once we do, we have no excuse for not making the attempt. If we don't give it our all, we're not being true to ourselves. We must be obsessed with reaching our full potential. Failure can be a growth experience; *laziness* is unacceptable. A phrase I've lived by my entire life is "persistence breaks down resistance." There's no substitute.

- **Continuous Improvement** — The moment we think we've learned all there is to know about a topic, we've set ourselves up for failure. Once we've stopped improving, we're absolutely going backward. *The world does not stand still.* There are always new methods, technologies and schools of thought. There are also people hungrier than us, and they're looking for an opening to take our place or to pass us by. Let's not give them one.

- **Recognize Our *True* Competition** — On the path to success, we're not competing with anyone else; we're competing with ourselves in reaching *our full potential.* Most people are either not living up to what they believe they can be, or they've set their sights too low. The moment we become comfortable is the moment we stop growing and start falling behind.

- **Embrace the Rules of Change** — Since almost nothing goes as planned, we should be ready to encounter the unexpected. First, it's necessary that we are **aware** of the situation; we can't be the person who ignores the reality to hold on to a fantasy. Next, we must **accept** that the situation is what it is; we should react to what's there, not what we *wish* was there. Finally, we must **act**. If things go sideways, we will adapt our existing plan to the current situation or develop a new one. We'll get the information we need, make our decisions and then carry out our plan.

- **Harness Our Fear** — Many years ago, I asked one of my mentors what he felt was the main reason he became a multi-millionaire. He wasn't raised in a wealthy family, and he didn't have wealthy relatives or friends before he found his financial success. His answer initially surprised me until I understood and internalized it. The reason he gave for his success — and why he continues to push daily — is *fear.* Fear of not being able to continue providing for himself and his family in the manner they'd become accustomed to. Fear of living the life of his mother and father, who struggled financially their entire lives. Fear of losing what he had worked hard for decades to gain. Fear of falling behind his competitors. Fear of letting people down who counted on him and who looked to him for inspiration. He credits fear for his competitive spirit. We shouldn't *avoid* our fear; we should *face* it. It can give us the edge we've been searching for. Embrace it. Use it. Transform it into *action*.

We shouldn't *avoid* our fear; we should *face* it. It can give us the edge we've been searching for.

Our Calling

THE MINDSET OF THE most prosperous individuals I've encountered is that they don't obsess about money. Instead, they push themselves *to be the absolute best in their field so they can dominate their competition.*

Eustace Wolfington once said to me, "Chris, don't worry about money. *If you're the best at what you do, the money will come."* It takes energy to worry about things; it drains us and still accomplishes nothing. If we put that energy to better use, becoming more skilled in our field or dealing with what's causing us stress, we'll get *results.*

High achievers have also taken the mental inventory and have embraced the idea that they're doing what they were meant to do. *Doubt will hinder our progress and our potential,* splitting our focus and keeping us from living our best life. One of the things we can ask our mentors is how they knew for certain that they were on the right path.

> Eustace Wolfington once said to me, "Chris, don't worry about money. If you're the best at what you do, the money will come."

One sign that we've made the right call is when we stop seeing our careers as work. *The most successful people see their career as a sport where all they crave is the winning result.* It's on their mind as they eat, sleep, dream, shower or exercise. This becomes a deep-rooted passion for them. It becomes exciting. It becomes fun. They're fanatically obsessed — in a good way.

Let's take a moment and define our values, separate from money. What do we stand for? What are acceptable and unacceptable attitudes, behaviors and actions? It's important to answer these questions; otherwise, our morality may slip when the cash comes in. Success with money is meaningless if we hate ourselves. It is possible to earn an amazing income without sacrificing the values we hold important. *In fact, good values make for great business.*

We believe it's crucial to find the purpose — our "why" — that drives our lives, and make sure it provides us with happiness and fulfillment; if it doesn't, it's not our purpose. This is not a selfish question. *We can't love others if we don't love ourselves.* When we live our best life, it will also benefit our children, our spouses, our families, friends and coworkers.

It is possible to earn an amazing income without sacrificing the values we hold important. In fact, *good values make for great business.*

We Are In Sales

ALTHOUGH THIS IS NOT a "how to sell" book, selling ourselves when it comes to managing our business and finances is the first step in excelling in this area. The toughest sale we will ever have is selling ourselves. If we don't believe in ourselves, our product and our idea, no one else will believe, either. My mentors and I believe our ability to excel in life will be determined by our power to sell our point of view.

> The toughest sale we will ever have is selling ourselves. If we don't believe in ourselves, our product and our idea, no one else will believe, either.

I've been in sales my entire adult life, so it comes naturally to me to see business and finance through this lens. No matter what field you're in or what your occupation might be, however, *you are also in sales.* Think about it: In any transaction, we are trading (selling) our goods, services or talents for compensation (money, barter or other benefits). Even if we're volunteering our services, we are still getting something from our time. Imagine if no one said, "thank you" or otherwise appreciated our contribution. Would we be motivated to continue?

In the *traditional* sales transaction, the salesperson is trying to get the most compensation possible while the customer wants to pay the least. With *The Theory of 5* sales transaction, however, the goal is to *find a win-win situation for everyone involved.* Rather than an antagonistic exercise, the best deals are partnerships, with each side providing something the other needs and neither going away feeling used or as a loser.

I have *never* felt like I was selling; rather, I was guiding and supporting someone to fill a need, want or desire. I've always believed I am a *problem solver* or "*solutionist.*" I've sold myself on why my friends, relatives or customers would need or want certain products, ideas, theories or concepts.

If I'm not sold on something myself, if I don't believe it will make their life better after understanding their wants and needs, *I don't sell it.* While I might not need it myself, I have to believe it's an exceptional price value for the customer. This very book is born from this mindset and this passion. *I believe in my heart and soul every person on the planet would have a better life by living a Theory of 5 life.*

For those of us who don't consider ourselves in "sales"… *we are.* Within the next few hours, we will be in a conversation with someone selling an idea. With this in mind, here are some ideas my mentors and I have found helpful in the sales process:

- **Sell Yourself First** — In any transaction, we must build a relationship with our client. Whatever the product or service, if the person we're dealing with doesn't like us, they won't listen to us and the sale is over. If we can present ourselves as someone with their best interests in mind, though, they'll be open to listening to us, and they'll take our ideas to heart. Whatever we're offering, we need to make sure we understand it backward and forwards, inside and out. We must present ourselves well and put ourselves in their position; would *we* want to do business with us?

- **Listen More, Talk Less** — Knowledge of our product is essential, but it's not the only factor in our success. Many low-producing salespeople know their product well — and can't get over telling you how amazing it is. They go on and on about it. They won't shut up about it. *Exceptional* salespeople ask questions and listen to what their customers say. These professionals make it a point to ask open-ended questions (the "Who, What, When, Where, Why and How" questions). These are the questions that *start a discussion,* rather than just provide "yes" or "no" answers. They also use what I call "acceptance cues" ("I see," "yes," "that makes sense," etc.) to show they are listening and involved in the conversation.

  These sales professionals take notes, summarize and then clarify that **they understand what's most important to the customer**. They pay attention to their customer's needs from the start. Then, they do a *personalized presentation* of their product according to what meets or exceeds their customer's expectations. This builds trust. When the customer understands that we care, that is the beginning of forging a lasting relationship.

- **Understand the Person's Motives** — We should be sure we can answer the question, "Why does this person care or have an interest in what I'm selling?" How is our product or service providing value to them? The first step is to listen to *their needs,* and then build value in our presentation. To come to an agreement, the *perceived value* to the person must exceed the price they'll pay. We must build *value and trust* by: 1) discovering our customers' *wants and needs,* 2) listening to them and becoming their advocate in this selling process, 3) being able to demonstrate the value of our product or service and 4) providing evidence that the company we represent is the best choice for them. If we do all these things, we'll come to an agreement (see Figure 2).

- **Keep It Simple** — We shouldn't complicate our presentation just to "sound intelligent." The mark of a true sales professional is the ability to explain the product to the average person. Jargon, acronyms and complex terms don't "build credibility" with a person; they just build a wall and drive them away. We should keep our presentation simple and never talk for more than two minutes without asking a question or otherwise keeping them engaged.

- **Mind What You Say and How You Say It** — When conveying our message, our words are only part of the equation. *Neurolinguistic scientists have found our tone and body language can be even more important than what we say. Studies found that 55 percent of communication comes from body language, 38 percent from our tone of voice and only 7 percent from actual word choice.* The most successful salespeople make sure they're putting their message across in the most effective way possible. Keep this in mind when communicating through email, texts or any other medium where tone and body language are lacking. What might be a joke in person can come across as sarcastic or even hostile in a text conversation.

For any product or service, when value exceeds the price, price is no longer the issue. By making ourselves the best in our field and becoming experts in communicating our ideas, we'll build a relationship and create customers for life.

Price

Traditional Sales
Mindset

Value

Theory of 5
Sales Thinking

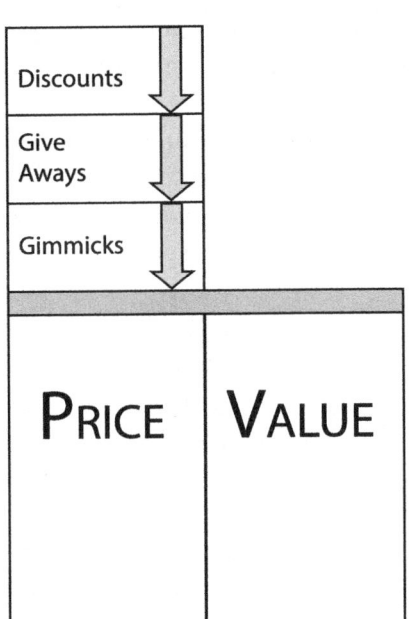

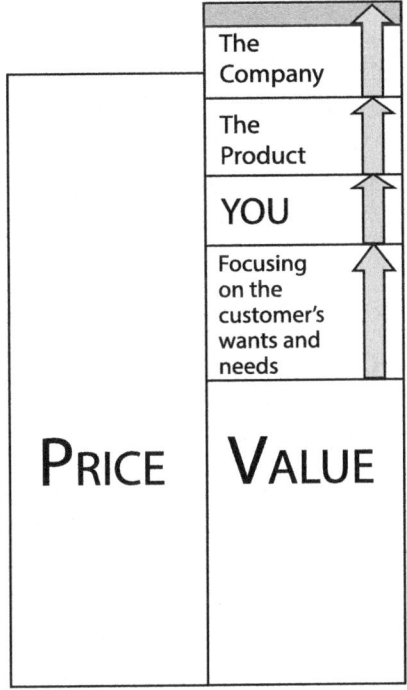

*Figure 2 — In the **traditional sales mindset,** where price is the only consideration, there is a "race to the bottom" with the competition because only one company can have the lowest price. Discounts, giveaways, gimmicks and other tricks are used to drive down the price. What many salespeople don't realize, however, is that the **perceived value** of what's being sold — along with the value of the salesperson and their company — also drops.*

*In **The Theory of 5 way of sales thinking,** the price doesn't drop; our value and the value of our product and our company **rises**, along with the perceived value of what we're selling. This is because we've listened to the customer's **wants and needs, adapted to what we've learned. As a result, we earn their trust. Once the perceived value rises higher than the price,** sales are made and customer go away feeling enthusiastic, knowing that they received a great price/value.*

Three Questions All Buyers Need Answered

When selling any product or service, Eustace Wolfington once shared with me three basic questions that every person will have, either consciously or subconsciously. These are questions we *must* answer before coming to an agreement.

Let's imagine we have a magic stone to sell, and our asking price is $1 million. We hold it in our closed hand as we approach our potential buyer. After hearing our price, they are shocked until we answer three questions:

- **Question No. 1: What is it?** — We can't come to an agreement if it's not clear what the person is purchasing. While answers to this question can be simple (in this case, "It's a *magic stone*"), some services or products are more complex. If so, clearly spell out what's being offered.
- **Question No. 2: How does it work?** — To justify the price and establish the value, the potential buyer needs to understand not only what it is, but how it works, at least in a general sense. *How does the magic stone work?* We tell them it will create their best life in each area of The Theory of 5. Once they understand its function or purpose, they will become fully involved in the discussion.
- **Question No. 3: What will it do for me?** — This is the step where we can paint a picture and they can internalize ownership. People buy because they *need* or *want* the object or service; it creates a solution in their lives.

"What will the magic stone do for me?"
"You will always have spiritual clarity. You will have a perfect relationship with your spouse or partner. You will raise children who will *thrive* in the world. You will excel in your career and have excessive wealth to support and influence family, friends and charities. You will be in peak health and physical conditioning for the rest of your life."

Engage their imagination. Have them share with us their desires. *They* will *work with us* to make the sale.

When the person we're speaking with is an active participant in the sale, both parties win when it's time to come to an agreement. *Involvement equals buy-in.*

Perfect Practice

The adage "practice makes perfect" is inaccurate. As legendary coach Vince Lombardi pointed out, "Only *perfect* practice makes perfect." If we're practicing and rehearsing with bad information or poor form, we're only reinforcing the wrong behavior.

When first starting out, word tracks can be valuable aids for getting our foundational skills in place. We can see what wording is effective and build our confidence as we work on our tone and other skills. It's a good habit to ask our leaders and mentors for their appraisal of what we're doing well and what needs to be polished. Once we see what makes an effective sales experience, we can then change some of the wording and make it more our own. Memorize, then personalize.

> The goal is to make every transaction a win-win. We should treat each customer the same as we would a family member or our best friend.

Speak Up

It's no surprise that the best businesses receive lots of referrals, have repeat customers and never stop marketing. We never know if the next person we meet will need our goods or services. While we shouldn't become the "pushy salesperson" everyone wants to avoid, we shouldn't hesitate to offer our services when the time is right. If people need or desire what we offer, they'll be glad to have us in their circle. The goal is to make every transaction a win-win. Treat each customer the same as we would a family member or our best friend. When we do this, people will see us as *a trusted professional or friend* instead of a "salesperson."

Our Circle of Confidence

While we should always be developing new skills, we'll inevitably have an area where we're at our best. This area plays to our strengths, where we understand how to put our skills to their best effort. Billionaire investor Warren Buffett calls this "business sweet spot" the "circle of competence"; we could also call it our "circle of *confidence*."

Knowing where our passion lies and where our game is strongest is key to determining this circle. This is where we have an edge over all the other competition. This is how we will dominate the business world.

Something odd can happen, however, when people confront their circle of confidence. Instead of embracing it, they can turn *away* from it and try to find something different. Perhaps it's a "grass is always greener" perception, or a lack of self-confidence ("If *I'm* good at it, then everyone else must be, too"). We shouldn't take our strengths for granted. If some things come easier to us than others, it's because those areas are where our passion and natural abilities meet. Take advantage of our strengths to grow and dominate.

Note: As I mentioned at the beginning of this chapter, this is not a "how to sell" book, although what you've just read is an excellent basic introduction to sales. There are *many* excellent sales books and material available. Do some online research and you'll find resources that will support your growth you no matter what your experience level.

We shouldn't take our strengths for granted.
If some things come easier to us than others,
it's because those areas are where our passion
and natural abilities meet.

Training Ourselves
to Lead Others

As WE BUILD OUR careers in the business world, at some point we may decide we want to work into a leadership position or are asked to take on this responsibility. This may or may not be a natural fit for us. Some people thrive on leading a team or business while other people tolerate it and look at it as a necessary burden. Whatever our outlook, we owe it to the people on our team to provide them with the best leadership we can give them.

> The right people make the difference between having a winning championship team and a losing "chumpionship" team.

The best leaders I've ever known have seen their role as an opportunity to serve others. Where average-to-poor managers seek to take advantage of the situation, great leaders have a code of ethics and the desire to watch and support their team members grow and prosper.

Great leaders understand that human capital is their most precious commodity when building a winning team. They understand it's all about recruiting, hiring, training and retaining the right people. Once they have those people in place, their team needs two things from them. They need leaders to oversee the day-to-day business while also providing them with — and continually reminding them of — the "big picture" vision. The right people make the difference between having a winning championship team and a losing "championship" team.

With newer, less-experienced leaders, it's crucial to be clear from the beginning, and explain what we want the team to do and *why* it needs to be done. It's also imperative that they understand what the benefits of these actions will be for them as key individuals, for their team and for the end user or customer, as well. With leaders new to the position, we continue to provide them with the tools and training needed to get their job done and grow the business. We want to share with them how their effort makes a difference for them, their team and the company. This is where the real day-to-day work gets done.

Great leaders bring a spirit to his or her organization and provide an example to their team. Leaders create a mission, vision and values that provide everyone on their team with a sense of calling and of making a difference. As leaders, always provide your team members with the reason — the "why" — of what your company does and why it does it. Sharing that vision makes a huge difference, and allows them to participate in the overall mission.

In an atmosphere where each team member is appreciated and understood, where there's genuine care and support, amazing results will be achieved. This atmosphere starts with the leader and starts from Day One. The culture we generate determines what happens each step of the way. Culture dictates behavior. *Behavior and daily activity determine results.*

Actions Create Culture

The best leaders push harder when "average" leaders have had enough. These leaders do so, however, by working *with* the team, not cracking the whip to bleed every last bit from their employees. By building a *team* mentality, great leaders can get results their people didn't even realize they could achieve. "Bully" bosses, especially as the Millennial generation takes its place in workforce, are seldom as effective as those who show real empathy and caring for their team. Which atmosphere would *you* rather work in?

Great leaders also never underestimate the power of a sense of humor. While we don't have to do a joke a minute or be the "funny" boss, it's just more fun to come into an office where things aren't always grim and dire. In the words of Dwight D. Eisenhower — a man who knew something about motivating people to do what they considered to be impossible — "A sense of humor is part of the art of leadership, of getting along with people, of getting things done."

But, just as the right actions can set our team up for success, there are other actions that can completely derail an organization. Great leaders will never allow...

The Seven Culture Killers

These behaviors, if practiced by the leader or permitted to exist in the office by the leader, will make our business a miserable place to work. They will absolutely kill office morale. These behaviors are so destructive that, if allowed to take root, they will run off the talented individuals we want on our team. These culture killers are:

- **Big Ego and Arrogance** — This is especially true if it's the leader displaying this quality. There's a difference between confidence and arrogance. People *like* confidence; *arrogance* cultivates a "me vs. you" mentality that will break a team apart or prevent it from forming at all. Additional obstacles are leaders with the "I, Me Mine" mindset we mentioned in the marriage section of *The Theory of 5*. These are the leaders who believe every great idea is theirs and will take credit even if they don't deserve it.

- **Micromanaging on a Consistent Basis** — Consistently hovering over our people when they are properly trained and can do their job makes everyone uncomfortable and less productive. While micromanaging actually *does* have a place in the leadership mindset — it's important to take a hands-on approach in guiding people when they're first starting out in our organization — know that uncontrolled micromanaging will chase off talented team members.

- **Gossip** — There are only two words necessary to address gossip in the workplace: "STOP IT" (perhaps three more: "OR YOU'RE FIRED"). Gossip is a workplace cancer — once it's discovered, it needs to be excised aggressively and immediately. Gossip is a tool small people use to make themselves feel powerful at the expense of others. It is *not* to be tolerated.

- **Office Politics** — Our teams have enough to deal with when building or operating a company that excels in its field; they shouldn't have to deal with life being made harder in their own office because of useless rules or petty power plays. We should make sure our team is just that — *a team*. We all pull together, or we go nowhere.

- **Dishonesty or Lack of Transparency** — Our employees need to depend on us as a leader and their peers as their teammates. As soon as that trust is broken by someone's lie or by a change in the rules they didn't see coming, the best and brightest start looking to take their talents elsewhere. People can respect those who make mistakes and take responsibility. They can understand when policies change if they know the reasoning behind it. What they *won't* accept is being lied to or blindsided.

- **Lack of Recognition or Equal treatment of Unequals** — We'll touch on this in more detail but treating hard workers the same as those content to skate by on the bare minimum sets a dangerous precedent. By treating everyone the same — even though some are more deserving of praise, promotions, bonuses and the other good things that come with putting in the time and effort to go the extra mile — we dampen down enthusiasm and reinforce laziness. We should *never* penalize the hard workers and reward the unmotivated.

- **Unresolved Issues** — Every office has its challenges. Things will go wrong from time to time, with equipment, personnel, policies or other elements. When things need our attention, we must take care of them. Don't put off getting necessary equipment repaired or replaced. If a change is needed in our process to make it run smoother, make it happen. When disagreements between co-workers are causing problems in the office and there is no sign of it stopping, get involved. Model the behavior to get things done in the company.

As leaders, part of our commitment to our people is to give them a place to work where they can fulfill their potential and go further than they ever thought possible. One way to support them is to make sure our office or our company runs smoothly. These culture killers must be avoided, and that requires paying attention and making sure none of them take root in our businesses.

Handling Conflict

When leading people, dealing with conflict is part of the job. Any two people will disagree from time to time; the more people we add to the mix, the more often conflict will become a factor. Effective leaders understand when to let people work things out on their own — and when they need to step in.

Most people in a conversation or a conflict are trying to get their point across or make themselves heard. If both sides are listening and working towards a compromise, it might be best to let them work it out. When both sides dig in and refuse to listen or if time becomes a factor, leaders need to take an active role.

I've found that most conflicts can be settled by bringing the two sides together and engaging them in a conversation. Instead of allowing them to wait for their turn to talk without listening to the other's point of view, we should *make* them participate in a conversation. We can encourage them to employ logic and empathy, and give each the forum so they are heard and understood; often, this is all they wanted.

Leaders can facilitate the conversation to the point where both sides agree. If they can come to an understanding, this helps the team dynamics and may lead to

> Conflict, by the way, isn't necessarily a bad thing. When handled properly, it absolutely can create chemistry and clarity between team members.

an atmosphere where future disagreements are easier to settle. If they can't, that's when we, as leaders, need to use what we've learned from both sides and make the decision for them. When we follow this process, they've at least felt heard and valued, even if the result didn't go their way this time.

Conflict, by the way, isn't necessarily a bad thing. When handled properly, it absolutely can create chemistry and clarity between team members. My relationships with some of my favorite business associates have grown after resolving a conflict. We had major debates and disagreements, but once we realized we had the same goal, we resolved our differences and developed a great respect for each other.

Leading and Teaching

There are six major leadership concepts my mentors and I have found to be true:

1. Team members do not quit a *company*; they quit their *leader*. If we've provided a valid vision, our team will follow us for the long haul.
2. *Leaders must lead.* Just as a parent isn't their children's friend — at least before they become adults — a leader must not lose sight of the fact they are there for a purpose. Our teams are looking to us for direction; we must make sure to provide it.
3. A leader isn't afraid to push his or her team to perform *actions or*

behaviors the team might not want to do. These leaders do this so their team can hit goals they might not otherwise think possible and see the *benefits* of their efforts.

4. Leaders must set *clear, specific daily expectations for behaviors, actions and results.* We can't make our team guess what we want. We must hold our teams, including the team leaders, accountable for the *results* to which we've all agreed to when they were hired or promoted.

5. Team members need consistent, usable feedback about their attitudes, actions, behaviors and results. This doesn't have to be a detailed review; a quick, specific conversation or counsel is a wonderful training and teaching tool.

6. Leadership is about creating positive change and constantly facilitating long-term growth. *Leaders must care enough to give their team the tools, resources, authority and training to grow, improve and excel.* Great leaders are always searching for ways to make their team members *better*, and are naturally driven to make a difference.

Equal Treatment of Unequals

In our society, we're all equal under the law (or at least, we should be). We are entitled to the same opportunities no matter our age, gender, race, religion or economic background. We all have rights, and we all have responsibilities. None of us are inherently better than anyone else simply because we're drawing breath.

That doesn't mean we're all equal.

We mentioned this concept in the parenting section of *The Theory of 5*, but it applies just as much in the workplace. *When it comes to our behaviors, actions, attitudes and choices, the idea of "equality" should stop and the idea of "merit" should begin. I believe that there's nothing quite as unfair as the equal treatment of unequals.*

Imagine you have two employees. Mr. Eagle gets to work early, strives to improve himself, helps his team whenever he can and regularly goes beyond what's expected. Mr. Donkey regularly comes in late, infects everyone else with his rotten attitude, does the bare minimum (if that) and watches the clock for his chance to blow out of the office. Would you treat them as equals? What message would that send to Mr. Eagle — and all your other employees — if he got the same bonus check as Mr. Donkey?

How motivated would anyone be to put in the extra effort? How motivated would the outstanding team members be to find another job where their effort was appreciated, rewarded and recognized?

It is crucial that we are aware of the message we're sending by our treatment of each of these team members. The best leaders build amazing teams by rewarding those who go above and beyond, and not tolerating those content to hang on. There will always be people who believe they are entitled to special treatment they did not earn or deserve. The time they spend whining would be put to better use by doing the work necessary to improve themselves and make contributions to the company and their fellow team members.

Ultimately, our workplace will be more efficient, happier and have increased production when we clearly let people know that the *individual* results, attitudes and behaviors of each team member will dictate their rewards, bonuses, recognition and opportunities for growth within the company.

Empower Those Who Lead for Us

To avoid the trap of micromanaging, trust those managers working with us with a *proven* track record of results. This requires another level of leadership, one where we *empower* those who lead teams in our organization. *Holding a person accountable for results without giving them the tools they need to get the job done is beyond frustrating.* We might as well just chase them out the door and save everyone the time and effort.

This, however, is the reality of many businesses. A title means nothing and an office doesn't make sales or encourage excellence in a team. Leaders without the necessary tools aren't leaders at all; they're really puppets of their managers.

The Theory of 5's definition of empowerment is this:

Authority + Necessary Resources + Shared Responsibility = Empowerment

We need all three elements to achieve success.

- **Authority:** If we plan on holding a leader accountable for his or her results, then we must empower this person. Not doing so is setting them, and us, up for disappointment. Imagine (or remember) being put in charge of a department but never receiving the proper authority. That's a sure-fire recipe for failure and a dysfunctional team.

- **Necessary Resources:** If we give a leader authority but not the needed resources (tools, knowledge, skills, finances, advertising, inventory, etc.), we are again setting them up to fail. There's no such thing as magic. Some teams might struggle — and occasionally even win — with inadequate resources, but we shouldn't expect our team to be a group of miracle workers.
- **Shared Responsibility:** If we've given our leaders the authority and the resources they need, we still need to remember that we are all part of the same team. Just as they lead their people, we lead them. At this level, they need our facilitation and involvement rather than being directed what to do at each step of the way. As they strive to reach their best, they should still receive coaching, training, feedback and support from us as we expect them to give to their team.

Our Turn:
Leading and Mentoring with The Theory of 5

When we become business leaders, this is the time when we are best equipped to repay the kindness and generosity that our mentors gave us. Remember the value you felt when a more experienced, successful leader took notice of you? We can repay that by becoming a mentor to someone else who's in the right place to take our lessons to heart.

Not only is this the right thing to do, but mentoring someone can make a difference for us, as well. In the process of mentoring someone, we'll be forced to examine the details of our own lives. The best leaders understand they are continuous students of the business. They know they must focus on growing in all areas of leadership, as well as the other areas of The Theory of 5. They also appreciate we can't truly understand a skill or concept unless we can teach it to someone else. When we teach, we also internalize. When we internalize, we hold ourselves accountable for our daily actions and behaviors.

By becoming a mentor, we'll also make ourselves better leaders and coaches. It provides us with a source of empathy — putting ourselves in our team member's place and seeing things from their point of view. We will also discover ways to improve in areas we may have previously taken for granted by seeing them from a different perspective.

Steps to a Prosperous Life

BUSINESS AND FINANCE ARE, without a doubt, fascinating but complex topics. As a way of summing it up, here are some of the most valuable lessons I've learned from my mentors. They might be considered "common sense" by some but, unfortunately, common sense isn't always that common:

- **Persistence Breaks Down Resistance:** *In our experience, persistence is the common trait of all prosperous businesspeople.* There is *no* substitute for persistence and relentlessness. Talent without drive is useless. Education by itself accomplishes nothing. Drive, dedication, determination and discipline are all necessary to find and keep our best lives.

- **Decide Who Gets Our Time and Attention:** The people around us will influence our thinking. Billionaires think differently than millionaires and millionaires think differently than broke people. Healthy people have a different outlook than sick people, and happy people unquestionably view the world differently than miserable people. There will be people we love who might have a negative mindset, and I'm not saying we should abandon them. We *do,* however, need to be aware of the effect they can have on

> Billionaires think differently than millionaires and millionaires think differently than broke people. Healthy people have a different outlook than sick people, and happy people unquestionably view the world differently than miserable people.

us. We shouldn't get distracted by battling things that don't really matter. If the battle isn't between us and what's standing in the way of our success and vision, then it's a distraction. I beg you, *don't take the distraction bait.* We should strive to build a circle of people whose attitudes, actions, habits and behaviors we value and respect.

- **Live a Grateful Life:** While it's important to focus on improving ourselves and our business, it's vital to take time to be grateful for what we have, especially for the people in our lives. Never forget our friends or take our spouses for granted. Keep focus on our children (they won't be children forever, and we won't get another chance to know them at their current age). Be the bigger person every time we get the chance — we'll never regret it. Our careers need constant attention, but so do those who matter most to us. Through The Theory of 5, we will find that balance and harmony.

The focus on gratitude is one of the most personal and important aspects to me and to The Theory of 5. I've found that the happiest people in the world are grateful and appreciative. Daily gratitude lays the mental groundwork for higher levels of enthusiasm, determination, energy and quality of life. We'll have better interactions with people because appreciation reciprocates. I've also seen that grateful people have less stress, as well, because they're not focused on the negative aspects of life. **Embrace the importance of gratitude — it's one of the most essential attitudes we can cultivate.** This outlook makes a difference in how we interact with the world, and how the world interacts with us.

Note: For more information, some of my personal favorite leadership authors, coaches and role models are Dave Anderson ("Learn to Lead") and Stephen Covey (*The 7 Habits of Highly Effective People*).

Financial Philosophies of the Wealthy

The way wealthy people think about money is different than how the poor do. The wealthy can examine the subject more clearly and without the desperation that those living a hand-to-mouth existence must endure. This clarity allows them to truly consider how best to make money work for them, rather than the other way around. My mentors have shared the following ideas with me when it comes to growing — and keeping — their wealth.

- **Get Focused:** What do we *really* want in life? My mentor Harvey Ritter once said to me, "Chris, do what you've got to do *daily* so you can do what you want to do *in life.*" Many people seem unable to let go of short-term pleasure and never do what it takes for sustainable happiness in life. When we build something real, we can enjoy our success by living the life we want and deserve.

- **Make, and Keep, a Budget:** If we only have a vague notion of where our money is and how it moves through our life, we can't control it. We shouldn't *wonder* where our money goes; we need to *understand* where it goes and then make decisions on how to grow it. One way to do this is to start saving and investing for retirement early on. It's easier to build wealth for later years if we begin early. Saving for retirement, by the way, can include rental properties, a business, savings, 401(k) plans, stocks, or a combination of all of these. By having a discussion with our financial mentors and advisors, we will determine how best to put our money to work and grow for us.

- **Spend Less Than We Make:** It's simple, but in today's credit-driven society, it's tempting to live a lifestyle we can't afford. We can fake it for a short while, but the bills always come due. It's a much happier life when we know we can pay *all* our bills on time every time instead of deciding which bill we'll be late on that month. *We should also make a point to avoid bad debt and credit cards;* the financially uneducated are always paying high interest rates while the top 10 percent *earn* interest.

- **Pay Ourselves First:** Two of my mentors, Harvey Ritter and Robert Kelly, discussed and reinforced the idea of making savings a *priority.* Every month or every paycheck, we should decide how much we'll save, and take that off the top — even before groceries. This should be a realistic number, but we must take it seriously. Downturns will happen in life. If we've got a margin of safety, it gives us a sense of security. All my mentors unitedly agree that saving 10 percent or more of our net pay is a goal that has been passed down from generation to generation *because it works.* Without savings and good credit, it will be challenging to take advantage of financial, business and investment opportunities to grow our net worth.

- **Budget in Some Fun:** It's much easier to create and maintain the discipline needed to live on a budget if we've made room for fun. Make it a realistic number, but it's okay to give ourselves permission to go out to eat, go to the movies or have a hobby. If it's a budget item, it won't break our budget. We can't lose track of our long-term plan for short-term pleasure, though. This fun/entertainment budget should be *sacrificed* until we have a minimum base savings of at least five months of total household expenses.

  (This point, by the way, was a major debate among my mentors. Some thought five months was too high, while others thought it was far too low. One mentor put it like this: "Why would we recommend budgeting in 'fun' when you're only five months away from being bankrupt or homeless if they lost their income? This is an urgent issue in today's society." What they all did agree on was that our savings and investments should continue to grow and diversify as we age. As Warren Buffet advises, "One should never put all one's eggs in one basket." To accomplish this, we should seek counsel from a trusted financial advisor with a proven track record of success consistent with our financial goals and objectives.)

Protecting Our Net Worth and Assets

My financial mentors have always recommended that the way to protect it is through diversity and insurance. Proper planning now can save heartbreak down the road. The sister of one of my team members retired 15 years ago with $2.5 million in addition to owning her home. This was money she and her husband had saved their entire lives. This nest egg was to be used for their retirement, to enjoy life and to travel — the reward they had promised themselves for all those years of work. Soon after she retired, though, she had a debilitating stroke and had to go to a full-care facility. The facility cost around $10,000 to $12,000 per month. Her husband still had to maintain their home and his expenses, as well. Within 12 years their retirement fund was gone. If they would have had long-term care insurance, they could have protected most of their assets for her husband and their family. Instead, they died penniless.

Once we have wealth, we need to protect it with insurance and investment diversity. Those with a measure of wealth can also find themselves with a target on their backs; they need to get with an insurance professional and investigate umbrella policies to protect what they've earned.

Diversity is also critical for maintaining and protecting wealth. Stocks in one company, for example, can fall with one bit of bad news, wiping out years of saving. By spreading out our resources, we can ride out waves of uncertainty. Real estate is often a great way to protect and grow our net worth and can provide a source of reoccurring revenue or passive income; *work with a professional, though, in all matters of investment that are not your field of expertise.*

Common Estate Planning Mistakes

There are common mistakes many people make, through inaction, inattention or just not wanting to face their own mortality, that put a burden on their family after their death. These mistakes can easily be avoided, but it takes a little knowledge, a little effort and a little planning:

- **Get Legal Documents in Place** — We should make sure we have a legal will and a healthcare directive in place. We can't make our family guess what we would have wanted or face a legal fight because we didn't put our wishes down in writing.
- **Update and Regularly Review Those Documents** — Circumstances, both ours and those of our beneficiaries, can change over time. Experts recommend that, over the age of 40, we should revisit our will and other documents every three to five years, or when our circumstances significantly change, i.e. promotions, retirement, job changes, death, divorce, etc.
- **Properly Title Assets** — We should make sure, in the event we pass on or become incapacitated, that someone we trust can access our bank accounts, home deeds, business information and other assets.

It's important to discuss these matters with a trusted advisor who is an expert in these matters. Financial topics are often emotionally charged, and never more so when dealing with an estate after the person has passed on. Having a third-party expert involved will help this. Smart planning and

communication beforehand will help avoid conflicts and misunderstand-
ings. Ultimately, we all want our financial legacy to *enhance* the lives of
our children and beneficiaries, rather than create strife.

Good Debt

What's that? Debt can be good?

It *can* be — but it takes planning and long-term thinking, and risk
has to be figured into the equation. Most of my mentors and I believe the
simple rule of debt is that, if it increases our net worth or has future value,
it's good debt. Some examples include:

- Real estate investments and revenue-producing properties
- Business loans (especially if we are buying or investing in a business we have been working with or a family business with a good
  reputation and a track record of profits)
- A home mortgage, if we plan on living in the same home for five
  or more years

There are some differences of opinion when it comes to the subject of
good debt. A friend of mine, a well-known author, speaker and business
consultant, has said that buying a home is a bad investment. He believes
that you should only buy property that can generate an income, and own-
ing a house ties you down. I've debated that with him, giving him the
example of my daughter and son-in-law. For them, taking out a mortgage
helped them to grow up and mature. Instead of spending money to go out
with friends or buying another surfboard or pair of shoes, they looked at
it as being able to buy that kitchen table or stove they've had their eye on.
Instead of taking a vacation, they can re-do the patio. Their outlook on
life dramatically changed, and their relationship has grown because of it.

My friend makes a good point when you're older or want to be mobile
— a house certainly can lock us in. Finances and psychology are linked,
though. During certain periods of our lives, a mortgage can and will re-
direct our focus and teach us good financial habits that will serve us well
throughout our life.

Be Extraordinary

No one sets out to have an average life or average career. The decisions we make every step of the way, however, dictate the course of our lives. Not everyone will understand or take part in our desire to excel in life. We should make the most important decision in our lives by surrounding ourselves with like-minded people who embrace The Theory of 5 philosophy. Small, consistent actions and daily efforts make the difference between having an average life and an exceptional life.

And, just as we need to keep an eye on our financial fitness, our physical fitness is something that shouldn't be ignored. Without our health, all the money and success in the world can become meaningless, and long hours put in at the office can be detrimental for our health if we don't pay attention to what our bodies need to function at their best. In the next section, we'll take a look at how to care for our health to get the most out of our lives.

No one sets out to have an average life or average career. The decisions we make every step of the way, however, dictate the course of our lives.

By overcoming obstacles, we discover who we are and what we're made of. We must use our passion, enthusiasm, belief, focus, care and creativity to maintain the mental fortitude that will steer us through life's difficulties. Always drive towards success.

The Only Body
We'll Ever Have

It Can't Be Ignored

Good health is something that's easy to take for granted — until it's gone — but it's actually the keystone to a great life. Without our health, every other aspect of The Theory of 5 becomes exponentially more difficult.

If we're in constant pain or endlessly dealing with health issues, our money is worthless except to pay medical bills. It's harder to enjoy our family and friends and it's challenging to even think straight about religion or spirituality. I've known unhealthy people who have their whole existence revolve around doctor visits and dealing with health setbacks and major illnesses. They have a tough time thinking about *anything* else.

The thing about our health is that, without proper and consistent care and maintenance of our bodies, our overall health will eventually take a turn for the worst. That's just a fact. For a while, youth can make up for poor exercise and eating habits. As we get older, however, time starts to take a toll on our bodies and we pay the price for our old, bad behaviors.

Naysayers may point to someone they know, or someone they've "heard" about, who lived to a ripe old age, all the while smoking, drinking and indulging to no end of other bad habits. These examples *may* be true, but what if these "charmed" people had lived a healthier lifestyle? What more could they have accomplished in their lives? Were their senior years filled with visits to the doctor? What was their quality of life? While there are exceptions to every rule, they're just that — *exceptions*.

Hoping *we're* the exception isn't a good plan for our lives.

Our abilities, our energy, our very *lives* depend on good health habits. The longer we go without a plan to take care of our health, the harder it becomes to make the changes we'll need to maintain our health as we get older.

I count myself fortunate on this subject because, in all the areas of The Theory of 5, maintaining my health and fitness has always come naturally to me, and I've been able to maintain it consistently. My mother shared with me how, as a two-year-old from my playpen, I loved watching fitness and exercise legend Jack LaLanne on television. At five, I'd hang out with my older brother, Perry, and do arm curls with him. In my youth, I loved competing in wrestling, I became involved with bodybuilding, power lifting and trained as a certified fitness instructor in college. I also enjoyed and competed in karate in my mid-20s through my mid-40s. Exercise and fitness have been essential to me throughout my life.

That being said, everyone is different. Some facets of The Theory of 5 will come easier for us than others. For those areas that don't come as naturally, we can structure our lives and surround ourselves with people who will hold us accountable, and fitness is no different. In fact, it's one of the easier areas for maintaining accountability because health goals lend themselves to measurability (weight, measurements, time spent exercising, lab results from regular check-up exams, etc.). Whether or not it comes easy to us, it's important to not ignore or take our health for granted. *It's too important to be ignored. It's the only body we'll ever have!*

Hoping *we're* the exception
isn't a good plan for our lives.

Start Smart and Be Safe

BEFORE BEGINNING ANY KIND of workout regimen or lifestyle-altering path, speak with your doctor. This is especially important if you have health issues or haven't been leading an active lifestyle. Ask your physician's advice on which type of exercise and nutrition plan would work best for you. Don't be a "weekend warrior" who sits in a chair throughout the week and then launches into action on Saturday! That's a sure-fire way to injure yourself — or worse — and will put any plans you had for fitness on the back burner while you heal or recuperate.

If you're in poor physical shape, you didn't get that way overnight, and you're not going to fix it overnight. By embarking on a sensible, long-term health plan, however, you *will* improve. *This must become a lifelong process, so treat it as such, and you'll enjoy lifelong benefits.*

If you're in poor physical shape, you didn't get that way overnight, and you're not going to fix it overnight.

Our One and Only

A FRIEND OF MINE SHARED an analogy about health that has always stuck with me. Imagine if you were a 16-year-old and a wealthy person came to you and said, "Hey, listen. I'm going to buy you any new car you want. Price is not an issue. Say the word, and I'll have it in your driveway tomorrow." The catch? "That's the only vehicle you going to have *for the rest of your life.*"

How would we take care of that vehicle? We'd do all the proper maintenance. The fluids would all be topped off, the tires rotated and all the other items regularly checked off the list. We wouldn't put off taking it in for repairs when we heard an odd noise or noticed it starting to drive differently.

In short, we'd make sure that vehicle was clean — *spotless* even — because it was something we loved and would depend on for our entire life. That's no different from our health and fitness. We've got to maintain our bodies and minds the same way. If we would take care of a car that way, why wouldn't we take that kind of care of our own bodies?

Finding Those
Who Will Challenge Us

Like the other areas of The Theory of 5, we need to find both virtual and personal mentors and co-mentors to challenge us to become as fit and healthy as we can possibly be. We want to look for people who are *better* than us. We want to find those who make us continue aspiring to *be* better.

When we're in decent shape, it's too easy in our 40s, 50s and beyond to say, "Hey, I'm in better shape than most people my age." If we compare ourselves to average, *we're only going to be slightly better than average.* If we compare ourselves to the elite, however, we start looking at things differently. As my mentor Robert Kelly has stated to me many times, "Nothing is good or bad until you compare it to something else."

By looking at those we hold as outstanding models, we start telling ourselves we could do more.

We want to find the *elite* in fitness, just like we'd want to find an exceptional businessperson, a great parent, the best possible husband or wife, and the person who lives, rather than talks, his or her faith.

I've been exceptionally fortunate to have several older mentors who have made a huge difference in my life. There are two in particular who stand out when it comes to inspiration and motivation for fitness and health.

Bob Plarr, now 71, was my first real health and fitness mentor. I got to know him through wrestling when I was younger. As I mentioned in the Mindset chapter of this book, Bob, a former wrestler himself and a Recon Ranger in the U.S. Marines, was an extremely successful local businessman. He liked to challenge himself in his fitness regimen by inviting local athletes to work out with him in his personal state-of-the-art gym.

It was an honor to be recognized by Bob, but he didn't make things easy. With Bob, you started your workouts at 4:30 a.m. "Most people don't last for more than a week," he said. I decided to take him up on the challenge. We ended up working out for more than 10 years together, starting between 4:30 and 5 a.m. I not only enjoyed working out with him, but I enjoyed the way he thought about life. He is exceptional when it comes to health and fitness and has an extraordinary mind.

If we compare ourselves to average, we're only going to be slightly better than average. If we compare ourselves to the elite, however, we start looking at things differently.

I met **Lee Kemp**, now 64, through business dealings. He was a Ford dealer and is one of the owners and founders of Hire the Winners, a successful recruiting and staffing company. As a champion himself, it was an appropriate name for his business. As I mentioned in the business and finance section, the man has the art of goal setting down to a science, and has enjoyed a multitude of successes because of it. This includes being on the U.S. Olympic team that had boycotted the Soviet games in 1980 and becoming the head wrestling coach for the Olympic team in Beijing in 2008.

These two men are easily within the top 1 percent of the top 1 percent when it comes to fitness in men over 60 years of age. They are in great shape no matter *what* age range you compare them against. A report recently found that the average boy in high school has a tough time doing more than five pull-ups. Both these men can easily do more than 50 push-ups in 60 seconds, bench press their weight more than 20 times, run a mile in under nine minutes, do more than 15 pull-ups and have less than 10 percent body fat. *These* are the people I want to compare myself to. *These* are the people I want to challenge me. This is how I'll become better than "average."

Eustace Wolfington, the 90-year-old man I mentioned in the business section of this book, models what I hope to be if I'm fortunate enough to live that long. He maintains his health by working out five days a week for an hour. "My workouts are very different now than they were when I was your age," he has told me, "but they keep me active. They keep me going."

His exercise consists mainly of walking for cardio, stretching out and doing 10 to 15 minutes of very light weights. He also reads a minimum of an hour and a half a day for his mind and spends 15 minutes a day with crossword puzzles. "I'm exercising my mind as much as exercising my body," he said. "My mind is like a muscle. I read, I daydream and I find humor in life. I've found that, to have a healthy lifestyle, you should be grateful for everything you have in life — but not *satisfied*. I'm grateful, but I'm still pushing myself."

This man is keeping things in *motion*. He makes sure that his joints stay limber by stretching on a consistent basis. He makes sure he is eating better foods. "I make it a conscious effort to walk and sit with a good posture," he said. "It's a bunch of little things that make the difference."

I recognize that I am tremendously fortunate to have these men in my life. They are certainly on the extreme end of the fitness scale and, therefore, rare finds. But, if we keep our eyes open and put ourselves in the position to find role models and mentors, we *will* find them — they're out there. As I've mentioned before, we no longer have any excuses for not being able to find a mentor in today's online, connected world. We also have access to virtual mentors by way of videos, books and online media. As with the other elements in The Theory of 5, we should find people who have achieved what we want to achieve. These are the people who can teach us. How did they do it? What did they sacrifice, and what did they gain? I guarantee they had 24 hours in their day, same as us; how did they use their time and energy?

Uncommon Common Sense

Nothing I'm pointing out here is earth-shattering news. We all know that we've got to treat our bodies well by exercising and getting proper nutrition. And yet, there are so many otherwise intelligent people in our society who just won't take these simple ideas to heart — until it might be too late. Just by checking these items off our list, we'll be head and shoulders above a large percentage of the world's population:

- **Move** — Basically, *any* activity is better than no activity. We don't have to run a marathon to start living a healthier lifestyle. We don't need to run at *all*, for that matter. If we only walk 100 yards today, that's 100 yards more than the guy who sat on the couch, eating potato chips, drinking beer and smoking cigarettes did. The only way to get started is to *get started.*
- **Stretch** — Health and fitness experts agree that stretching is not only beneficial but essential to maintaining our fitness. Stretching increases our blood flow and circulation, gets oxygen to our brain and helps with our balance. It also makes it easier to maintain proper posture as we age, giving us a more youthful appearance and aiding our overall health. Keeping limber can help maintain the structure and health of the thoracic spine — the middle of the back — where it's common to develop aches and pain as we age. Most importantly, stretching out before exercise helps decreases injury, *allowing us to get the most out of our fitness program.*
- **Hydrate** — Drinking lots of water to stay hydrated is very important at any age. Most people don't drink enough water, and there are too many drinking too much soda. *Nothing is better for our bodies than water.*

- **Sleep** — Our bodies need to regularly restore themselves, and there's no substitute for a good night's sleep. If we use our bodies during the day, sleep comes easily during the night and we're prepared for the next. For businesspeople and others who are constantly traveling, working lots of late-night hours and finding themselves in hotel beds, this can be especially challenging, but no less important. *Good sleep improves our health and extends our life.*

- **Teeth** — Many don't realize how important it is to take care of their teeth and gums by practicing good dental hygiene and going to the dentist twice a year. Having teeth and gum problems as we get older can be a major health challenge. *Also, health aside, never forget that a great smile opens many doors.*

- **Food** — Some say that breakfast is the most important meal, but what we consume for breakfast is important, too. Is it fruits, egg whites or steel-cut oatmeal? Or is it a lot of bacon and eggs every day, or sweet cereal? Food is the basic and necessary fuel for great health.

  Making smart food choices begins in the grocery aisle. So, when is the best time to go shopping? My mentors and I believe we should never go to the grocery store on an empty stomach. Going when we're not hungry gives us the psychological boost to buy less food and make healthier choices. Also, if there aren't a lot of sweets and unhealthy food around the house, they won't be around to tempt us when our willpower might be running low.

  It's helpful to make a list of all the healthy food we plan to buy and review our fitness goals when making the list. One of my fitness mentors always views a photo on his phone showing what he looked like at his physical peak before making his food list. It keeps his motivation going when temptation strikes.

This isn't rocket science! We should keep in mind, however, that while these are necessary starting points, we'll always want to aim higher than "slightly above average."

Get Going Early

I've taken Ben Franklin's adage, "Early to bed and early to rise, makes a man healthy, wealthy and wise" to heart.

For me, the best time to work out is first thing in the morning. The details of your life or personal preferences may lead you to a different timetable, but I've found that getting up, getting active and getting it done has provided me with the following benefits:

> Getting our body engaged first thing in the morning wakes us up in a way that coffee never will.

- **Early Win** — As soon as we accomplish something first thing in the morning, we just feel good we got it out of the way. This is especially true if we're working 50, 60 or 70 hours a week. It leaves time for other key priorities in our lives, like our spouse, our children, our business and our spirituality.

- **Physical Energy and Mental Focus** — Getting our body engaged first thing in the morning wakes us up in a way that coffee never will. Our blood is pumping, our muscles are working and our minds are energized. While others are trying to get going when they get to the office, we're already working at peak performance. We've beaten inertia, and now inertia is working *for* us.

- **We're Less Likely to Skip** — An early schedule cultivates consistency and self-discipline. When we know that, every morning, we're getting up and working out, we gain that consistency and, when it comes to exercise, consistency makes a big difference. If we wait until lunch or the end of the day, life has a way of getting in the way. Meetings run long, unexpected events pop up and our time can get pecked away until something has to give. If we've already put our body through its paces, our health won't be the thing that gets skipped.

- **Better Sleep** — When we work out in the morning, we sleep better at night, which has several health and mental benefits. If we were up early, we'll be physically worn out by the time the day ends. When our heads hit the pillow, sleep will just come.

- **Metabolism Boost** — As our bodies become more accustomed an active lifestyle, our metabolisms will kick into a higher gear to accommodate the increased load. When we work out first thing in the morning, we'll burn more calories during the rest of the day.

- **Fewer Distractions** — If we're serious about maintaining good results, it's easier to do it first thing in the morning when the gym isn't as crowded. We'll spend less time waiting on this machine or that one, and there will be fewer distractions. The place is packed during lunch and in the evening. There are fewer people and fewer distractions at 6 a.m. then there are at 6 p.m. We also might start seeing familiar faces — those who are as committed to their health as we are; even if they don't become mentors, they can be a peer group that boosts our accountability to fitness.

- **Improved Mood** — When we work out, it releases endorphins — the "feel-good" hormone." If that happens the first thing in the morning, they are released right away. Nothing feels better than a good workout under our belt, especially if we're prone to blowing things off at night. It boosts our mood and gives us that sense of accomplishment. By achieving success first thing in the morning, we arrive at work ready to *conquer and dominate.*

Fitness and Our Children

It's much easier to live and maintain a healthy lifestyle if it's part of our life from a young age. This stops us from having to undo old habits and build new ones.

It was important to me to model a healthy lifestyle for my children early on, so I put a gym in my house right away; I wanted them to see their father working out and taking care of himself. They were often there at an early age, watching me. I wanted to show them that staying healthy was just a part of life: you have a living room, a bedroom, a kitchen — and an area where you work out.

They all got the message. While they might not be as passionate about exercise as I am, our children work out on a consistent basis. They've also become better than I've been with their eating habits.

Children learn what they see their parents do. If they see their parents sitting on the couch never doing any physical activity, that becomes their "normal." If they see their parents take an interest in their own health and make good choices, however, they're much more likely to model that behavior long after they've left home and have started making their own choices.

I wanted to show them that staying healthy was just
a part of life: you have a living room, a bedroom,
a kitchen — and an area where you work out.

Finding What Works for Us

To be successful in this area, we want to figure out what motivates us intrinsically towards fitness and health. Getting fit isn't a "one-time" thing we can achieve and then move on. It's a constant process and a lifestyle decision. If it doesn't come easily or naturally, we need to design a plan and process that speaks to us. That plan can evolve as we get older and the demands on our time change.

In my youth, competition was my motivating drive. Between 22 and 45, it was a habit that I was enthusiastic to continue with. When I hit 45, however, I started to look at it in a different way. I did it for energy and to feel good. I did it for health, so I could focus at work and in my personal life. I did it for my family, and I did it for personal pride and self-esteem. We all have to do what works for *us* — again, our "*why.*" That may take a little while to figure out. Still, I urge you to put in the time; it'll be well worth it for yourself and those who love you.

Sometimes, to reach a goal, it's helpful to set up what I call a **Mental Event Challenge** — or **MEC**. One MEC that works well for me is that of a deadline. I'll choose a future event to challenge myself to work towards. If I know I'm going to a convention, for example, I will push my workouts to another level. If I'm going to meet friends I haven't seen for awhile, I'll eat better in the weeks leading up to that, and have more intense workouts. My daughter's wedding date, for instance, was a natural goal line. Vacation and bathing suit weather are regular occurrences for many people as well.

Everyone has their own events where they'd like to be in better shape. I believe, when we make a deadline and set these kinds of MEC for ourselves consistently, we'll always have goals that will *intrinsically* motivate us for a specific event. When our willpower might otherwise be dipping, the MEC will now ignite our will and drive us forward.

214

Listening to Our Bodies

As I HAVE AGED, my exercise regimen has changed. I had always enjoyed karate and mixed martial arts, but at a certain point, I started to get injured. I began asking myself, "Why am I doing this?"

We want to do workouts that we enjoy and look forward to. If we find ourselves doing something out of habit — which was what I was doing with MMA in my mid-40s — we need to start reevaluating our work out. We need to decide what's important to us.

For me, there was a certain age where I realized I couldn't lift heavy anymore without injuring myself; people who can lift heavy into their 50s and 60s without injury are the exception to the rule. I realized that I wanted to be healthy and physically fit, and getting hurt wasn't the way to achieve that. I simply want to feel good about myself. I want to look and feel good. It's important for me to have the energy I need in order do the things I want and need to do.

Aging is part of life; it's going to happen. Deciding to put in the effort to becoming and staying fit and healthy, however, is a life *enhancement*, and one we can attain.

Go online and look for health and fitness information that deals with your age group. There are differences between our 30s, 40, 50s, 60s and so on. Don't trust it when someone says, "I don't care if you're 30 or 70, you need to do this." That's simply not true. When I go to a gym and see someone who's not a certified trainer putting a 70-year-old guy through the same workout as they just did with a 30-year-old man, I know that poor guy is about to get hurt. We have to do a personalized workout based on the condition we're in and our personal health goals.

Investing in Ourselves

MANY PEOPLE AVOID GOING to the gym because they don't know what to do or are too embarrassed to look "clueless" in front of others. The truth is that we're *all* ignorant about the things we don't know how to do. The only cure for ignorance is education, and the only way to learn is to do research and ask someone who knows.

Most gyms have in-house trainers and experts who can put us through our paces. They'll work with us to design a program and show us how to properly use the equipment. And, if we're truly serious about being our best selves, we can always hire a *certified* personal trainer, especially when we're first getting started.

To use the earlier car analogy, we spend money to have our car washed and waxed. We spend money to keep it serviced and running well. Likewise, investing some money in having a trainer show us what to do can be the best investment we'll make in this facet of our lives. We shouldn't be afraid to invest in our health and in ourselves. What better investment could we make? It's far more challenging to take care of other important people in our lives when we don't take care of ourselves. If we don't invest in ourselves, we may not be able to invest in the people we love.

Start Now

THERE'S A CHINESE PROVERB that states, "The best time to plant a tree was 20 years ago; the second-best time is *now.*" This is true for a lot of things, but nowhere truer than when it comes to our health. Would you like to tell your teenage self to take better care of your body? You can't, but you can bet Future You would like to pass that same message along to your present-day self.

There are too many people who say "tomorrow" or "next week." This is what too many of us said to ourselves *yesterday* and *last week. We can just start today.* We can get healthy and stay healthy. We can find our stride and what works for us. No matter how slowly we might walk or run, we can start walking or running. No matter how light a weight we lift, we can *lift that weight.*

I've heard people say they want to get in a little better shape before they go to the gym. That's a plan for failure if there ever was one. Even if we start with a 50-yard walk, *starting something now* is what's important. No matter how slow we walk, we're still walking faster than the guy sitting on the couch who says "tomorrow."

There are too many people who say "tomorrow" or "next week." This is what we said to ourselves *yesterday* and *last week. We can just start today.*

This Is It

WE EACH GET ONE shot at this life. *Choose your best life.* We all have our ups and downs. Our overall best life, however, is the one where we focus on the positives of life. It's where we focus on what we *can* do rather than what we don't — or *won't* — do.

While some are blaming others or finding excuses, we can be living *The Theory of 5 challenge and reap the rewards.* When we choose our friends and our mentors wisely, we can truly enjoy how awesome our lives can be. It will not be easy, but the best things never are. By working for the health and fitness lifestyle that we have always dreamed of having, *we make that our reality.* Live happy and healthy!

Interviews

On the following pages are interviews with some of the most exceptional individuals I personally know who are living The Theory of 5 lifestyle. With a combined net worth that exceeds $2 billion, these people are living proof that the lessons and philosophy contained in this book can help you achieve your best life. It's my hope that you'll take their wisdom and points of view with you as you chart your own course with The Theory of 5.

Dave Anderson

DAVE ANDERSON is president of Dave Anderson's LearnToLead, an international sales and leadership training and consulting agency. Before founding that company, Dave was a successful leader in the automotive retail industry for a number of years. In addition to leading more than 2,000 workshops, seminars and speaking engagements in the past 25 years on the topics of sales and leadership, Dave is the author of 16 books, some of which include *It's Not Rocket Science, How to Run Your Business by THE BOOK* and *Unstoppable: Transforming Your Mindset to Create Change, Accelerate Results, and Be the Best at What You Do.* He is also the host of the podcast "The Game Changer Life."

In addition to this, Dave, with his wife Rhonda, is the co-founder of the Matthew 25:35 Foundation, with the stated mission of "bringing food, shelter, clothing, education, healing and ministry to under-resourced and imprisoned people worldwide."

BUSINESS

What are some of the key traits financially successful businesspeople possess?

DA: They work within a budget. The most financially successful people I know have budgets and they stick to them. They live beneath their means. When people fail to do that, it causes a lot of trouble. We see it a lot in our business — even people who are doing well fall into this trap. No matter how well you're doing, you can't live above your means. They also pay themselves first. You've got to save, and you've got to pay yourself before you go spending on discretionary items.

One of the things I caution our clients on is not mistaking a bull market for brains. So often, these businesses start to rock in a great economy.

They think they've got it all figured out, money is cheap and they stop changing, stretching and working on themselves. They stop renewing and improving. They stop doing the things that got them there in the first place. That's something I'm very careful not to get sucked into and encourage others to avoid.

> As a leader, you've got to get people better or get better people. It usually takes a combination of both to get to the next level.

What is your personal motto or slogan you are known most for in your business?

DA: You know, I said a lot of quotes over the years, so it's kind of hard to pick just one. I suppose it would deal with the idea of accountability. As a leader, you've got to get people better or get better people. It usually takes a combination of both to get to the next level. Also, accountability is not something you do *to* someone; it's something you do *for* someone.

What businessperson do you admire most? What is it about them you most admire?

DA: I believe it would be Bert Boeckmann, who is the chairman and CEO of Galpin Motors. His dealership has been the No. 1 Ford dealer in the world for 27 straight years and has been the No. 2 Honda dealer and the No. 1 Mazda dealer for the past two years. I've known him for 20 years, and he's been a client of mine for that long. He started at that dealership as a salesperson in the 1950s. He's 86 now, and he stays engaged and stays relevant. He's there every day, and he's still humble.

When I go out there and hold classes for them, Bert is still sitting on the front row, taking notes, while I'm there wondering, "What in the *world* can Bert Boeckmann possibly expect to learn from *me?*" But there he is, engaged, available and accessible. He's not just a figurehead; he's kept himself relevant because he continues to work on himself even after his massive success. He's not content to rest on his laurels — and he certainly could. I love his energy. I love his engagement and his commitment to staying relevant.

What was the hardest thing you ever had to overcome in business or finance, and how did you overcome it?

DA: I would stay starting this business and getting it going — getting a foothold when nobody knows you. I ran a large dealership group in northern California that got purchased 20 years ago, and I got forced out over pay issues. I wanted to get started in training, but the field was crowded and there were some really well-established names out there at the time. How would we get noticed? How would we establish our foothold?

I decided to develop a niche and not to try to be everything to everybody. I think a lot of people do the opposite. They go in there with the "deli counter" mindset, trying to be everything to everybody and end up being nothing to anybody because there's nothing specific they do well. I knew we had to develop a leadership niche, which was our strength. That was the strength of the group I was with and it was the strength of my own knowledge base. We just had to do that really well, continue to work and get better at it and establish a reputation. It was hard building momentum and getting traction. That first year was particularly difficult. During that time, I was invited to start writing a column for a magazine, I published my first book and was invited to speak at a major convention. I was able to start getting some exposure. Galpin was my first client — we still have them 20 years later — and we made sure we did great work for them because you can't grow if you're not keeping the customers you already have.

I knew, though, that after being forced out of the dealership group I was in, I didn't want to work for anyone else. I didn't want to go through that ever again. So, even though it was hard, I thought, "All right, we'll just suck it up." My wife and I sat around our dining room table stuffing brochures and envelopes. I knew the first couple of years would be difficult, and they were, but getting started is the hardest part. That's what it took, and you do what it takes.

SPIRITUALITY

How has religion and spirituality enhanced your life?

DA: It's changed my mindset. I became a Christian when I was 12 but I never really got into applying the principles in a practical way until I became an adult and got into sales. I had just come out of selling insurance door to door, and I was a new, young, broke kid that got into car sales in Texas. My first thought was that I wanted to fit in with all these other salespeople who had been there forever and who all had their war stories. But after a while, I realized I really *didn't* want to fit in because they appeared to be very unsuccessful and very unhappy. They are *not* the type of people I wanted to be.

So, I thought I needed to be different than that. I knew that I didn't want to think the way they did. So, I started a very simple routine. I went to the Bible and started reading one chapter of Proverbs a day. There are 31 chapters, so, I got through the book in a month. There were so many practical lessons about sales in Proverbs, like "A soft answer turns away wrath," or, "He who answers a matter before he hears it is a fool." All that applied to sales and attitude. So, I just did it month after month after month after month. And then I thought, "Okay, well that's just one book, you know. There are 60-something more." I started really getting into trying to find out how that wisdom could impact my daily decision-making process, how I thought of the things I chose to do and the things I chose not to do. It really has become a tool to adjust my mindset and to create a different set of values and a different filter. It allowed me to set different priorities, and it carries on to this day.

Give us an example of how you use religion or spirituality in your daily life.

DA: I wrote about this in my book *Unstoppable*. I have a mindset routine that I work on in the morning. There's a verse in Romans 12:2 to that says, "Be transformed by the renewing of your mind." And I think that's an immense promise — that you can be *transformed*, not just "tweaked." When you're talking about transformation, you're talking about *everything* changing, and the way to do it is to renew your mind. *The fact is everybody renews their mind with something, and what they renew their mind with determines what they're transformed into.* I decided I wanted to renew my mind with God's word and be transformed into *that* type of person. I started with Proverbs and it has developed to where I will not start a day until I've gone through my mindset routine.

There are seven different devotionals that I go through. I have, I think, 112 of my favorite scriptures memorized so I can go over them again in my head just to clean my mind and get it focused. I have 56 different affirmations. Most of them are spirituality-based that I read over in the morning, and then I start the day with the gratitude journal. I think gratitude is a huge part of spirituality — being grateful for what you have while you strive for what you want. And I also record the things that went well the day before.

> People tend to experiment, jumping from thing to thing to thing, looking for some easy way to get a spiritual fix; that's just the beginning of disillusionment.

It takes about 90 minutes every day. When I started, it took about 10 minutes, but over 30 years it's developed to a big part of my life. Somebody just recently asked me when was the last time I ever missed it, and I said, "I honestly can't remember. There have been times when I had to cut it short when there was an emergency here or there, but it's a huge part of my daily life.

What are some words of wisdom for people who want to improve their commitment to spirituality/religion?

DA: I really believe you've got to spend the time to fully get it. It's like if you want to watch a movie but you're only watching two minutes at the opening, two minutes in the middle and two minutes toward the end. You really don't get the whole idea what's going on. Who's the good guy or the bad guy? What happened first? What happens next? Why are they're doing what they're doing? No one watches a movie that way, but that's how most people read the Bible. They'll take a little snippet here and a snippet there, and then they wonder why it doesn't make any sense.

I think if you don't read the whole thing, you don't get any of it. If you don't understand all of it, you really don't truly get any of it. It takes work. It's a daily practice, just digging into it and going through it. Don't look for a flavor of the month. If it's something you really want to add meaning into your life, to change your life, decide up front that you're really going to dig deep and make it a meaningful part of your life, and not just a hobby. Don't experiment. People tend to experiment, jumping from thing to thing to thing, looking for some easy way to get a spiritual fix; that's just the beginning of disillusionment.

What has been the most challenging thing in your own life that spirituality has helped you overcome?

DA: It's helped me with forgiveness. It helped me forgive the man who murdered my mother 15 years ago. The Bible says a lot about forgiveness and that when you don't forgive, you become bitter and angry and stressed. I know I needed that Biblical perspective. If I didn't have it, I wouldn't have understood that forgiveness was something I was really doing for *me*, to release myself from that bitterness. My forgiving him didn't make it right. It wasn't doing him a favor. He couldn't have cared less if I forgave him or not. It was something I was doing to release *me* from that bitterness to give it to God to deal with. I had a brother who didn't handle it well and basically drank himself to death. He couldn't let it go. After several years, he did manage to forgive and release it, but the damage had already been done to his liver and kidneys.

That's a drastic example, but there are examples around us every day. I see people get so worked up over minor offenses and grievances. They only get two "likes" on their Facebook photo and they pout for days. You've got to be able to move on and get over things. The mindset of forgiveness has allowed me to forgive people who didn't do me right in business and other areas. It's been a big thing for me to let go and not get caught up in negativity.

My forgiving him didn't make it right. It wasn't doing him a favor. He couldn't have cared less if I forgave him or not. It was something I was doing to release *me* from that bitterness to give it to God to deal with.

Dale Pollak

DALE POLLAK, a speaker, best-selling author and entrepreneur, founded vAuto in 2005 after spending 13 years as a successful dealer principal. Although visually impaired, Dale found ways to build a system that allowed him to judge ways to best stock used inventory for his dealership, and before the Internet became a true market changer, Dale recognized the value that technology could bring to the industry and began developing ways to harness it in the pre-owned vehicle marketplace.

One of the most recognized authorities on automotive management strategies, Dale is also the author of books such as *Velocity: From the Front Line to the Bottom Line*; *Velocity 2.0: Paint, Pixels and Profitability*; *Velocity Overdrive* and *Like I See It: Obstacles and Opportunities Shaping the Future of Retail Automotive*.

BUSINESS
What are some of the key traits financially successful businesspeople possess?
DP: Passion, focus and determination. If you're going to be successful at anything, you have to be passionate. I think that one of the downfalls of people in business is that they lack focus. They try to accomplish too many things at one time, or they're not laser focused on a singular outcome. I think having focus is extremely important because it keeps the primary objective at the forefront, and everything you have is channeled toward the achievement of that objective. And determination is particularly important because, inevitably, there are fits and starts, ebbs, flows and stumbles along the path to success. You get knocked down a lot, and you need that fierce determination, in spite of a lot of negativity, to get back up and keep going on.

Why do you believe you have succeeded in business when many others fail?

DP: My success has much to do with necessity. I have everything on the line, and I had no other options but to succeed. Due to my vision impairment, basically I'm unemployable. I had to make my own way. That was my only option.

> I tell my people all the time that "our best days are ahead." That credo works in both good times and bad.

What is your personal motto or slogan you are known most for in your business?

DP: I tell my people all the time that "our best days are ahead." That credo works in both good times and bad. When things are tough, it's a message of encouragement, and when things are good, it conveys the idea that, although they might be good, they could still be better and *will* be better.

What businessperson do you admire most? What is it about them you most admire?

DP: Two people have influenced me a great deal in business. One is my father, and the second is Mike Krupka. My father taught me the discipline of the automobile business. Mike Krupka, who is the managing partner of Bain Capital, has taught me more than anyone else the value of practical, analytical business thinking.

What was the hardest thing you ever had to overcome in business or finance, and how did you overcome it?

DP: The hardest thing I've done is to change a long-standing, deep-rooted culture of an industry. I think that much of my success in doing that owes to the fact that there have been very significant transformations in the auto industry. Change always creates opportunities for those willing to step in, I had the good fortune to have the vision and the right message at the right time. And I did it with the traits I mentioned earlier: passion, focus and determination.

PARENTING

What are the key traits or behaviors of a successful parent?

DP: I think that being present is absolutely essential. "Present" doesn't necessarily mean simply being physically present. I think it means a lot of things, including physically present, but it also means emotionally present. I also believe that possessing and demonstrating good values is extremely important, as well.

What person, as a parent, do you admire the most, and what is it about them you admire?

DP: I'd have to say my own parents. I got something distinctly different from both of them. From my mother, I learned the necessity and value of being present. She taught me the meaning of being physically and emotionally present. From my father, I got the lesson of consistency, values and happiness.

What is the biggest challenge a parent has, and how do you successfully overcome it?

DP: I think the challenges of being a parent today are many, and the things I've already mentioned are critical, but on a personal level, the greatest challenge I've had in being a parent is allowing my children to fail. It's something that I'm not particularly good at, but one of the most important lessons of parenting is that failures are inevitable, and failures provide important lessons. One of the hardest things in life a parent does is to allow their children to fail. I think, though, that it's important to do that, but when you do allow them to fail, be there emotionally, physically to help bring them back up. As I look back, I can see many moments when I came to the rescue when I should have let them fail on their own and take the lessons with them.

One of the hardest things in life a parent does is to allow your children to fail.

Evelyn Longsworth

EVELYN LONGSWORTH is an educator, motivator and subject-matter expert on business, leadership, management and coaching. Evelyn has consulted with dozens of multi-million and billion-dollar companies over her career.

A wife, mother and grandmother, Evelyn is a person who I consider to be one of the most positively influential people in my life. Her views on marriage and parenting have proved to be invaluable.

PARENTING
What are key traits or behaviors of a successful parent?
EL: I think one of the key things is that you unconditionally love your children and that you care about them. You nurture them, and you have to be there in the moment because that's when bonding occurs. That bonding occurs from the minute of conception. At their birth, you are engaged forever with them.

The other key thing about parenting, and I've told this to many friends, is that the reflection the child sees in your eyes is what that child becomes. If you are positive towards the child, that will carry through; if you are negative, that will also carry through. I'll use my own father as an example. When I was growing up, he always spent time with me and encouraged me to be a loving, intelligent, competent girl — and I tried to become that. He would tell me I could do anything; I just had to believe in myself. I believed him and was able to achieve a lot more than I would have without that encouragement. Also, as I grew up, my father took me everywhere. He talked to me, explained things to me and was constantly educating me. His love was unconditional, and that was a big factor in my development.

What person, as a parent, do you most admire and what is it about them you admire?

EL: It was my father, Emil Ortsey. He was a magnificent man. He was a loving and caring coach. He was always there for me. He constantly nurtured me and encouraged me.

My father had determination. He was a steelworker and, at that time, made very little money. He had a goal in his mind, though, and he never gave up: Both of his children would be educated. For my brother and me, it wasn't a matter of "if" we went to college. That wasn't the choice. It was "when" we went.

Also, if he lived today, he probably would have been diagnosed as learning disabled. He had a lot of difficulty reading, but he would spell words to my mother and she would tell him what the

> ...my father took me everywhere. He talked to me, explained things to me and was constantly educating me. His love was unconditional, and that was a big factor in my development.

word was. My oldest son, when he was about six, asked him why he did that. He said, "My brain doesn't work like it should and I have to struggle with that. And it's really difficult because reading is crucial. All the books have knowledge, but that knowledge comes through words." That made an impression with both of my sons; they both became excellent and avid readers. I think it had a lot to do with his grandparenting. He never gave up. He died at 82 and was still learning words in the English language.

What is the biggest challenge a parent will have (or you have had), and how can they overcome it?

EL: I think one of the biggest challenges is that you want to love your children for who they are. You want them to succeed and reach their potential. At the same time, you do not want to compare them to their peers, your relatives' kids or the neighbor's kids. You also have to nurture your own child and then let them go — and it can be difficult to know when to let them go. You have to be careful and constantly watchful about your children's peer selection and their activities. Parents face many challenges with drugs, technology and social media. Parents need to be constantly aware of everything that is going on. It is not easy when both parents are working and have careers. Raising kids today is very different than when we grew up and these new challenges have a tremendous impact on our children.

What are some common mistakes you've seen parents make, and how can a parent either prevent these mistakes or correct them after they've already been made?

EL: One of the things I often see parents do is try to be their child's friend. They don't really have rules, regulations and consequences in place, and that's a huge mistake. They are the parents; they are in charge. These parents tend to let the child run the show, and that will work against the child because they don't understand rules, regulations, consequences and follow through. Instead of being their friend, these parents should say, "Child, I love you. I'm doing these things *because* I love you and I want you to learn the right reasons for doing the right thing." Letting the child run the show can be *frightening* for preschoolers. They don't know their limits and they don't know the boundaries. Their parents have to define those boundaries. A lot of times people will discipline their child, send them to the room and then two minutes later run in, hug them, kiss them and let them go. What does the child learn? "This too shall pass." Because of those rules, regulations and unconditional love they've learned early on, parents and children can become very close as they get older and *become* a friend, but you can't separate that out early on.

Overpraising is another area that does not help a child as they grow up. The practice of giving everybody a trophy for participating and just showing up does them no favors. That's not how the real world works. When you work at IBM and don't meet your quota, you're not getting a trophy and you're not getting a bonus. I think we set these kids up early on with a sense that they don't have to achieve. "It's not that important," they end up believing. "If I just show up, everyone's going to clap and recognize me." To me, that is a demotivator for a young child. They need to learn that they have to earn things in this life. Hard work pays off and we are teaching children at an early age to be responsible and have a work ethic. It also gives the child a feeling of accomplishment. My father had a quote that he said often as we were doing chores: "Be the labor great or small, do it well or not at all." I found it annoying at times when I wanted to take shortcuts. He wouldn't allow it. He gently encouraged us to do it properly. Later I realized he was teaching me excellence.

The practice of "helicopter" parenting also harms children. These parents are trying to protect the child by hovering around them, but what it does is breed a distrust in their child's own ability to make decisions. They're actually eroding the child's development, self-esteem and confidence. Children learn through experience; parents constantly hovering, always ready to swoop in, actively works against developing the child's competency.

MARRIAGE
What are some behaviors or actions that make a marriage successful?

EL: When I was a teenager, my mother said to me on several occasions, "Make sure the man you marry is a man you also like," and I didn't get it. How could you *love* someone and not *like* them? I didn't have the wisdom when I was a teenager to understand what she was talking about, but the truth became clear as I got older. My husband and I liked each other as well as loved each other; that makes a difference.

Before saying "I do," it's also important to know each other's values. Are your priorities the same as theirs? Trust is also important in marriage, both in yourself and in that other person. And perhaps the biggest thing in marriage is communication. You have to show appreciation for each other and not take them for granted. Sometimes that means just the two of you going away for the weekend or taking special trips as a way of saying that our relationship is very, very important. It can be hard to do that, especially if you have young children, but you have to make the time to do it. It provides a way of reconnecting with your spouse.

What do you see as the biggest challenge today when it comes to marriage?

EL: It goes back to goals and values, I think. Do we understand the other person's values, their priorities, their interests and their goals? Did we discuss these things before we got married?

Take careers, for instance. If both of you are working, whose job takes precedence? What if your spouse gets transferred and you have a good job? What happens then? Couples can find themselves at a crossroad where one starts to think, "Wait a minute — I didn't sign up for this. I don't *want* to leave my job. I don't *want* to move." I've seen couples struggle with this and I've seen couples divorce over this. You have to have these discussions early, and you have to have ongoing communication.

It's also important in a marriage to give each other space. Each partner needs their own alone time — time either with friends or hobbies or interests. I think it makes you refreshed and more interesting when you come back together. I've never been one to believe that you have to spend every waking moment with your spouse. That might work for some people, but it wouldn't work for me.

What's the best recommendation you have given or been given when it comes to building or maintaining a successful marriage?

EL: In addition to what my mother told me about making sure the person you love is the same person you like, I think the other thing is that you have to be a team. You have to have goals. You have to discuss short-term, middle and long-term goals. Are you on the same page as your spouse? He might be thinking about saving money for long-term investments and you've got a credit card and you're spending like crazy. That's going to be a problem. It's also important to know where your mate is emotionally. What is he really feeling? What's he experiencing? How is his career going? And all of that comes back to communicating, and I think you have to talk sooner than later. One of the mistakes I see people make is that they let issues fester, thinking, "Oh, well, it's not that big of a deal. I'll just overlook this today." That doesn't work out very well.

I'm fortunate that I had good role models. My parents had a wonderful marriage. They always talked, and that's where I learned how important constant communication was. They also had similar goals. They had limited income, but they always knew what their priorities were and what they wanted for us.

What was the most difficult thing you experienced in your own marriage and how did you get through it?

EL: This sounds kind of odd, but during our marriage we really didn't have issues that were super challenging. We had our share of ups and downs, disappointments and so on but nothing we couldn't work through. The greatest challenge occurred at the end of our marriage when he was diagnosed with Alzheimer's Disease. It's a debilitating, devastating disease. You watch the person that you've known and loved slip away. We fought it for seven years and I was able to get through that because I had two fabulous sons. I had good friends and I had some caring neighbors. I joined support groups that were very helpful, and they were very necessary for me.

> Each partner needs their own alone time — time either with friends or hobbies or interests. I think it makes you refreshed and more interesting when you come back together.

I was able to go through those seven years and, after my husband eventually passed away in 2012, I thought the worst was behind me. When my son died in 2014, I learned that wasn't the case.

It's very, very difficult when you lose a child and you never get over it, but you have to seek help — whether it's professional support, whether it's from a group or it's from someone else who's gone through it. When my husband died, my older son had said, "Mom, one foot in front of the other, one day at a time. That's what Dad would want." That's what I tell myself every morning and every night because that's what my son would want me to do, as well.

Losing a child, you'll go to your grave feeling that void, that emptiness. You think of the things he wasn't able to achieve. He achieved a tremendous amount in a short life, but I just feel bad that there are other things he didn't get to do. I sit back sometimes, though, and I think that I have more to be thankful for than most people. I had a great husband and a wonderful marriage. I had two wonderful sons, a wonderful daughter-in-law, Susan, and three fabulous grandchildren. My three grandchildren helped me immensely through that time. They came just at the right time, and they continue to bring me joy every single day. I think about all the wonderful times, the vacations we had, the memories. It's the memories, over time, that really help you get through it.

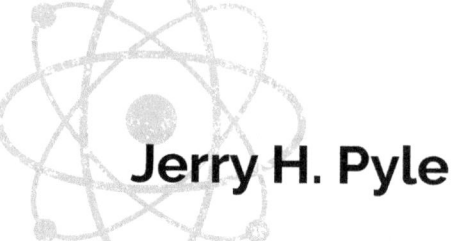

Jerry H. Pyle

JERRY H. PYLE is the executive vice president of the Friedkin Companies in Houston, Texas, one of the world's largest independent Toyota distributors. A Harvard graduate with an MBA from Wharton, Jerry began his automotive career at Ford Motor Company, spending 16 years there and eventually leading the Eastern Region of the Ford Division. Invited by Lee Iacocca to join him when he left Ford for Chrysler, Jerry became Chrysler's vice president of sales and marketing. Jerry has also been a board member of J.D. Power and Associates, a member of the Board of Managers for the Power Information Network and a board member of New Hope Housing.

BUSINESS

What are some of the key traits financially successful businesspeople possess?

JP: It starts out with being able to deal with the right numbers. Not every company I've worked for generates good numbers. Ford was the best. I worked my first 16 years with Ford and my highest job was being in charge of the eastern half of the United States for the Ford division. When Lee Iacocca left Ford, he invited me to join him at Chrysler, where I became the vice president of sales and marketing. That gave me a real insight for numbers, and I saw that Ford's numbers were much better and more topical than those of Chrysler. So, leaders need to be suspicious of the numbers.

Then, when you have a way to get good numbers, thank the people who are providing them. Even some of the good, big, publicly owned companies generate fuzzy numbers. We all know that people make the difference, but companies, especially publicly owned companies, are judged by their numbers. Good numbers provide you with information about your earnings, your turnover, your retention and other factors you need to know about.

The biggest danger, though, is to over-use numbers and hide the most valuable information. At Chrysler, for example, after the group vice president I worked under had a heart attack, I wound up reporting directly to Iacocca for about a year. Iacocca could gobble up numbers but had an unbelievable way to look at a spreadsheet and only see the numbers that made a difference. In manufacturing meetings, he would listen, but I could see a point where his eyes would glaze over and he'd start to look disinterested. At the end, however, he would ask two or three questions and the manufacturing guys would say, "Mr. Iacocca, we just don't know. That's a great question." He could always pick out a reason to use a number to make a point. Without numbers, you've got no way to compare yourself to the competition.

And, once you've got good numbers, you've got to use them to motivate, not to condemn. It's like that old saying, "You praise in public; you kick ass in private."

You've really got to have strong people in that part of the business. And, once you've got good numbers, you've got to use them to motivate, not to condemn. It's like that old saying, "You praise in public; you kick ass in private."

What is your personal motto or slogan you are known most for in your business?

JP: It would be, "With Pyle, there's always a second chapter." When someone would come in with a marketing or advertising presentation, for example, I would listen and keep my mouth shut. In the end, *I would always try to send them away with something to build on from what they brought me — Chapter Two.* It will lead to something bigger and better. Because of this process, we're going to have a great advertising campaign, a great car, a more effective workforce, a better Christmas party... Whatever it was, give them a second chapter of which they can be a part.

What businessperson do you admire most?
What is it about them you most admire?

JP: I think the businessperson I admired the most was Ben Bidwell. He was my mentor at Ford. He was a gifted writer and speaker and was easy to like/love. The dealers loved him because he was easy to talk to, was good with a wisecrack and was just a really good guy. He also looked out for me. When I was the advertising manager for Lincoln Mercury, the head of human resources at Ford Motor Company asked me if I would consider working for Ford overseas. I was still building my career at the time, and I told him I would consider anything. The offer was to go down to South Africa and be the head of sales and marketing. I told Bidwell about the conversation and he said, "Are you freaking crazy?" After that reaction, I looked up what their marketing budget was and the department I was in was spending almost a week what the South African budget was spending annually. I turned it down. Ben got me back on track.

What's a piece of business advice you'd give to someone?

JP: Mentors are the best people to learn from, but I promise you can learn as much from a bad manager as you can from a good manager. Bad managers will take the wind out of your sails and make you go home and tell your spouse that you've got to get out of there, but there's so much you can learn from a bad manager. He or she will do the things you couldn't possibly think anybody would do, and it causes you to see *why* they would think that way. A lot of it is narcissism and all those kinds of bad personality traits, but a lot of it is because of bad judgment and using bad numbers. Wherever you are, you're going to end up with bad managers — people who don't know the right thing to do or the best thing to do or the most productive thing to do. Learn from the bad managers — what do they do and why?

The second piece of advice would be to ask questions of everyone with whom you come into contact. Take the time to listen to their responses and acknowledge their responses. When you do this they'll feel heard and you'll often learn something.

What was the hardest thing you ever had to overcome
in business or finance, and how did you overcome it?

JP: I've never stressed about the actual job. You just have to know what you're doing. If you're well trained — and bless Ford for training me well — you know you have to be the first one at the meeting, know where all the switches are, smile, know what you're supposed to know and love the people who help you.

Probably the most difficult time was when I left Ford. I had been there for 16 years and was head of the entire Eastern Region of the Ford Division and I knew I had upside potential. I get the call from Iacocca and he said he'd made me the vice president of sales and marketing for Chrysler. I was 40 then, and that was a big, big jump. I called Ben (Bidwell), who was my boss's boss, and he said, "Jerry, that's the dumbest idea I have ever heard. They have no products. You don't know Iacocca that well, he's tough to work for...you've got to rethink it." This was about 8 o'clock at night. I appreciated what Ben said, but I still wanted to do it, so I called my boss and told him what I was doing. He asked me if I remembered everything that Ford had done for me. I didn't feel that I owed them any favors. "Before this," I told him, "you had me running the Northeast region which was the toughest job at the Ford division." It was about 10:30 at this point, and I was still upset as my wife and I were getting into bed, and then the phone rings. It's Ben. He says, "Jerry, I just want to tell you, if I were you and at your age, I would do exactly the same thing." I thanked him and knew I could then get some sleep.

HEALTH

What is your health and fitness philosophy?

JP: I'm not a health and fitness nut, but I weigh exactly the same as I weighed in college. My wife is the same way. We eat well, we exercise, we like to have fun. I think there's no better blessing than health, but look what's going on in our country. Upwards of 50 percent of our people are obese. How can that happen?

I used to be a runner until I had to have my hips replaced. I still do about 45 minutes or so every day on the treadmill. I do 30 minutes on weight bands, and then 15 minutes on some machines. I do this from about 5:30 to 7 a.m.

I might be a little paranoid about my health, but ever since I was 24 years old, I've had annual physical, and I chart all the metrics. I chart the cholesterol, weight and so on. It matters to me. Again, it's using the numbers. What are the right numbers? Are you above average or below? If you're too high, how do you get it down? If you're too low, how do you bring it back up? In this way, health is a lot like running a business.

Part of your overall health is also keeping your mind fit. Both my wife and I are inveterate readers. She reads a book a week and I read three books a month. That keeps our minds active, and it also gives us things to talk about. Reading is an excellent way to keep your mind fit.

How do you make fitness a priority during busy or stressful times in your life?

JP: Early workouts work for me because I never have meetings at 5:30 a.m. Sometimes I have a 7 a.m. meeting so I might have to cut my workout down to an hour then, or just start at 4:30 a.m. When I'm on the road, most of the places I have meetings also have a nice gym available. Like anything that's important to you, it's a matter of discipline.

My wife and I travel overseas at times, and we go on walking tours. We go on hiking trips for vacations and it mentally stimulates us, being in different countries, having to deal with different languages. That's the stuff that really keeps you cooking. About five years ago we went on a big hiking trip through France, and I had someone come to my office twice a week to teach me French. Learning a language is as good as exercise, I promise you. If I ever get to the point where I actually retire, I plan to spend two or three days a week learning another language. It's terrific exercise for your brain.

MARRIAGE
What do you think the biggest challenge is for marriage today?

JP: The pace of our society is a challenge. My wife and I have a favorite Chinese restaurant near our apartment in Manhattan. It's upscale, black tie, expensive and good. The last time we were there, around Thanksgiving, we sat at a two-top — just us, chatting. We saw a well-dressed guy and a really lovely woman sitting near us, probably both in their mid-30s. In the hour we were there I noticed that they probably didn't say five words to each other. What were they doing? They were both staring down at their phones. It's such a waste to go to a good restaurant and not pay attention to the food or your companion. It's so prevalent now. I see it with my grandkids. It's changed society. It's made communications faster and better, to be sure, but it's also grossly disturbed interpersonal communications. It's offensive.

A few years ago, we gave our top managers bonuses, but also a gift. We found wonderful wooden boxes and put stationary engraved with their names along with envelopes in them. It was really beautiful. When we presented it, we said, "Computers are great, but write a thank-you note and occasionally a love note to your wife or husband. Write it in hand, address it, put a stamp on it, put it in the mail and you will change your relationship." There's nothing wrong with sending your wife an email or text saying you're going to be 10 minutes late to get home. But *write* a love note. When your best friend does something for you, write a note. Put a stamp on it. I think it helps people stay human.

Early workouts work for me because
I never have meetings at 5:30 a.m.

David Boice

DAVID BOICE is an entrepreneur and financier who has owned numerous companies in the technology, real estate, marine and automotive industries. David has co-founded two of the largest technology and consulting companies (AutoMark and CyberCar) in the automotive industry with an enterprise value of $200 million. He is also the co-founder and current CEO of Team Velocity Marketing and an owner and founder of Tier10Marketing.

BUSINESS

What are some of the key traits financially successful businesspeople possess?

DB: The most successful people I know in business and finance have a passion and energy for what they do. I believe it is a combination of those two elements that help drive success. Some people are passionate about something, but they don't have the energy it takes to bring it into the end zone. Then, there are those who are very energetic but lack the passion it takes to see them through the difficult times. You need a balance of both to succeed.

Confidence is another key trait that I find to be the most consistent among successful business people. I think people who are generally exceptional in business and finance possess a confidence about them. Not an arrogance or cockiness, but a definite sense of confidence. They have a belief that they are better than other people in a certain area, that they're more capable. And, when the time is right, they are the ones who consistently continue to deliver successful results. I think we see that manifest itself in sports all the time, but it's not often seen in business because it's not as evident or televised.

Add in discipline. It's difficult to be successful in business and finance without it. It is one thing to possess the passion, confidence and energy to be successful. But when you add in self-discipline, it is like adding in the glue that binds it all together allowing you to stay focused on moving forward. The most successful people are those who are self-disciplined enough to stay focused on their vision and say, "Look, I can't take this vacation right now," or, "I can't do this thing that I really want to do, even though I know it would be more fun." It takes a lot of discipline to stay focused on your goals and solve the issues that have the highest payoffs first. These high-payoff items tend to be the most difficult as they often take a longer time to complete.

> It takes a lot of discipline to stay focused on your goals and solve the issues that have the highest payoffs first.

What is your personal motto or slogan you are known most for in your business?

DB: We have a saying in my family: "Change, whether good or bad, is resisted with equal intensity." We are seeing this in the (automotive) industry right now. Our industry is changing, our consumers are changing, and I am amazed at the number of very bright people who are resisting inevitable change with great intensity, as if it's not going to happen. I'd like to be known as someone who recognizes that change is inevitable and as someone who is able to lead in an evolutionary way.

I think to be a leader today, you have to be able to be innovative and adapt and embrace change. One of the most important things, I believe, is that you have to realize many smart people will resist change with equal intensity. As long as you know that going in, it helps you become more realistic about the things that you have to accomplish to get your organization in a position to win in a changing environment. I don't think that's ever been more true than it is today.

What businessperson do you admire most? What is it about them you most admire?

DB: I'm in the technology and automotive industry, and from an outcome perspective, it's hard not to admire Steve Jobs the most. The sheer number of industries he disrupted and changed is amazing. He achieved so much at an early age before his death. He overhauled the computing industry against a lot of odds. He overhauled the phone industry. He overhauled the music industry. It's remarkable. His focus was always on the products his company delivered. He wasn't known as a finance guy or a brilliant inventor. He was really known best for delivering world-class products at price points that no one had ever heard of before. The new iPhone costs $1,000 — that would have been impossible without Steve Jobs. He was a fanatic about controlling the experience of the consumer.

He also didn't build technology that could integrate with a lot of things, which was in fashion at the time. That's how Microsoft built its empire. Jobs went about it in an entirely different way. He controlled the experience, down to the weight and feel of the box, to make it a world-class experience.

In the auto industry, if I had to choose, I'd say I admire Alan Mulally from Ford. I've had the chance to spend a lot of time with people who were at Ford during his reign. I found his leadership through the recession and post-recession incredible. He outperformed others and put his brand in a position to come out ahead during a tough period of time.

What was the hardest/most challenging thing you ever had to overcome in business or finance, and how did you overcome it?

DB: Thinking back to the early years of my company, the biggest challenge we had to overcome was a lack of capital. Being under-capitalized, no matter how good your idea, is something very difficult to do. We had to build our business in a very old-fashioned way by today's standards. When starting a business with next-to-no capital — whether it's a car dealership, a technology company serving car dealers, or even a bakery, for that matter — you have to behave differently. It takes far longer to do things than it otherwise would. You come up with a lot of creative ideas to overcome the fact that you don't have the funds to buy a certain piece of equipment or hire a person who would be much better at doing something than you are.

I had to find creative ways of financing my company without borrowing money or taking on investors. I used to sell pre-programmed computers to auto dealerships. These were the days where dealerships didn't *have* computers, so we had to provide them. Back then, in the early 1990s, PCs were very expensive, so we had to go into the dealership and ask them to pay us for the PCs upfront. On our end, we'd finance the computers over 12 months, and that would give us some working capital we could use to buy more computers, develop software or hire more help. To make this work, I had to make really good products that would stay in the dealership for at least 12 months. Looking back, I can see how risky that was, how hard it was and what kind of pressure it put on our organization. I'm proud of the fact that we overcame it. While I'm grateful for the lessons learned, I don't know I'd do that over again. It has made me debt adverse, and on a financial level that's made for a much stronger business today — we have large reserves of capital on hand as a result of those early lessons.

> There are a lot of situations that they'll go through and they need to have somebody in their corner at all times who has their back and their best interests at heart.

PARENTING

What are some of the key traits or behaviors of a successful parent?

DB: First, I think your kids need to feel from you an unconditional love. It makes for the best relationships. It doesn't have to be an unconditional friendship, but love is powerful, and they need to feel it consistently. There are a lot of situations that they'll go through and they need to have somebody in their corner at all times who has their back and their best interests at heart. They need to know you are someone who they can really count on.

The second thing is that a lot of people raise their children to be great children — to be perfectly behaved, get good grades, have the perfect manners and so forth. The approach I've taken with my children that, once they got to a certain age, *I wanted to raise them to be great adults.* I think it's a different approach and it's an approach that revolves around rewards and consequences. As adults, if we work hard, take good care of ourselves and we do the right things, there are a lot of rewards for us.

But if you don't, the consequences as we get older are significant and can be permanent. These mistakes start early in life. What I've tried to do is to raise my kids to be very productive young adults, so they could be successful and independent on their own.

What person, as a parent, do you most admire and what is it about them you admire?

DB: I'd have to say my mom and dad. I certainly modeled my parenting style after my combination of my mother and father. They were just the perfect parents because my mom was very much oriented around us as children and my father was very much oriented around teaching us the lessons of life that we'd need as adults.

There are also some friends of mine who I consider to be amazing parents who raised children who were ready to take on life. My executive assistant Lisa Hutchens and her husband Doug have raised two sons. One is in the National Guard and the other has his own business — and they're both exceptional people. I can see that their success is a direct reflection of the way they were raised. Their sons really stand out from the crowd in a very positive way.

What is the biggest challenge a parent will have (or you have had), and how can they overcome it?

DB: One of the things I think I was most challenged with as I was raising the girls and having success in my business was deciding what level of disclosure to include them in. I love my children and wanted to spend as much time with them as I could. Of course, that meant that I wanted to include them in the things that I finally had an opportunity to enjoy in life. I wanted them to have those same successful experiences. I wanted to show them that by working hard and making sacrifices you could enjoy and experience things like flying first class, staying in beautiful hotel suites, having a private driver and attending VIP events.

On the surface, that sounds like something that every adult who's achieved a level of success would like to experience with their family, right? The biggest thing I had to overcome, though, was that I didn't want them to think that this type of experience was just included in life. I certainly did not want them to feel that they were *entitled* in any way to this lifestyle that I myself had worked so hard to achieve. This way of life is something that's been earned over a long period of time with hard work and many sacrifices. Since they hadn't been born yet to see those struggles, they had not been exposed to the long road it took to get here. How do you teach someone grit and determination? I think that's a big challenge for parents who enjoy some levels of success. They love their children and want them to share in their own personal successes. But you can very quickly create an entitled, bratty kid who thinks they are entitled to possess the same privileges and experiences as you. That's not how the real world is, and they did not personally earn these privileges. I just choose to "share" them with the ones I love. I also define my success by raising happy, independent children who will go out and make a difference in the world using the knowledge and awareness I worked hard to instill in them. I think we have found a nice balance.

What are some common mistakes you've seen parents make, and how can a parent either prevent these mistakes or correct them after they've already been made?

DB: I hate to say parents are too involved today but that seems to be the case. I see so many parents completely controlling their children's lives and schedules and not giving them the freedom and the independence to make mistakes. My dad was very successful in the military — that meant we moved a lot. I went to 13 schools in 12 years and I went to three different high schools.

I understand change and being accountable for myself because I was constantly moving and changing environments, changing languages, and sometimes even "changing" religions just to get into a private school because we couldn't afford real private schools — sometimes we were Catholic and sometimes we were Lutheran. My parents really threw me out there into the deep end of the ocean, saying, "Hey, we're going to a new school." I had to figure out a way to survive in an environment that was changing every year — new teachers, new friends, new surroundings. Fortunately, for me, sports were an answer to that. I learned to play just well enough to always be able to make the teams no matter where we lived.

A lot of kids don't get a chance now to go out and skin up their knees on the playground. There's this constant contact between parent and child;

especially now with cell phones and GPS devices. My parents allowed me to make my own mistakes — I made plenty — and then I had to pay for those mistakes with consequences. Parents today don't seem to allow children enough freedom to go out on their own and figure things out. By making their own mistakes they find great pride in their own successes.

I think the most common mistake I see is that there's too much parental control. When these kids go to college, they're so unprepared to be independent that they often fail. For many of them, *it's the first time they've ever experienced failure* because their parents never let them fail before.

We all see it in sports, right? Nowadays, we call them participation trophies. I was at a tournament the other day with my daughter, who's an accomplished horseback rider. I was amazed when I saw all the trophies they gave away. They gave trophies and ribbons all the way up to 14th place. *That's not the way the world works — 14th place doesn't count unless it's on the* Forbes *list.*

I also think parents very much want to be *friends* with their kids. I've suffered from that too. I really enjoy my children and being with them, but I think that establishing very clear lines in the family hierarchy of who the parent is and who the child is critical. In some families, it's flip-flopped. When the children start to make the decisions of where the family is going to dinner, what time we can eat, what activity we are doing, when grandma can come in for Christmas, etc., that is a problem. I think it is okay to let the kids have some influence, but I also think parents often put them in a position to make decisions they are not yet capable of making.

They gave trophies and ribbons all the way up to 14th place. That's not the way the world works — 14th place doesn't count unless it's on the *Forbes* list.

Chip Perry

CHIP PERRY has been a leader in digital media and helped to pioneer online automotive sales efforts. A graduate of Harvard Business School, Chip became the first employee of AutoTrader.com in 1997 and served as the company's CEO from its start through 2013, at which point it was the world's largest online marketplace, with $1.5 billion in annual revenue, 16 million unique visitors a month and 3,500 employees.

Before AutoTrader, Chip was a vice president of new business development at the *Los Angeles Times* and led the team in the early 1990s that launched TimesLink, one of the first major newspaper online services. Chip retired as the president and CEO of TrueCar in 2019, and is now CEO of Sotheby's Motorsport and operating partner of Automotive Ventures.

BUSINESS

What are some of the key traits financially successful businesspeople possess?

CP: I would say an innate curiosity is key. Curious people are always asking, "Why? What's the driving force behind this phenomenon?" They're always digging. Really sharp financial people will ask good questions, and good questions are driven by a curiosity about how things work and what makes them tick economically. What are the causes and what are the effects? They're able to pull a problem apart and unpack it. You can't skim across the top of an issue; you've got to dive down into the data and see what the underlying problems are — and what the underlying opportunities are.

What is your personal motto or slogan you are known most for in your business?

CP: My motto would be, "It's important to be a good S.O.B." In this case, that means "student of business." If you're really good at figuring out how

249

things work, you're a good S.O.B. Again, I've preached for many years about how important curiosity is. You've got to be innately curious to be a good S.O.B.

I would also say another motto of mine would be, "The secret to a company's success is the people; the people are the secret sauce." Without the right people, the company doesn't work.

What businessperson do you admire most? What is it about them you most admire?

CP: I would say the businessperson I admire the most is Amazon's Jeff Bezos. I admire him because he's so focused on building long-term value and he's willing to invest ahead of profit to build those long-term values. I find that quality in him amazing, not only because he sees great opportunities, but that he's willing to invest for the long term to build them. That's reflected in the fact that Amazon's profits aren't all that big, but their value is huge. The market believes all the things he's working on *will* be huge. I don't admire him because of his wealth but because of his approach to business. I met him once back in 1999 when someone like me could actually meet him. I was struck by his curiosity about the auto industry and his desire to create a delightful experience for consumers in whatever category he offered.

What was the most challenging thing you ever had to overcome in business or finance, and how did you overcome it?

CP: The hardest thing was starting AutoTrader.com from scratch, a company that, when I left, was worth $7 billion. AutoTrader was about building something from the ground up, taking the spark of an idea and building a team who created a business model and a value proposition around it. It was about developing a sales team, a marketing team and an organization from scratch. That was big selling. The way I went about it was to attract really good people who were passionate about the mission we had — which was to improve dramatically how people buy and sell cars across America. They were on fire about it and worked with me to build that vision.

The second hardest was assuming the helm at TrueCar and figuring out how to turn it around. The company was already up and running but had encountered some difficulties with its customers. It was having slowing revenue growth and a crisis in investor confidence. What I did there was to pull together all the good people in the company and created a common vision about what it would take to turn the company around. We then focused all our energies on three or four big programs or initiatives that enabled the company to a resume its growth and start to produce positive results for our customers, investors and employees.

Both efforts, by the way, required a lot of 100-hour weeks.

Attitude is so important in situations where you're building something. When-ever I'm with people in a problem-solving setting or in a business meeting, I always try to help them walk out of the meeting *built up* and *fired up* about what they're going to do next, rather than torn down. It's so easy, as a boss or a supervisor, to ruin somebody's day by providing criticism or input in a way that's more demoralizing than motivating. The key is to develop a mindset of having an interaction with this person where, afterward they'll walk away and say, "Yeah, I took my best ideas in, but I came away with an even better idea and I'm excited about going after it." I'd much rather have that outcome as opposed to someone leaving after just being *told* what to do. That's the way I want to lead.

I've evolved through trial and error as a leader. I realized along the way that I was being a bit too abrasive, too quick, too brusque, not explaining myself and not being patient enough. I learned this by watching the effect that I was having on people. I saw some people become demoralized because of my actions. I realized that was not what I intended to do, and that I needed to fix it. I worked hard to change how I interacted with my people, and it made a big difference.

> Whenever I'm with people in a problem-solving setting or in a business meeting, I always try to help them walk out of the meeting *built up* and *fired up* about what they're going to do next, rather than torn down.

HEALTH

What is your health and fitness philosophy?

CP: My philosophy is to be observant about how my body changes as I get older and to try to be mindful of food intake and proper exercise programs I need to get into shape and maintain my fitness.

What or who has influenced you the most when it comes to health and fitness? Why?

CP: I had a personal trainer about 10 years ago who I worked with for five years. He taught me about the importance of fitness and the benefits of a healthy lifestyle. That was important because I had never really had an exercise plan before. He also taught me the basic principles of what's called "functional fitness training." Activities like bodybuilding and weightlifting are more for cosmetic purposes. Functional fitness training is to improve your general physical health with specific, functional goals in mind. My hobby, my activity, is golf, so I built my fitness program around developing the flexibility and strength needed to improve my golf game, with the long-term goal of being able to "shoot my age" someday when I play. If you can live into your 80s and shoot into the 70s, that's an amazing life achievement. Not many people are able to do that, and I'd love to be able to. I've learned that strength and flexibility are important to be able to pop the ball out there far enough to be able to break 80. If you don't keep your body working and flexible, you can't do that.

What are some tips or encouragement you'd give someone who wants to improve their fitness and change their lifestyle for the better?

CP: Get help from a professional. I don't believe this is something most people can do from reading a book or watching a tape. Maybe some people can get in front of the TV and follow it, but I've tried and I've found that I need to have the discipline of an appointment with a professional trainer. A trainer can also coach you and make sure you're in the proper position when working out. The precise position is very important; the difference between "Position A," where you're slightly off and "Position B," when you're perfectly on, can be huge. The right position can be dramatically more effective because it's hitting all the right muscles. It's important to find someone to help you get it right.

How do you make fitness a priority during busy or stressful times in your life?

CP: I think it's best if you can pick a time do it when it's best for you. For me, it's at lunch. I work out, and then I eat. Exercise and then food intake is a good sequence. That discipline is important.

Susan Givens

Susan Givens started her career as an advertising representative at *AutoSuccess* magazine at its inception in 2001 and worked her way up to become publisher and owner of the company in 2008. She is now a group publisher at Babcox Media. Susan has also worked in several different capacities to increase the role of women in the automotive field in both sales and leadership roles.

BUSINESS

What are some of the key traits financially
successful businesspeople possess?

SG: The most successful people I know don't *react* when they know something difficult or challenging happens. Instead of reacting, they take a second and pause to think of a solution.

Business can be a very fast-paced environment, and so many people get mad or frustrated when something doesn't go their way — and that can happen daily in a business setting.

Successful people don't give in to anger or frustration. They stay humble and think it out before moving forward. They are also able to gather a supportive group around them to accomplish their goals. They know that they will all be working together toward a solution, rather than just getting mad and walking away.

What is your personal motto or slogan you are
known most for in your business?

SG: I don't know if it's a slogan, but I think one of the main things I try to live by is surrounding myself with people who I *like* to do business with. In the past, I've wasted a lot of time surrounding myself with people who didn't want me to get to the next step, which made me not want to help them. I've learned from that and make sure that the people around me are positive, like-minded individuals who have good intentions. I've learned just how important that was, and that's made a huge difference for me and those in my life.

What businessperson do you admire most?
What is it about them you most admire?

SG: I got into the automotive industry right after college, and one of the first people I met was Sean Wolfington. He was already successful when I met him, and I've seen him grow and grow and build this awesome empire. And what I really admire about him is that, no matter how successful he's become, to this day he still takes the time to ask me how I'm doing, how my business is going and how I feel about things. That's a great trait and one that I try to take with me when working with other people in the business.

What was the hardest/most challenging thing you ever had to overcome in business or finance, and how did you overcome it?

SG: When I first started at *AutoSuccess*, I started working my way up and eventually bought a bit of the company, and then a little more. I had a partner who, as I mentioned before, wasn't very positive. There was a lot of negativity, in fact, and a lot of personal demons he was fighting with. Dealing with these things really started to take a toll on the business. In February 2008, I knew I had a decision to make. We would either lose our jobs or someone was going to have to buy this business and turn it around. So, I bought *AutoSuccess*. I remember going to meet my old partner and handing him the check to buy him out, and on the way home, asking myself how I was going to make this work. It was a great business model, people loved the magazine and people loved working there. During that car ride, I told myself "This will not fail." And I lived by that, from then through now. On that ride home, in fact, I sold four covers. We'd never sold that many covers in one day, and from there on, it was a total turnaround.

> During that car ride, I told myself "This will not fail." And I lived by that, from then through now.

One of the things I'm proudest of is that we have people at *Auto-Success* who have been there for 10 or 15 years, and we've become a small family. We watch out for each other and have built the business to where it is today. In April 2017, we'd built it to the point that we were acquired by Babcox Media and we've grown exponentially since then, with more resources available to us than ever before. That ride home in 2008, though, was the turning point for the entire company.

PARENTING

What is the key trait or behavior of a successful parent?

SG: The No. 1 thing in parenting is love, and to make sure your children know that love, especially in the world we live in now. A close second would be finding and keeping a balance in your family life. My husband and I both work full time and there's a lot of traveling involved with both of our jobs, so we needed to strike that balance where we didn't miss out on family time because childhood only lasts so long. You'll have a job until you retire, but they're only little for so long, and you really want to take advantage of that time. Work will always be there, but you don't want to miss the basketball games or sleepovers.

What person, as a parent, do you most admire and what is it about them you admire?

SG: I admire my mom. When I was 17 years old, my dad died unexpectedly, and she had to become both the mom and the dad to two teenage girls. Raising two teenage girls alone is far more difficult than anything I'd ever want to go through, so I certainly admire her for doing that, for keeping us alive, making sure we were educated and giving us the tools to become the people who we are today.

What is the biggest challenge a parent will have (or you have had), and how can they overcome it?

SG: When my middle son was born, it looked like he had a bruise on the back of his leg that ran down to his knee and just wouldn't go away; we didn't know what it was. It took us about nine months and numerous visits to doctors to find out he had a condition called Capillary Venous Malformation. Where we live, there weren't any vascular pediatric doctors, so we had to travel to the University of Cincinnati Children's Hospital for treatment and found that it was something he's going to have to deal with for the rest of his life. We did find out what it was, though, and how to treat it. One of the biggest challenges as a parent is just remembering that you have to be your child's biggest advocate. Nobody else is going to fight for your kid like you will.

What are some common mistakes you've seen parents make, and how can a parent either prevent these mistakes or correct them after they've already been made?

SG: I don't think there are any perfect parents out there. We all make mistakes, and I guess that's one of the keys: If you make a mistake, *learn* from it. One of the mistakes I think parents make is not establishing a routine, and that's something I try to live by. Kids need routine. They need to sleep eight or more hours a night, go to bed at a certain time, wake up at a certain time, eat at regular times and so on. It's simple, but it's really important; it helps them work out their day. Also, it's something that might not seem like a big deal but reading to them is huge. Their minds are like sponges, especially when they're younger, so it's important to take that time. For us, it creates both a bonding time and an educational time. I don't think parents put enough importance on that.

The other thing that I believe parents should focus on is making sure your kids take part in a sport or activity. If your kid isn't sports oriented, that's fine. Give them an instrument, get them into art or some other activity. It teaches them how to be social and it gives them a chance to develop discipline because they are listening to a coach or other leader. It can provide them with lifelong lessons as they get older, and it gets them moving. My kids really don't have an interest in video games because they'd rather be outside playing or with their friends.

One of the biggest challenges as a parent
is just remembering that you have to be your child's
biggest advocate. Nobody else is going to fight
for your kid like you will.

Lee Kemp

LEE KEMP is an internationally recognized world-class athlete in the sport of wrestling. He is a three-time Gold Medalist in the Wrestling World Championships, a four-time Gold Medalist in the World Cup of Wrestling, a two-time Gold Medalists in the Pan American Games, a seven-time national champion and was named the United States Wrestling Federation's "Man of the Year" in 1978. Lee was inducted into the International Wrestling Hall of Fame in 2008, one of the seven athletic and achievement halls of fame he has been included into as of this writing. Selected but unable to represent the U.S. in the 1980 Olympics because of the United States' boycott of the USSR, Lee got his chance to fulfill his Olympic dreams by being selected to coach the U.S. Wrestling Team in 2008.

Lee, an entrepreneur with an M.B.A. from the University of Wisconsin-Madison, is the subject of a film documentary on his life, *Wrestled Away: The Lee Kemp Story*, released in 2019.

Lee is also the founder of Hire the Winners, one of the fastest-growing hiring and recruiting companies in the U.S. and, following his passion for health and nutrition, co-founded the nutritional company FORZA by Kemp, which addresses the nutritional needs of wrestlers and athletes.

Fitness

What is your health and fitness philosophy?

LK: My philosophy of fitness is to die healthy. If God blesses me with old age, I want to be healthy as long as I live. I want to maintain my ability to be physically active as I age embodying flexibility, strength, movement — bending, twisting, squatting, lunging, crawling — and emotional well-being.

I spent some time recently working as a personal trainer, so I got to work with the general population on their general fitness goals. I worked at an upscale health club, and one of the things I did with my older clients (those over 60) was to tell them to get down on the floor. I wanted to see how they got down and I wanted to see how they moved. You'd be surprised by the people my age or older — many simply couldn't do it or told me they didn't *want* to do it. They didn't understand why I was asking them to do it, but there's a simple reason. To me, that is a basic movement pattern. Before we walk, we crawl around, and we bend and twist and learn how to stand up. Then, we get to old age and many find they just can't do that anymore. To me, that's the total opposite of fitness.

> As we get older,
> especially if our jobs
> keep us at a desk,
> we don't bend. What's
> worse is that some
> people feel like they've
> earned the *right* to
> not move when they
> get older.

As we get older, especially if our jobs keep us at a desk, we don't bend. What's worse is that some people feel like they've earned the *right* to not move when they get older. They say, "I've earned the right of leisure and luxury and I can pay people to do all the other stuff that I don't want to do." This starts to include moving their own body.

I'm always impressed with an older person who's lean and in shape because that doesn't happen by accident.

Who has influenced you the most when it comes to health and fitness, and why?

LK: Almost everything I've ever done successfully in my life I've done through observing people who are already good at the thing I wanted to be good at. When I was 22, I was at the University of Wisconsin, training to make the 1980 Olympic Wrestling team. I was finishing up a workout and saw an older man biking. When I got close enough, I recognized him — Jack Heiden, father of Olympic speed skater Eric Heiden. Eric's drive for success had been one of my motivations to become a world champion in wrestling. So, I had this opportunity to strike up a conversation with his father. To a 22-year-old guy, someone in their forties seemed old — the arrogance of youth and all that. Even so, he seemed very fit, and I knew I could learn from him. We talked about his lifestyle, his exercise process and his diet. His view on eating and nutrition had a huge impact on me. We didn't speak for very long but during that brief time he taught me lessons I still use to this day.

After that change in perspective, I started to project my life way beyond the 1980 Olympics. I looked at a lot of the older people around me and saw they were out of shape and seemed content with it. When I got to my fifties, I knew I wanted to look like Jack Heiden.

Another of my mentors is Terry Shockley. He was a former wrestler and a booster to the University of Wisconsin wrestling program. He's 78 now, and if you saw him, you'd think he was 60. He can still do wrestling drills. Terry is a successful businessman who owns several radio stations and still manages them all. He travels extensively and carries a pretty heavy workload. He's a physical role model to me, a business role model and is just a good man with a lot of character.

A third role model was my father. My dad, who was a farmer, was in his early 60s when I was in high school. One day, he challenged me to a foot race. He was older, still had his boots on, and I was a state champion athlete. I told him he didn't want to do that, and I didn't want him to get hurt. He still challenged me — *and he won.* I knew he was fit because he did a lot of work around the farm, but I had no idea he could sprint like that. When I asked him how, he said, "I just keep myself at a certain level where I know I can do it. If someone challenges me, I'll know I can do it." That's stuck with me ever since.

What are some tips or encouragement you'd give someone who wants to improve their fitness and change their lifestyle for the better?

LK: It all starts with focus. What I mean by that is, you can have someone motivating you and telling you to decide to make a change. For that moment — maybe during the pep talk, the conference or the workshop — maybe you *do* want to make that change. If you don't have the focus to follow through, though, it won't last. The time when you *really* change is when you start focusing, when you finally decide that you really want to

260 The Theory of 5

be good at something. Now you're not just a bystander going through life anymore. Now you're fully engaged and involved.

You've also got to know *why* you're doing what you're doing. If you don't have a purpose, it's hard to know what you should be focused on. Most people don't want to spend time thinking about what their purpose should be. If I'm trying to motivate someone, sometimes I'll ask them a hard question: "What one line would you like to go on your tombstone?"

Some people don't have anything on their tombstone, but others, because of the life they've led — because of their legacy — will have an inscription. What do you want yours to be? Some people will look at me after I ask that question like they've just seen a ghost. They just don't want to think about it. But give it some thought. What do you want said about you after you're gone? Whatever those things are, you've got to start getting busy working on your tombstone inscription by creating a life and a body of work that will guide people.

And, while focus is important, you've also got to learn how to balance your life. When I was in college, I was 100 percent focused on wrestling. I didn't really care about anything else. I worked on my grades just enough to stay eligible for the team. When I went to graduate school, though, I had to drop my classes after the first mid-term because I didn't do well. When I went back the next semester, I started to identify who the good students were, and I started to observe their behaviors and what they did. I spent time with them and started to study more. My study routine was about three times a day, and so was my exercise routine, so I found a way to make it all fit.

You will *develop habits in your life, so make sure they're* good *habits.* This applies to anything in life you want to successfully accomplish. The habit gets you into a routine. I became a successful athlete because I made it part of my total lifestyle. I wasn't just an "in-season" athlete. A lot of my teammates couldn't wait until the season was over so they could go drinking and do the other things they couldn't while they were training. When the season came around again, they had to fight their way to get back into shape. I decided that I just want to stay shape all the time. Rather than having to get *back* into shape, it's easier to stay in shape and form the right habits and routines keep you where you want to be.

 # Jim O'Connor

JIM O'CONNOR is a retired Group VP at Ford Motor Company, having served the company for more than 40 years. A Villanova University and Harvard Executive Course graduate, Jim came up from his first job as the regional field representative for dealers in Jacksonville, Florida to serve as the executive director of marketing in the United States, the CEO of Ford Canada, president of Lincoln Mercury and president of the Ford Division. Among other things, Jim currently serves on the board of the Kelly Management Company, is an owner and partner of Kelly Ford and is on the board of directors for KEEPS, Inc. and Dynatron Software.

Business

What are some of the key traits financially successful businesspeople possess?

JO: First, I feel every leader needs a clear vision, where he or she wants to take the organization and they have to be very consistent in communicating that strategy. You can't just put up a slide on January 1 and say, "Okay, here's the strategy" and hope the organization understands it. You've got to constantly reinforce your strategy through *good communication.*

Second, leaders need to know financial reporting, all the numbers and how to make a profit. Finance is the language of business and all successful leaders really understand the numbers backward and forward. They need this ability so they can communicate the importance of everyone being on the same page and understanding how to make a profit.

Third, successful leaders surround themselves with highly talented people. They spend a lot of time building their team and, if they have to replace someone, they make sure that the replacement is qualified to execute the responsibilities of the job. At Ford, we did anywhere from $8 to $10 billion a month in revenue, so we couldn't have lightweights. Leaders

262 The Theory of 5

had to delegate to people who we knew could get the job done and who were passionate about the company, the brand and their responsibilities.

What is your personal motto or slogan you are known most for in your business?

> Leaders should not work on "minnow" issues; they should only want to work on "whale" issues because they have the greatest impact on performance.

JO: The people who know me the best know that I talk a lot about "minnows and whales." Leaders should not work on "minnow" issues; they should only want to work on "whale" issues because they have the greatest impact on performance. As the president, I didn't have time for "minnows" — those were things I delegated to others. One must manage their time each and every day to be productive. Ford had 283,000 employees worldwide and I was one of the Top 15 decision makers in the company. It was important for me to keep my focus on key strategies and things that were going to leverage our business.

Another one of my mottos was "You have to put the elephant issues on the table in the meeting." I wanted people to talk about what was *really* going on. I didn't want them to sweep things under the rug and talk about it next time or discuss it out in the hall after the meeting. I never got involved in politics; you have to put the issues on the table and discuss what needs to be done in a clear and consistent manner and work to show results.

My other motto was, "If you're working with me or for me, you need to know that there's no *right* way to do the *wrong* thing." I don't tolerate people cheating the company, cheating others or doing anything unethical to get ahead. I push *ethics* all the time. There really is no right way to do the wrong thing.

What businessperson do you admire most?
What is it about them you most admire?

JO: I admired Harold "Red" Poling (president of the Ford Motor Company between 1985 and 1987, vice-chairman in 1988 and 1989 and CEO and chairman from 1990 until 1993) a great deal. He was the most decisive CEO's that I ever worked for at Ford. We could be going through the darkest day and have a discussion with him, and he would always have a clarity about the issue at hand. There wasn't a lot of minutiae. He was always very pointed in his strategy.

Another businessperson I admire, and whom I met with several times but never had the opportunity to work for, is Alan Mulally (Ford's CEO from 2006 to 2014). Mulally was also a very decisive leader. He set out a strategy called "One Ford, One Plan, One Team," where there would be no "chimneys" but, instead, One Team. He also put in place a "Red, Yellow and Green" review process that took place globally *every Thursday* to measure performance against key metrics. It was very simple. "Green" meant go on to the next issue. "Yellow" meant there were areas that needed improvement. "Red" meant that additional team members would come in to assist. Mulally was a strong executive. There was a book written about him titled *American Icon* which went into the steps that he and his team took to come out of the 2008 recession without having to take a government bailout like GM and Chrysler did. I was very impressed with him and wish I could have had the opportunity to work with him.

What was the hardest thing you ever had to overcome in business or finance, and how did you overcome it?

JO: There were many issues in my 40-year career. One example was when I took over Ford of Mexico. The peso devalued and interest rates jumped to more than 100 percent in Mexico. In our business dealers need to keep an inventory — usually a 60- to 75-day supply of new vehicles. At Kelly Ford, we keep an inventory of about $12 million worth of new cars and trucks and $2 million in used vehicles. If your interest rates suddenly jump to 100 percent, you can't carry that kind of inventory, and our Mexican Ford dealerships were faced with that crisis. I decided to hire five guys who had worked for me and retired and asked if they would spend six months in Mexico for me. With the company's approval, we bought back every single unit in the country and put them on Ford's books. We were paying around 8 percent interest at the time, so our cars and trucks got a lot more attractive when the rest of the industry in Mexico had a disaster on their hands. The finance companies were all upside down on their loans, so we went in and bought each of the dealer's finance companies, as well. We saved every Ford dealership in Mexico. Other brands had a major disruption in their distribution channels.

PARENTING

What is the key trait or behavior of a successful parent?

JO: It's important to communicate and show love to your children. It's also important to be very consistent in your application of discipline. There are times you have to give your children the "tough love" and send them to their room or what have you, but they need to respect you and they need to know that what you're doing you are doing out of love.

From my own experience, my father was not around — he walked out when I was two. My brother and I are 11 months apart and we are very close. What we *did* have was a mother who showered us with love even though she worked two or three jobs most of the time.

What person, as a parent, do you most admire
and what is it about them you admire?

JO: Clearly, that would be my mother. She was an orphan, actually — something we didn't find out until after she died. My daughter was doing some genealogy research on our family and found that out. My mother was hardworking, religious and extremely compassionate. She never said one bad word in my entire life about my father. She always let my brother and I know that we had her full support. She would say, "James, anything you want to accomplish, *you can accomplish*." She was always positive and supportive. She was a school teacher in Newark, New Jersey for 33 years. It was a real tough inner-city environment. She had to take two buses to get there because she never drove. Just a very loving, very positive person, and that's something I've tried to emulate with my own family. I saw my mother struggle financially all her life, so as I got older and got to a certain level at Ford, I made sure to take over paying all her bills and provide her with true comfort.

What is the biggest challenge you and your wife have had
as parents, and how did you overcome it?

JO: The biggest challenge was, because of my career, we had to move the family 16 times over 40 years. That's was a huge challenge and I give my wife all the credit. For example, when we moved from the New York region to the California region, I would still I just go into an office that had basically the same process I had in New York. I was at a higher level looking at the problems or opportunities a bit differently, but it wasn't that different for me. Each move required us to buy a house and put the kids in a new school. It was different for them because the kids around them already had cliques and it was harder for them to meet and make new friends.

My wife, Judith, was the one who looked for and selected our new home and also had the difficult task of getting the kids settled. Part of being a partner is building your relationship with your husband or wife. You really have to work as a team. I would focus on the workplace while she was in charge of making the decisions about the home. She knew I would always be there to support her and the kids, but she was the class mother, the Brownie leader and made sure the kids were always happy. She handled it perfectly.

What are some common mistakes you've seen parents make, and how can a parent either prevent these mistakes or correct them after they've already been made?

JO: Probably the biggest mistake is not talking or communicating with their children. You've got to find out who your children are as people, and they've got to know who you are. Kids are all different — some are introverted, some extroverted — so you've got to know what works for them as individuals to communicate with them effectively. Many families don't keep those lines of communication open, and the kids just drift off. You can't let that happen.

You've got to find out who your children are as people, and they've got to know who you are.

Grant Cardone

GRANT CARDONE is an internationally renowned business and sales speaker, teacher and coach who specializes in sales, marketing, branding and entrepreneurship. Named "The No. 1 Marketer to Watch" in 2017 by *Forbes* Magazine, Grant provides his audiences and students with fresh ideas on leadership, the economy, small business, retail sales, employment and other topics dealing with business in the modern age. The creator of the 10X Revolution, his 10X Conference is one of the largest business conferences in the world.

Grant is also the author of seven sales and business books, including *The New York Times* bestseller *If You're Not First, You're Last.*

BUSINESS

What are some of the key traits financially successful businesspeople possess?

GC: Number one, they focus on offense, not defense, meaning they focus on the top two inches of a financial statement and not the next 17 pages. The power of the top two or three inches of an income statement — or the first page, depending on how complicated the business is — is more important than the expenses of the business. Failing businesses are focused constantly on management rather than entrepreneurial activity. A growing business focuses on the top lines, not the bottom lines. It's why there's so much disruption in the marketplace today. The big companies get successful, and then they get conservative and start trying to save money. Then, the small companies come in and are focused on expansion — producing new income — and less on expenses. That's how they go and grab market share. So, during the first 25 years I was in business, I was focused on saving money when I should have been focused on using money to expand the market. This applies to the solopreneur and it applies to Amazon. *Expand the top line.*

Managing expenses is not an entrepreneurial activity. I spend 95 percent of my time on offense, producing income and five percent of my time managing the expenses. Most people are already fairly disciplined when it comes to spending money; where they're not disciplined is producing income. The emphasis should be flipped. We were all brought up by fairly conservative parents who taught us to save money. The major issue in America is not saving money; it is producing new income. The mantra, the idea, the constant attention is on saving money, saving money, saving money — invest in your Keogh plan, pay off your loans, buy a house and so on. Buying a house, by the way, is not how to make money; it's how to save more money. Everything is about moving money to some safe place as opposed to using it to grow your top line.

We have five businesses here and the accounting department never tells me what to do. We don't even include them in meetings most of the time. In our real estate division, I just closed a deal worth $80 million. We used $27 million in cash, and I'm going to keep this deal for 10 to 15 years. Our accounting person who "controls" our real estate investments is telling me about what she thinks the returns are going to be. I asked her, "Why are you even spending time on this?" When she asked me what I meant, I said, "I don't need a report. I've already bought the deal. My job is to now increase the income on the property." She thinks the returns are limited to the way it has been performing in the past, believing that I cannot move the income. She is focused on the last 15 pages of the financial statement while I'm only focused on the top two inches. I am not going to *lower the expenses* at the property. My effort is going to be to *increase the income* of the property. I am not going to try to "manage" the property better. Management is not an entrepreneurial activity.

This is a different way of thinking. The best companies are always the ones that are focused on growing revenue. They're not focused on these other things. They outspend. They outmarket. They have bigger inventories. They end up dominating the marketplace. Amazon doesn't do return on investment studies. They're willing to lose money to grow the top line. We were all taught by middle-class parents to save money. Saving money does not work today because the money doesn't earn anything.

People don't cost money; *not making income* costs money. Advertising doesn't cost money; *not being known* costs money.

When it comes to income and expenses, which one can you grow the most? Which one can you affect the most? Let's say my expenses are $10 million a year. How low can I get that? I can only get it down to zero. Now, let's say my income is $10 million a year. How *high* can I get it? I want to control the one that doesn't have a limit. I can only reduce my expenses so far. I have taxes, I have employees. I have marketing and advertising. I don't want to "manage" downward. I want to "entrepreneurial" upward.

> Let's say my expenses are $10 million a year. How low can I get that? I can only get it down to zero. Now, let's say my income is $10 million a year. How *high* can I get it? I want to control the one that doesn't have a top.

I had two very successful companies for 25 years. I have dwarfed the amount of success I've created in the last nine years by flipping this concept. I used to heavily manage my expenses. Managing expenses means you are going to stay small. We don't do ROI studies here. I've never done a return on investment study. I don't care if there's a return on the investment. I care if I make more money. I care if I get more customers and if I acquire a bigger share of the marketplace.

What businessperson do you admire most? What is it about them you most admire?

GC: Elon Musk has got to be one of the guys because his thing is massive. He's not thinking about net profit today. He's not thinking about what it costs. He's thinking about the upside. They don't know what it's going to cost to go to Mars. They don't know how to get there and they don't know what's there if they do get there. And he still says, "Yeah, we should do this." By the way, just because he's a rich guy doesn't mean he has enough money to pull that project off. He does not have enough money to do it. So, his attention was on what? "Hey, if the purpose is great enough, the idea is big enough, we can raise the money."

I like Warren Buffett. I don't always agree with what Warren says, but I like the way he invests. When he invests, when he takes a position, he takes a *massive* position. He does not diversify. Warren also isn't extravagant. He's bought one house his whole life. Where he once thought flying privately was a waste of money, however, he realized that, in his situation, it was the best way to travel because he could get more places.

These are the guys I'm studying. I'm not studying guys who barely made it or did really well. I'm studying the guys at the top of the food chain. I'm studying guys who are thinking big, and I'm not just studying people in my industry. Take the case of car dealers. Car dealers who only study other car dealers are going to get crushed because of it. Who does Warren spend his time with? Who does Bill Gates spend his time with? Who is Elon hanging with? They're not hanging with other people like them. They're hanging with other people who are doing bigger things than them.

What was the hardest/most challenging thing you ever had to overcome in business or finance, and how did you overcome it?

GC: The economic collapse of 2008 was a major turning point for me and my career. I said to myself, "Okay, this will never happen to me again." I miscalculated the downside. I miscalculated just how ugly something can get. I was taking what I had done for granted. I didn't think, "Oh my God, the economy could get cut in half." I was too dependent upon one vertical. I knew I had to expand into other fields. It had been a problem for years, by the way. If you look at my career from 2008 to today, I have dwarfed everything I did the 25 years before that.

I've gone from having 80 people in a conference to 12,000 people at my latest 10X Growth Conference; counting online attendance, it was closer to 18,000. Also, the audience in the room was no longer employees but owners and operators and entrepreneurs from every walk of life from across the country. In fact, I believe there were people from 22 different countries at the conference. I remember when I'd come to Philadelphia and I couldn't get 100 people in the room. And it wasn't because my pitch was bad; it was because my audience — made up primarily of car dealers — was wrong.

There comes a time when a person needs to say, "Wait a minute — maybe I have the wrong product. Maybe I'm in the wrong industry. Maybe I'm in the wrong vertical. Maybe I'm too dependent upon this. Maybe this is a broken audience." Look at the car dealers who don't really want to invest money in their people but wants to spend money on advertising.

Why was I calling on this audience? So, you see, my business plan was broken in the beginning. I was passionate to educate salespeople because I was a salesperson, but the guy who hired the salesperson didn't want to spend or invest money in them. It was just a broken model right from the get-go. I didn't observe the reality of the situation and I went for what I was initially passionate about, rather than what turned out to be much more successful opportunities.

PARENTING

What is a key trait or behavior of a successful parent?

GC: First, I think you have to be a good person yourself. I had to ask myself, "Well, what does Grant have to do to be a good person?" One of my mantras is that "Success is my duty." I need to have success for me, so I feel good about me. If I don't feel good about me, I'm not going to be a good dad. If I'm not making my dreams come true, how good a dad am I? If I'm worried about money every second of every day, how can I really be with my kids? So, I probably spend more time with my kids than any other person I know. I don't know of anybody who makes more time for their spouse or their kids than I do. But I've created a life where I can do that.

Second, I ask myself, "What am I doing with my kids? What am I doing with them when I'm with them?" I know that, when I was a kid, I was very frustrated that my parents didn't let me help more. Kids want to be grown-ups. It's an interesting thing. The kids want to do what Mommy and Daddy are doing — pushing the shopping cart, driving the car, playing with the phone... whatever the parents are doing, the kids want to do. So, one of the things we do at my house is that we let the kids help a lot. We get them involved in stuff I'm doing. My six-year-old spoke to 10,000 people at my conference in Las Vegas. My eight-year-old spoke to 10,000 people in Vegas. They were *required* to do it. They *had* to get on the stage. It was a job. We gave them a job. And it was a good thing for them to do. The self-esteem of being able to do that is an unbelievable power flow.

My wife and I want the kids to exteriorize. We don't tell our kids to "be careful." I've never told them to slow down. We want them communicating and expressing. We've never told our kids not to talk to strangers. We encourage them to talk to strangers and introduce themselves. It's *my* job to make sure they're not around unsafe people. It's not their job to worry to treat everybody like they're a threat. My job as a parent to make sure they're in an environment where they're not going to hurt themselves and where they can introduce themselves to strangers and not be hurt.

We want them to go out; we don't want them to go in. My kids see me go online every day. I think Facebook and YouTube and Instagram are places for me to set an example for my kids that I'm interested in all people. I'm willing to communicate my opinion and I'm willing to show up over and over and over again until I build an audience who wants to support me — and my kids see me do that. We don't talk to our kids about success. They see success happening in our family.

> We've never told our kids not to talk to strangers. We encourage them to talk to strangers and introduce themselves. It's my job to make sure they're not around unsafe people. It's not their job to worry to treat everybody like they're a threat.

What person, as a parent, do you most admire and what is it about them you admire?

GC: A good friend of mine, Doug Dohring has five kids and I believe 13 grandkids, and he is one of the best parents, best friends and best example of a human being I've ever met. He and his wife have been married since 1979 and all their kids are sane, independent free thinkers. He's a very successful businessman — he owns a digital education company called ABCmouse — who works on self-improvement and makes time for his family. He doesn't have a lot of "noise" in his life that's counterproductive.

What is the biggest challenge a parent will have (or you have had), and how can they overcome it?

GC: I think the biggest challenge people have today is that they're operating with bad information. I know I did. I just had a lot of information from my own upbringing that was incorrect. It might not have been incorrect for my family, but it was incorrect as time went on. So first, I needed to get rid of some of the false data that I was operating with. If the programming is wrong, then the calculation is going to be incorrect and you can see that in our culture.

Our kids see everything we do. There have been studies where kids were watching TV programming and getting an educational class and were compared to kids who were focused on just the education. There was an *increase* in learning with kids who were playing with toys, watching TV and learning. There was an increase in the comprehension of data. The kids see everything and learn everything. Everything is being imprinted. My kids could watch a TV show, be playing on a phone and still know what my wife and I were talking about in the other room. I think parents underestimate the power of the child. The child can do more, contribute more, give back more and learn more. Kids are curious. I treat my kids like they are grown-ups already. I don't think that I'm talking to an eight-year-old. I think I'm talking to a little spiritual being who could literally dwarf everything I've ever dreamed of doing.

MARRIAGE

In your opinion, with a divorce rate over 50 percent, what is the today's biggest challenge when it comes to marriage?

GC: Number one, I believe that talking about what happened yesterday, three days ago, or last week is never going to improve my marriage — what she did or didn't do a week ago, what I did or didn't do. I think in marriage, like in business, that never helps. I'm going to damage my marriage if I spend time in the past.

Number two, we need a place to go to, and I don't necessarily mean a physical place. Humans do best when they have a destination. My marriage is best — we fight less, nag each other less and have fewer problems — when we have a big target that we're trying to achieve together. Times when I don't have activity, when I'm a little bored and there's no place to go to, when she's off doing her deal and we don't know what each other's deal is anymore — that's when we have trouble. So, once a week on Sundays we meet and, when we're doing it right, we go over what we're doing and where we're going. Again, we're focused on the windshield, not the rear-view mirror.

What would your recommendation to an engaged couple be in order to build a strong, successful marriage?

GC: I would tell them to clarify what each of them, individually, has as their dream. Nobody wants to give up their dreams — and nobody should. Those are innate to the individual.

Say "Jared" and "Sandy" get together. Jared has his dream. Sandy's got hers. They need to clarify what parts of those dreams are really important and which parts they would be willing to give up.

You've also got to examine and re-examine those dreams. My wife, Elena, wanted to be an actress and she was — she made those dreams come true. But, especially for women in Hollywood, at some point, it's going to stop. Unless you're an aberration like Meryl Streep, you're not going to be an actress forever; there's going to be a younger actress to replace you. For a long time, I wanted to be a public speaker and I was, until I realized that it wasn't really what I wanted. It was destroying my life, going around, traveling everywhere to speaking engagements. I couldn't even have a family because I was on the road. Every day, the individual needs to clarify their dreams and never give up on the ones that matter most to them.

I would tell that couple, "Hey, you guys need to lay out the dreams you *have* to make come true." Or maybe make a list of the dreams that maybe — *maybe* — aren't really that important to you. You need to share with your spouse which one of these dreams you are not — no matter what — going to abandon or drop. If you are married and one of you gives up on your dream and then doesn't have a dream, it's going to be a *problem*, because everybody needs to dream. Everybody needs to wake up in the morning and have something to live for.

...we're focused on the windshield,
not the rear-view mirror.

Sean Wolfington

SEAN WOLFINGTON is chairman and CEO of The Wolfington Companies and owns businesses in the automotive, technology, marketing, real estate and film industries. In the automotive technology field, Sean was chairman of VinSolutions — one of the fastest growing technology companies in the world — and has built some of the leading digital marketing companies, include BZ Results and Cyber Car. Sean is currently the founder, chairman and CEO of CarSaver, a board member of Data Driven Holdings and Team Velocity Marketing, and owner of Los Angeles Honda, one of the top 100 dealerships in the country.

In addition to these ventures, Sean also is the co-owner of One Media Group and produces motion pictures, including *Sound of Freedom, Self Medicated, The Mighty Macs, Little Boy, Hold On* and *Bella* which, in 2006, won the Toronto International Film Festival's People's Choice Award.

BUSINESS

What are some of the key traits financially
successful businesspeople possess?

SW: The most successful people I've met in business, first and foremost, are mission driven. They are people whose passion comes from the fact that they're really living and working for something bigger than themselves. Typically, their mission is other-focused, working to make life better for their employees and for their customers. That type of passion is rocket fuel, not only for the leaders but for those who follow them. Everybody wants to be part of something great, of a mission bigger than themselves.

A second trait would be that they have a crystal-clear vision of what their end goal looks like, even if they don't know at the time how they're going to get there. They have a sense of what success will be, and that's key in reaching their goal.

Another trait is that they typically are very strategic, or they know how to surround themselves with strategic leaders who can create a clearly defined plan — a way to get from "here" to "there."

Successful people are also doers. You might make a great plan, but if you don't execute it, it's not going to be worth anything. Along with that drive is resilience. They never give up, and that's partially because, for them, it not just about business or about making money. They want to make a *difference* because their mission matters. They also have an addiction to excellence, because why would you want to promote something that isn't great? From the product to the way it's delivered to how they treat their customers and employees, an addiction to excellence is important.

Finally, the most successful people I know are high-character, high-integrity people who recognize that doing the right thing is the only thing that matters. Their integrity engenders trust in the people who follow them and who they work with.

What is your personal motto or slogan you are known most for in your business?

SW: I would say "Love and Gratitude." To love God. To love others. To love what I'm doing and who I'm doing it with and for. To love building and delivering greatness in whatever form. I believe love is the most powerful force in the universe, but it definitely doesn't get the attention it deserves. For me, it's the driver in my life. I think it's crucial that people are loving and kind to the people they interact with at work and at home. If people used that as their primary focus, a lot of our problems would dissolve or be avoided, and a lot more good would be done in this world.

As for gratitude, I think it's critical. We are all incredibly blessed. If we can stand, see, hear, breathe and live without pain, then we should be grateful — it's vital to becoming a happy, fulfilled person in all areas of their life.

What businessperson do you admire most? What is it about them you most admire?

SW: There are so many, but I'd have to say my biggest business mentors are, oddly, both named Eustace — my uncle, Eustace Wolfington, and my cousin, Eustace Mita. The thing they both have in common is they are extraordinary husbands, fathers and servant leaders to everyone they work with, with the highest level of integrity and a pursuit of perfection in everything they do. They are also both well balanced in their lives. They do an extraordinary job at work and at home. The one common theme that makes them great in everything they do is that they are humble, loving and kind to their colleagues, employees, customers, wives, children and extended family.

What was one of the most challenging things you've ever had to overcome in business, and how did you overcome it?
SW: The difficult thing is when you have a team of people who put everything they have into achieving a mission and you don't accomplish everything you set out to attain. Along the way you'll always have valleys, pitfalls and roadblocks. When you're on the side of the road with a flat tire, clouds of doubt and storms of fear and worry roll in. It's in those moments when I get quiet and call the "Help Line." I ask God to give me peace and clarity to make the right decisions, and inevitably it all works out. When I was younger I learned the phrase, "This too shall pass," and it always does. In hindsight, often, when I get to the peak, I look back on all the valleys and thank them for what they taught me. I also thank God for helping me not to lose faith in those moments when I'm tempted to quit. To be clear, I don't thank myself for not quitting or losing perseverance. I don't pat myself on the back. I thank the "Help Line," because that's where I get my support.

SPIRITUALITY
How has religion and spirituality enhanced your life?
SW: For me, spirituality is the trunk of the tree, and everything else is the branches growing from that center. My faith is almost like oxygen — what oxygen is to my body is what faith is to my soul. At a pretty early age, I'd say in the first 20 years of my life, I used my time and talents in pretty selfish ways. But then I started to ask questions like, "What am I here for? What's my purpose in life?" I was eager to understand how I could be successful and what that success would look like. As I studied and I learned, I came to the conclusion that success wasn't just making money, but instead was making a difference in the time that I have on this planet.

So, I wanted to be a better person, in every area of my life, but then I realized that it was hard because I was very flawed and had a lot of weakness. The first thing where my faith played a role was in helping me come to the realization that I'm human. I mess up often and am in desperate need of forgiveness. What I'm most grateful for in my faith is that when I call the "Help Line" and ask God to forgive me, I get unconditional love and grace and forgiveness, that helps me begin again even after I fall. And, because I experience that forgiveness, I can give it, as well, because inevitably others will mess up and need that from me. Sometimes, their actions can hurt me or my family, but it gives me the opportunity to give what I receive. My faith has allowed me to be faster in apologizing when I mess up and faster to forgive when others do.

> For me, spirituality is the trunk of the tree, and everything else is the branches growing from that center. My faith is almost like oxygen — what oxygen is to my body is what faith is to my soul.

Give an example of how you use religion or spirituality in your daily life.

SW: The old ad for American Express was "Don't leave home without it," and I believe the same goes for faith. For me, life and work are not easy. It's like when you play golf; you're going to end up in the sand traps from time to time. It's not a matter of "if" but "when," so the question is, how are you going to handle the sand traps of life? For me, I handle it by calling the "Help Line" and ask God for help, and I do it in a number of different ways. First, before even heading out in the morning, I call the "Help Line" to be proactive and to be still, not only to thank God for everything He's doing but also to listen. Then, throughout the day, whether in the fairway or in the sand trap, I'm checking in to ask for guidance. That's what's made the difference in my life.

I've had six successful businesses in my life, and people have asked me what my secret was. How does that happen? Other people ask me how I met my wife because my wife is amazing. The answer is the "Help Line." Everything interesting in my life is because of that. If you want to reason for the mistakes and the biggest mess ups in my life, it usually because I wanted to go out alone. Don't leave home without your faith. On days when I'm "too busy" to spend the quiet time I normally do with God, that day is going to be uphill. The days when I do spend that time aren't without their problems, but I have the clarity to react properly, and I'm more likely to be patient, to be kind and to handle things more effectively.

What are some words of wisdom for people who want to improve their commitment to spirituality or religion?

SW: In my case, it started with me saying, "Hey, God, if You're out there, help me — help me be the man that You created me to be." And, inevitably, God started to show up in my life, because when you ask Him, He does. You know, if you were to interview the 20-year-old Sean and ask him what his dreams and goals were, they would pale in comparison to what God's been able to pull off through my life, even despite my many weaknesses.

I can't tell others what to do, but what I do is let go of my plan. I trade my plan in for God's plan and I constantly call the "Help Line" and ask, "What do You want from me?" I believe that I didn't create myself, so how am I to know what I'm here for? I have to constantly ask.

And that's led to a pretty wild, adventurous journey. I could never have imagined I'd meet a Spaniard girl in London who would eventually become my wife and the mother of our four children. I could never have imagined I'd be running successful companies. I could never have imagined that I'd be making movies — that had never even been an interest of mine growing up. All the biggest successes in my life have come because I've felt called to do them. I've started businesses where I could have written an entire business plan on why that wouldn't have been the time to do it, but the deepest part of my soul was called to do it. My soul gets me into stuff. My heart, my hands and my feet get me through it, along with the compass of my soul. The bottom line is that, if anyone thinks that Sean Wolfington is the reason Sean Wolfington has had success, they're wrong. It's all been dependent on the "Help Line."

What was the hardest thing in your own life that spirituality has helped you overcome?

SW: I can't speak for everyone, but I know I came standard more selfish, more impatient, quicker to anger, less forgiving and less humble than I'd like to be. Really, faith has helped me overcome the lower parts of myself and rise above by the grace of God to be more *like* God and less like *me*. It also helps us rise above the fears that gang up on us whenever our soul is asked to do something great for God or others.

And it's also allowed me to forgive those who have hurt me and to apologize for those I've hurt. It's helped me to become more aware of myself and others in the effort to become a more loving, kind, patient, honest and forgiving person. I'm not saying that I've arrived, but I'm aware. I firmly believe that if God can change me, He can change anyone, because I was an adventurous young lad, to say the least. I didn't have bad intentions, but often had bad impacts without consciously meaning to, being unaware of the wake I was leaving behind me. The calendar is based on what came before Christ (B.C.) and what came after (A.D.), and so is my life. If you looked at "Sean B.C." and "Sean A.D.," he's a different guy. There are people who know me from both times, and they'll say, "Yeah, that old guy's been gone for a while."

MARRIAGE
What are some behaviors or actions that make a marriage successful?

SW: First and foremost, both people need to be aligned in their deepest beliefs and values. In our case, that is our faith. One thing we both agreed to from Day One is our marriage is that all we want is God's will and not our own. That's been helpful because, throughout the peaks and valleys of our relationship, when we face challenges, we both call the "Help Line," pray together and ask for God's help. That's our foundation.

Secondly, I'm crazy in love with her, I'm incredibly grateful for her and I do my best to express that as often and as effectively as possible in a way she can receive it. Different people are wired differently and need different things to hear that message. For her, that means quality time, and that's also critical for my relationship with my kids. I read once that love in a relationship is spelled "T-I-M-E." Being someone who has always been a workaholic, I really had to re-engineer. It didn't happen overnight, but it happened over time. My wife and I try to make a date night every week, where it's just her and me, and we have our time before bed. My evenings are sacred because it's the time I have dinner with my family, hang out with them, put my kids to bed and spend time with my wife. Sometimes work does come up, but I never want to miss putting them to bed, because that's a sacred time for them and for me.

A lot of guys are not very expressive in telling their wives or their kids that they love them. If anything, I *overexpress* to my wife and my kids that I love them. I believe it's important for them to live under a waterfall of love. That can be done with words, or it can be done through physical touch — hugging or kissing. I just don't want to hold back because I know one day I'll be on my deathbed and I don't want to think that I wasted any time not expressing to my wife and kids how much I love them and what they mean to me. I'm *not* going to have that regret.

With a divorce rate over 50 percent, what, in your opinion, is the today's biggest challenge when it comes to marriage?

SW: There are a few things. One is selfishness in general. Both people come home and they wonder why the other person isn't doing what they're supposed to do and wondering why they're not appreciated and respected. The opposite would be both coming home and saying, "What can I do to show my spouse that I appreciate, love and respect them?" The remedy to selfishness is *selflessness*, to love and serve each other and put each other first and not just meet half way. Each person has to be willing to go all the way to the other because there's going to be a moment when they need you do to that. Sometimes to do that, though, you need help. I think the gravity of our nature — or at least my nature — will pull us down. Again, that's why it's critical I go to the "Help Line" whenever I have an issue with my wife.

My wife and I have developed a "move" for those times when we're at risk of having anything but love and gratitude for each other. The person who recognizes it goes and presses the other person's nose like a button. That "reset" button is us reminding the other to not get caught up in the quicksand that could keep us from loving each other, to protect the joy that we have. We even made a game of it to see who would do it faster than the other. It's a tactile thing that starts with a commitment and understanding that we want to realize how ridiculous is it that we waste so much time doing anything but loving each other and being grateful for one another.

In addition to selfishness, there are obstacles that you might not even realize are having an effect on your relationship. The phone has become one of these obstacles, and I'm speaking as a recovering addict of my phone and of work. That little blinking light on my phone can be a challenge. I've got to choose quality time with my wife and kids or that little blinking light. And, for most of my kids' lives, they've seen me choose that little blinking light over them. I've changed and matured, and I've realized

> Each person has to be willing to go all the way to the other because there's going to be a moment when they need you do to that.

my own nature, that sometimes I can't sustain the temptation. So now we have a rule: No phones at the dinner table. They're just not allowed. Too many distractions flow through that phone — not just work, but social media and mindless entertainment. It can threaten the quality time with the ones who you should be spending your time with.

What was the most difficult thing you've had to overcome in your own marriage and how did you get through this?

SW: We've been blessed that we haven't had any challenges or issues that have put us on the ropes. Probably the biggest challenge we've had was my lack of maturity at the beginning of our marriage. Because I lead at work, sometimes I would bring that attitude home and felt that my voice or my opinion was more weighted than hers. I also think that work took up too much time and caused me to neglect my wife and my children when they were very little. Early in my marriage, I wasn't as good at handling those minor skirmishes, so they became bigger battles. Now, I have a better perspective. I was able to change, though, and I'm confident that if I hadn't made those adjustments of striking a balance to invest quality time and connect with my wife and my kids, it would have been the beginning of something tragic. If not physical separation and divorce, then an emotional separation between me and my wife and my children. Fortunately, I was able to see all the factors. There haven't been any huge challenges; it's just the day-to-day challenges that are like water against a rock. If you don't handle them properly, they can draw your further and further from the people you love.

The time when you *really* change is when you start focusing, when you finally decide that you really want to be good at something. Now you're not just a bystander going through life anymore. Now you're fully engaged and involved.

Afterword

Life as It *Should* Be

CONGRATULATIONS! YOU'VE TAKEN THE time to read *The Theory of 5* and are ready to take your next steps into a world larger and more wonderful than you've ever thought possible.

This is just the beginning of your journey — now the planning work and action begins.

Here, at the end, I ask you to take time and think about what I, my mentors and co-mentors have shared with you. On the face of it, The Theory of 5 is a simple concept: Find people living the life you want to live in key areas, befriend them and ask them to guide you on your journey.

Simple, but life changing.

By taking this lifestyle and making it our own, we set ourselves up to experience success in ways we never dreamed possible.

Several years ago, at a dinner meeting with five of my friends, mentors and co-mentors, we entered into a detailed and emotional conversation about life.

During this discussion, one of my friends said, "What surprises me most about life in general is that most of us are willing to sacrifice our health in order to increase our wealth. Now, years later, we will sacrifice our wealth in order to regain our youth and health!"

This was a deep thought and, unfortunately, it is very true for many people. All of us sitting around the table knew we were guilty of this — or were heading in that direction

"You're right," another friend said. "We are all so anxious, nervous and concerned about what may happen in the future that we forget to enjoy the present."

I've often thought about this conversation and one day a realization hit me like a bolt from the blue: Most of us live like we are never going to die, or forget that we all have an expiration date on our lives.

At that dinner meeting, we agreed that many people we know already will die never having lived the life they should have had — the life that they dreamed about. "Most people are living a life where they daydream about what they want," one of us said. "Unfortunately, they never take the daily actions needed to make it happen."

We often give up our purpose, our passion and our "why" just to make money. We are plagued with indecision and lack of vision. The most common prison in the world is the one without bars. It's a prison most people are not even aware they are living in; therefore, they have no idea how to get out of it.

> This is the prison of the daily routine that we are sentenced to if we don't have a vision.

This is the prison of our daily routine that we are sentenced to if we don't have a Theory of 5 vision. Many people live for the weekend and are too tired to enjoy it. Think about this: Many of us do not have time to eat dinner with our loved ones; we end up dining alone if we even take time for dinner at all. We eat on the go, sleep on the go and even meet on the go.

We are told this is *normal.*

But *should* it be?

Stop for a moment. Imagine a world where we are clearly aware of our PURPOSE — and we have the passion and determination to live it. Envision what will happen when we live a Theory of 5 life.

- We would be better partners.
- We would be better parents.
- We would have the career of our dreams.
- We would have better health.
- We would have more patience.
- We would have more passion.
- We would be better *people.*

Here's the truth of the matter: *We all have this potential.*

I am confident that The Theory of 5 is the key to the happiness and prosperity we all long for and deserve. There is absolute power in people

286 The Theory of 5

because, when we surround ourselves with like-minded people with passion and purpose, our dreams will come true.

Make this a priority in your life: Spend the majority of your time with people who nourish and inspire you. Make the time for people who believe in you and support your dreams and vision.

And make time to be there for them. Support them. Inspire them.

Stay positive, even when it feels impossible to do so. Learn to believe in yourself. Love yourself for who you are now and who you know you will become. Be relentless in pursuing your dreams. Never forget: You are the author of your own life. Choose your friends wisely, build your circle of five and live the life others only dream of.

It's your life.

There is absolute power in people because, when we surround ourselves with like-minded people with passion and purpose, our dreams come true.

Acknowledgments

WHEN I LOOK AT the network of partners, mentors and role models who have been there for me, it's easy to see why the concepts detailed in *The Theory of 5* came into focus in my life.

First, I must thank my family; without them, my life would have no meaning. My wife, **Lisa Saraceno**, for her patience and support over the last few years while I worked on *The Theory of 5* on our evenings and weekends — I couldn't have done it without your support and patience. I would also like to share how blessed, appreciative and grateful I am that my daughters, **Tia Saraceno Dorsett** and **Taylor Saraceno Williams**, grew to become the women I knew they would become when I first held them in my arms as newborns.

I'd also like to thank the rest of my family for the impact they've had on my life:

Angelo Saraceno
Wanda Saraceno
Perry Saraceno
Kathie Saraceno
Michael Saraceno
Nick Saraceno
Mark Saraceno
Scott Dorsett
Owen Benjamin Dorsett
Greyson David Dorsett
Tyler Williams
Sophia Saraceno Williams

Adam Hartle
Madison Hartle
Rex Hartle
Roman Hartle
Sloan Hartle
Ashton Young
Brandon Young
My wife's entire family,
   The Rodriguez family
My aunts, uncles, cousins and
   grandparents

In the business world, I've been fortunate enough to have access to exceptional minds. These tremendously successful business associates have inspired me and held me accountable to achieve what otherwise might have been impossible for me to attain.

In addition to my exceptional friends and business partners **Greg** and **Tim Kelly**, along with our CFO **Adam Smith**, the Kelly Automotive Group has a board of directors/advisors made up of:

- **Robert P. Kelly** — The chairman of the Kelly Automotive Group, and one of the founders
- **Jerry H. Pyle** — A Harvard graduate, former president of Friedkin Corporation and CEO of Gulf States Toyota, Inc.
- **Eustace Wolfington** — Founder and chairman of Half A Car, as well as a real estate investor, movie producer and entrepreneur/business investor
- **James O'Connor** — Former vice president of the Ford Motor Division, a partner in Kelly Ford and a business investor
- **Vince Sheehy** — President and CEO of Sheehy Auto Stores, as well as a board member of several automotive organizations
- **Joseph S. Holman** — A chairman of the board for Holman Enterprise, a multibillion dollar company

Also, as founder of dealerElite.com, I've had the pleasure of partnering with:

- **David Boice** — The founder of Team Velocity, a partner in Tier10 Marketing and an investor in a dozen other companies
- **Sean Wolfington** — The chairman and CEO of Carsaver, a partner and investor in a dozen other businesses, a film producer and winner of numerous business awards

In addition, I'd like to thank **David Lewis**, owner and founder of DLA Training, for decades of friendship and tens of thousands of hours of business conversations and debates.

This book would not exist without these people, along with dozens of other business associates and friends, people I know I can call at a moment's notice when there's a question I need answered or council on a decision I need to make. These people include:

- **David Falkirk Davis:** Writer/Author/Friend/Co-Mentor
- **Dave Anderson:** Business/Marriage/Spirituality/Fitness

- **Grant Cardone:** Business/Health/Marriage/Spirituality
- **Susan Givens:** Business/Marriage/Parenting/Spirituality, and for encouraging and challenging me to write and share the philosophy of Theory of 5 thinking
- **Lee Kemp:** Fitness/Parenting
- **David Koder:** Website design/Marketer/Friend/Co-mentor
- **Evelyn Longsworth:** Marriage/Parenting
- **Steve Munyan:** Spirituality/Marriage/Business
- **Chip Perry:** Business/Marriage
- **Bob Plarr:** Fitness
- **Dale Pollak:** Business/Parenting
- **Marty Raymond:** Spirituality/Business/Family
- **Keith Shetterly:** Business/Brilliant Mind

These people have exemplified not only exceptional business practice, but also have been good role models for the other areas of The Theory of 5. My life would be lessened for not knowing each and every one of them, and The Theory of 5 would not have taken shape.

I'd like to give special thanks to **Andrew Schultz,** who is the managing partner of The Theory of 5 University (www.Theoryof5University.com). Andrew is a lifetime educator who puts his heart and soul into teaching and coaching, and I (and his students) admire his passion for sharing with our clients the secrets of the world's most happy and prosperous people.

Finally, when you stop and really think about your life, it can be staggering just how many people make an impression. This is by no means a complete list, but I'd like to thank the following people for making a difference in my world:

Charlie Algieri
Jim Alhquist
Ed Bachert
The Backenstoe Family
Tom Ball
Cliff Banks
Jim Barndt
Kelly Bender
Brian Benstock

Joseph Berrios
Chuck Bostic
Cheryl Boyer
Karen Bradley
Sean Bradley
Rick Brobst
Anthony Brock
Brian Brown
Charlie Brown

Richard Bustillo
Joe Cala
Serena Cape
Doreen Carl
Ron Carl
Bill Cariss
Scott Chlebove
Lisa Copeland
Jeff Cowan
Hayden Craddolph
Phil Crammer
Kristen Davis
Sue Davis
Andrew DiFeo
Kyle Disher
Mike Disora
Nancy Ettle
Charlie Etzweiler
Karen Feldman
Kurt Feldman
George Gabriel
Ron Glassic
Sandy Griener
Gerald Grillo
Bill Hamlin
Greg Hilt
Jesse Holder
Dave Howard
Mike Kaunitz
Alicia Kelly
The Kelly Family
Dave LaBar
Brian Longehagen
Terry Longmore
Julie Lundy
Leslie Lundy
Marty Lundy
Steve Lundy

Steve Lundy Jr.
Frank Marr
Rick Martis
Jim Mayben
John Melsheimer
Steve Melsheimer
Ivan Mendez
Shahrokh Merhrker
Jon Miller
Brad A. Modrich
Chrystal Mohr
Lynn Munyan
Monsignor Murphy
Greg Noonan
Jim Onushco
The Onushco family
Brian Pasch
Carrie Pasch
Juanita Peters
Mark Peters
David Plummer
Tom Powers
Don Pryor
Tye Reed
Brad Ritter
Brian Ritter
Bruce Ritter
Dale Ritter
Larry Ritter
Ron Ritter
Jerry Roberts
Marian Rohrbach
Dave Rothrock
Mike Salavati
Fred Saracino
Amanda Schneider
Ben Schneider
Andrew Schultz

Gloria Schultz
Arnold Schwarzenegger
Art Silfies
Adam Smith
Eric Sparrow
Sylvester Stallone
Tony Tarsi
David Villa
Ken Walls
Fred Webber
Harris Weinstein

Sally Whitesell
Keith Williams
Glenn Wood
Paula Young
Richard Young
Tom Young
James A. Ziegler
Promise Keepers Organization
The Saturn corporation
The older Italian gentleman I met
after marriage classes in 1985

I'd also like to take a moment to thank the dogs in my life (dog people understand). The reality is that my dogs have truly supported me with their calming effect, loyalty and love through some of the most challenging times in my life, from my childhood through today. Thank you to Gidget, Taffy, Pepper, Bingo, Teeny, Rocky, Adrian and Apollo.

A Note to My Children and Grandchildren

My dearest hope is that you all will work together to continue to update and tweak The Theory of 5, sharing your own talents and experiences to encourage happiness and prosperity for everyone. I love you all!

About the Authors

CHRIS SARACENO is a business, real estate investor, speaker and leader who has, over the past 36 years, discovered what surrounding yourself with happy and prosperous people, coupled with hard work, can bring over a lifetime.

A vice president and partner in the Kelly Automotive Group, he has been a partner in 14 different automotive franchises and founder of the online community DealerElite. com, Chris is also the co-owner of the coaching, mentoring, training, and consulting company The Theory of 5 University, which has worked with individuals and companies on five continents.

Chris has been a featured speaker and author, and is a former advisory board member for AutoTrader, DealerRater, Hire The Winners, and Cemboo Film Distribution, as well as a co-founder of the training company Team Builders, Inc. He was a member of the launch team for General Motors EV1, and one of the three original Saturn Corporation lead trainers, where he helped develop Saturn's "one-price" selling process, which influenced how vehicles are now sold. Chris is also an executive producer and co-writer of the hit song, "The Theory of 5 Song."

Chris lives in Merritt Island, Florida, with his wife, Lisa, and has four children and six grandchildren. He is committed to giving all of them his best energy and guidance, and to providing an example of what will be accomplished when you have support and an exceptional attitude.

For more information, visit www.TheoryOf5.com.

DAVID FALKIRK DAVIS is a writer, author and editor. He lives in Indiana with his wife, Kristen. David is also a fiction writer and is the author of the *The Joined World* trilogy, *The Death Effect* and the *Fast 40* series of flash fiction. For more information, visit www.DavidFalkirk.com.

Made in the USA
Middletown, DE
13 October 2023

40442153R00169